THE MAKING OF A MEDIA PRINCESS

On February 4, 1974, two black men and a white woman pushed their way into a Berkeley, Calif., apartment. Minutes later, they sped away, firing wildly. With them went Patricia Hearst.

Thus began an unprecedented real-life drama, resulting in an incredible media barrage which kept millions of Americans in suspense. In journalistic terms, it was easily the biggest kidnaping story since the Lindbergh case in the '30s, but with a bizarre twist: the SLA's demands insured that the media would give space to SLA propaganda, and in the interests of protecting Patty's life, would suppress or soften unfavorable stories about SLA members.

The vast media empire had become a pawn of the SLA . . . and, inevitably, of the Hearst family, desperately trying to gain the release of their daughter. PATTY/TANIA goes beyond the headlines to examine not only the bare facts of the Hearst kidnaping, but its larger implications, including the role of the media in political kidnapings, the adequacy of press coverage under terrorist-imposed censorship, and much more.

WITH SPECIAL APPENDICES CONTAINING
- A complete capsule chronology of the Hearst kidnaping
- Full texts of SLA ransom documents
- Complete transcripts of the Patty/Tania tape recordings

PATTY/TANIA

Don West and Jerry Belcher

PYRAMID BOOKS ▲ NEW YORK

PATTY/TANIA
A PYRAMID BOOK

Pyramid edition published January 1975

ISBN: 0-515-03727-3

Library of Congress Catalog Card Number: 74-25050

Printed in the United States of America

Pyramid Books are published by Pyramid Communications, Inc. Its trademarks, consisting of the word "Pyramid" and the portrayal of a pyramid, are registered in the United States Patent Office.

PYRAMID COMMUNICATIONS, INC.
919 Third Avenue
New York, New York 10022, U.S.A.

TABLE OF CONTENTS

Acknowledgments

The authors wish to thank all of the people who generously cooperated and volunteered information about this complex story. There were those from the underground, some from radical and revolutionary groups, police investigators, friends and relatives of those personally involved and chance acquaintances. Many cannot be identified and listed without endangering their lives. More merely want to avoid the limelight of publicity.

We owe a special debt of gratitude to our colleagues on the *San Francisco Examiner*, who assisted immeasurably. These include, but are not limited to, Sam Blumenfeld, Gale Cook, Steve Cook, Lance Gilmer, Ed Montgomery, Don Martinez, Baron Muller, Carol Pogash and Harold Streeter.

Ella Swarth's kindness and skill in typing our manuscript must be gratefully acknowledged.

Thanks, too, to the Belcher kids for their constant support and occasional silence.

And the greatest debt of all is to Nancy Belcher—who contributed significantly to researching this book —and Marion West, the authors' infinitely patient and understanding wives. They endured this work—and us—with great grace.

Preface

The abduction of Patricia Campbell Hearst on February 4, 1974 was the first political kidnapping in the history of the United States. It was and will be much more than that, for its aftershocks will be felt for years to come.

Theatrical from the outset, the Hearst case became a bizarre multimedia mix of whodunit-spy-suspense-cops-and-robbers thriller, Greek tragedy, incredible operatic libretto. And, on a few occasions, even comedy. At one time or another the principals employed such props as poisoned bullets, "Mission Impossible" orders issued through tape recordings, a U-2 spy plane over-flight, messages pinned to red roses, stagy disguises. A Hollywood scriptwriter would be handed his pink slip if he tried to foist off such a gimmick-ridden, melodramatic and implausible plot on his producer. Yet fantastic as it seemed, this was the stuff of real life. The terror, the violence, the fear, the mind-bending, the heartbreak and the blood—all were real.

In journalistic terms, it was The Big Story, certainly the biggest kidnaping story since Bruno Hauptman abducted and murdered little Charles A. Lindbergh, Jr. in 1932. It can be argued that it was the biggest kidnaping story of all time. It *was* the most intensely reported of all time. One of its climactic and violent scenes was witnessed, live and in color, by millions of Americans.

As a political story, it was one of the biggest of the decade. In revolutionary, counterculture politics, at least, it rivals the Watergate scandals. Here, too, it can be argued that in the long perspective of history, the Hearst case may have a greater impact and deeper significance than Watergate. If, as there is some evidence to indicate, the kidnaping of Patricia Hearst was the germinal act of a new American era of no-holds-barred political terrorism, then it will almost surely overshadow Watergate. Unquestionably it will loom larger than Watergate in the historical view, if, as the Symbionese Liberation Army and its sympathizers would have us believe, the seven-headed cobra is not merely a freaky-mystical symbol of an isolated group of sociopaths, but the vanguard emblem of the Second American Revolution.

Even if one wishes to consider the SLA only as a band of desperate and deluded criminals, and Patricia Hearst as a poor little rich girl gone wrong, the story still is one of the most fascinating of our time. In telling it here the authors—who, as newsmen working for the *San Francisco Examiner* covered and wrote news accounts of much of the action—do not claim it is the full story. Some of the facts will remain hidden forever, not because the facts were not sought out, but because some of the central figures are dead, others are still too terrified to tell what they do know, and others refused to talk for reasons, legitimate and otherwise, which they alone are living with.

Some of the material presented here took three years of digging and investigation. The story began long before the birth of the Symbionese Liberation Army, and long before Patricia Hearst moved to Berkeley.

Wherever possible the facts have been checked, double-checked and checked again. Interpretations have been considered, debated and reconsidered before being committed to these pages. Within the limits of our time frame and our abilities, this, then is the story.

CHAPTER ONE

THE REAL PATTY HEARST—I

I

Patty Hearst looks happy. She is smiling—not a full smile because she may be a little self-conscious about being photographed by a professional from her father's newspaper. Or perhaps the self-consciousness stems from her feelings that this is all kind of corny, conventional—kind of Hillsborough-socialite-snobby. Still the smile, though restrained, seems genuine. Her eyes are in slight shadow, but she is looking directly into the camera. The set of her head is confident.

Her face is oval in shape. A high, clear forehead, nose perhaps a trifle too prominent for movie-star beauty. Her hair is golden brown, but in this black and white photograph it appears dark. It is just beyond shoulder length. Backlighted, her hair creates a half-halo around her head.

She is wearing a simple, light-colored mini-dress, long-sleeved, the hem at mid-thigh. The dress is tasteful, conservative and perhaps slightly out of style—in no way ostentatious. It shows off a slender junior miss figure, good legs.

Patty Hearst is walking across the beautifully kept

13

lawn in the back garden of the Hearst home in Hillsborough. Her left hand is in the right hand of Steve Weed; their fingers are entwined. He is nearly a head taller than she. He is not smiling. Behind his round steel-rimmed glasses, the eyes look distant, preoccupied. His hair is blond. It touches his collar. His dense moustache appears to have been trimmed for the occasion. He is wearing a dark blazer, a wide patterned necktie, light-colored shirt, light-colored slacks flaring slightly at the cuffs.

Patty is happy, some would say radiant. Steve is serious, some would say uncomfortable. The photograph was made December 19, 1973. It was the day Patricia Campbell Hearst, daughter of Mr. and Mrs. Randolph Apperson Hearst of Hillsborough, announced her engagement to Steven Andrew Weed, son of Donald Everett Weed of Palo Alto and Mrs. Stanley Pepper of Santa Rosa. The young woman was 19 years old. He was 26 years old.

Tania looks grim. Her mouth is in a thin tight line. She may be a little self-conscious because, as a photographer herself, she knows her stance in this photo is posy, melodramatic. The photographer now is an amateur, a member of the Symbionese Liberation Army.

The oval face is in three-quarter profile. This is a color photograph. Her brown eyes are opened wide, staring. There is a lack of depth in the eyes, a vacancy. She is wearing a black and red knit cap. Her hair, descending from beneath the cap, touches the canvas sling draped around her neck.

The sling is attached to a short-barreled automatic weapon fitted with a curving ammunition magazine and a cylindrical gunsight. Her right hand grasps the rear grip of the gun, her forefinger on the trigger. Her left hand is cupped just forward of the weapon's magazine. On the third finger is a ring.

She is wearing a brown military shirt, open at the neck, and brown military pants. The photo is not full-length but it shows that she is in a slight crouch, her legs set wide apart—classical stance of the gunslinger ready to shoot from the hip. In the background is the ensign of the SLA, the seven-headed cobra.

Patty is grim, some would say sinister.

Exactly where, when and by whom the color photograph was made could not be determined. The Polaroid print was delivered to San Francisco radio station KSAN on April 3, less than 24 hours after an SLA message sent (along with a dozen red roses) through an underground newspaper. The "Red Roses" message promised that the time and place of their prisoner's release would be announced within 72 hours.

With the Polaroid print came another tape recording. The voice was the voice of Patricia Campbell Hearst. The words were the words of Comrade Tania:

"I have been given the choice of, one, being released in a safe area, or, two, joining the forces of the Symbionese Liberation Army and fighting for my freedom and the freedom of all oppressed people," the voice said. "I have chosen to stay and fight."

Which is the true portrait? Or is the picture of the young woman clutching the gun somehow implicit, undeveloped, just beneath the surface of the photograph of the young woman holding hands with her fiancé?

II

Winter fog slipped in over the eastern hills early in the evening. Now, shortly before nine o'clock at night, the city of Berkeley, California, lay quietly under the cold overcast.

The gibbous moon was obscured. The night was almost windless. When it did stir, the movement was barely perceptible—two to three miles an hour. The temperature stood at 48 degrees, but because of the damp fog it seemed colder. A dark, chill night. Not a pleasant night for wandering along Telegraph Avenue, where by day Berkeley's restless, antically costumed "street people" congregated to buy or rip-off second-hand denims and thirdhand books, to trade ideas, gossip and dope. Not a pleasant night either for strolling on the huge University of California campus, where Telegraph dead-ends a stone's throw from Sproul Plaza. Sproul Plaza: where the Free Speech Movement was born in the mid-1960s, the politicized launching pad and occasional battleground of the American counter culture.

At this hour, on this night, Telegraph and the campus were almost deserted. A few merchants were closing their shops, a few students heading home from night classes or study sessions. Night walking, even on balmy nights, was no longer a big activity. Rapes were not rare now, muggings not infrequent. The cautious traveled in groups, carried police whistles, knives, cans of Mace. Often students were accompanied by large, well-trained dogs.

By day, regardless of weather, Berkeley swarmed with some 30,000 students plus faculty, street people, tourists. By day Telegraph and the campus were always bright with color, swirling with movement and movements—some highly vocal and visible, some underground and only whispered about by the radical cognoscenti.

For Berkeley—always exciting, often tumultuous and occasionally violent caldron of the counterculture—this was a quiet Monday night. It was almost inevitible that what began this night would begin in Berkeley. The date was February 4, 1974.

III

Five blocks south of the campus, Patricia Campbell Hearst and Steven Weed had just finished a late supper and were watching a TV show called "The Magician" in their neat, comfortable two-bedroom apartment at 2603 Benvenue Avenue. Their place, Number 4, was one of two units in the rear of the twin-building rustic-modern fourplex. The young couple shared the $250 a month rent. Although they were not married, they

16

leased the apartment under the names Mr. and Mrs. Steven Weed. She received $300 a month allowance from her father, newspaper executive Randolph Apperson Hearst. He earned $444 a month as a teaching assistant at the university.

The fourplex was one of the newer structures on the 2600 block of Benvenue, an old residential neighborhood now in transition. Once a strictly family neighborhood, solid and middle-class, it was evolving into an almost exclusively student enclave. One by one the older homes were being demolished and replaced by boxy modern apartment buildings. Nearly all the householders in the older homes, retired people most of them, rented one or more rooms to students. The fourplex at 2603 Benvenue, flanked by two older homes, was the handsomest of the new buildings on the street, contemporary in design with large sliding glass doors and dark brown shingled exterior.

Number 4, shielded from street noises by the two-story twin structure which fronted on Benvenue, was a fine place to be on a chilly, foggy night. Warm, quiet, secure and private.

Steve and Patty, as they were called by almost everyone who knew them, shared in their life together a well-developed sense of privacy. They had only a few close friends, and even they did not call often at Number 4.

Patty's sense of orderliness also was well developed. She kept the apartment clean and well organized. In other student apartments, dormitories and communes in Berkeley, revolutionary posters, peace-and-love posters, funny "put-on" posters were the usual decorations. They were absent here. Instead, the walls were hung with tasteful art prints and photographs. Some of the photos were Patty's. Photography was one of her interests, and she was considered an accomplished amateur.

The apartment was furnished in eclectic style with antiques Patty and Steve had picked up at flea markets in the San Francisco Bay area, Persian rugs bought at bargain prices, secondhand furniture that they had carefully refinished.

The supper she and Steve had lingered over tonight was also tasteful. Patty was an accomplished cook, and proud of her skill.

Patty and Steve were, at the moment, happy and content. They had met in the fall of 1970 at Crystal Springs School in Hillsborough, California, where Patty's parents lived. She was a student, he a math teacher. But they had not become "involved" until after her graduation, when she enrolled in Menlo College. Steve and Patty had been living together for the last 18 months. They had their problems, and their living arrangement was one of them.

Patty's parents had been upset in the beginning. Her father did not make moral judgments about such living arrangements. He was a casual Catholic, a convert-by-marriage from the Episcopal Church, and reasonably open-minded about new youthful life styles. But he had worried about whether Patty would be happy with young Weed. Her mother was a conservative socially and politically, and a devout Catholic. She disapproved in principle of what her generation called "shacking up." But now Patty's parents were coming around, beginning to accept Weed. Patty and Steve had announced their engagement the previous December. They planned to be married in June.

They were not typical UC Berkeley students, but neither were they wildly unconventional in their life style for this time and place. Steve was 26 years old, a teaching assistant studying for his doctorate in philosophy. He wore his blond hair moderately long and cultivated a moustache that almost covered his mouth. Patty was 19 years old, an undergraduate majoring in art history. She was attractive, with a small, trim figure, long golden brown hair. Some people considered her beautiful. They were better off financially than most Berkeley students, lived more comfortably and kept to themselves more than most. They smoked marijuana, and at this moment had a stash of the stuff in the apartment. Both liked wine. To eschew either pot or wine, in Berkeley, would be considered hopelessly establishment or eccentric. They shared a quiet domestic-

18

ity, a quiet love, that seemed more mature than their years.

IV

Three miles northwest of the Benvenue apartment, Peter Benenson braked his ten-year-old Chevrolet Impala convertible to a stop in the driveway of his small stucco home at 1304 Josephine Street. Benenson was 31 years old, a mathematician specializing in environmental studies at UC's prestigious Lawrence Laboratory. He was a bachelor and did his own cooking and shopping. He had just returned from the Berkeley Coop supermarket five blocks away with his weekly supply of groceries.

The time was 8:50 P.M. At that moment, as Berkeley Police investigators later reconstructed events, occurred the first violent act of a night filled with desperate and deliberate violence. Two young women sprang out of the darkness, taking Benenson completely by surprise. The neatly bearded mathematician was five feet, eight inches tall and weighed 155 pounds. The two women were smaller, but they were determined and skilled in assault. One slugged Benenson with a pistol. The two bags of groceries in his arms spilled onto the driveway.

The stunned Benenson was quickly and expertly blindfolded, trussed with a nylon cord and wrestled into the back seat of his own convertible. One of his assailants got behind the wheel, started the car, backed out of the driveway and drove off at a moderate rate of speed. The convertible headed toward Benvenue in convoy with a white 1964 Bel Air station wagon.

On Benvenue, the driver of the convertible backed into the driveway sloping down into the spacious garage beneath the front unit of the fourplex at 2603 Benvenue. The station wagon parked nearby. A dark-colored Volkswagen sedan with at least two people in it had been staked out on the street for several minutes before the arrival of the other two cars. Its license plate was carefully covered over.

From one of the cars, two men and a woman emerged and moved purposefully up the concrete pathway on the south side of the shingled fourplex. The pathway was well lighted by three globular outdoor lamps mounted on the wall of the fourplex.

The woman went directly to the door of Number 4. The patio between the two buildings of the fourplex also was well lighted. The woman's two companions fell back into the scant shadow of a bamboo plant near the door. On the sliding glass door was a decal: "Warning—Protected by ADT Residential Security System."

The woman pressed the doorbell to the left of the glass door. Weed and Patty both responded to the two-toned chime of the bell. He was suspicious of the figure he saw through the translucent door and Patty seemed alarmed as she stood behind him. They rarely had friends over; they were expecting no one tonight. Their place had been burgled once before—thus the alarm system. Still, Weed opened the door.

The woman was slightly hunched and had one hand over her face. "I just had a car accident out front," she said, "and could you. . ."

She didn't finish the sentence.

Instantly two men burst in behind her. Both were armed. Within seconds Weed was thrown to the floor. Then he was being kicked in the face and head with heavy boots.

One of the gunmen slammed Weed in the back of the head with a wine bottle. Weed's blood puddled on the hardwood floor of the hallway. His hands were tied behind his back, quickly and not too securely. One of the men demanded his wallet. "Take anything," Weed told him. "Just leave us alone."

"Where's the safe?" one asked.

"We don't have a safe."

The gunman seemed to accept that. Weed, face down and groggy, got only glimpses of the invaders. He heard one of them moving about the apartment. He neither saw nor heard it when one of the three placed

20

or kicked a box of twenty-five 9mm bullets under the bookcase in the hallway. The tip of each bullet had been drilled and filled with cyanide. Cyanide bullets were the trademark of terrorism.

Weed did hear Patty's voice somewhere behind him. She was making frightened, whining sounds.

Steven Suenga, 26, a UC student who lived in Number 3, chose that moment to walk out of his apartment. The two black men dashed out, grabbed him, pulled him into Number 4 and battered him to the floor. They tied him and placed him beside Weed.

Weed's consciousness was going in and out of focus. But the voice of the woman pierced the haze. "We've got to get rid of them," she said. "They've seen us."

Weed heard the metallic snick of a weapon's bolt being shoved home. He got the message: In another instant he and Patty and his neighbor would die unless. . .

Weed thought: "I've got nothing to lose." He shot to his feet, sprinted down the hallway, across the front room, out the sliding glass door at the rear of the apartment, then to the six-foot fence at the back of the rear patio.

V

At that moment, 21-year-old Rocky Brown* was in the older home next door at 2607 Benvenue, where he rented a room from Mrs. Ruth Reagan. He and four other UC students were at the dining room table cramming for an upcoming midterm examination in genetics. Their concentration was shattered by a scream, then a blast of gunshots.

"What happened was, we were sitting there. . .and we heard a really sharp, distinct scream," he recalled.

* Rocky Brown is a fictitious name. Like a number of other witnesses in the case he asked that his true name not be used because he fears for his life. All fictitious names will be marked with an asterisk.

21

"And at first we thought maybe there were just some people fooling around, or somebody was arguing. But it didn't sound like a normal, just-an-argument scream. It was very intense."

Then: "We heard three shots. Like, *bambambam!* Real quick, real sharp shots. And we weren't sure if it was firecrackers or what. None of us was familiar with gunshots."

Brown and the three other young male students at the table leaped up, and dashed down the hallway and onto the front porch of the Reagan home. Their young woman companion stayed in the dining room.

From the porch Brown and his friends could look down into the driveway 20 feet away. They saw a convertible with its trunk open and a jumble of figures moving rapidly toward the car.

"We looked over the side . . . I saw her, Patty Hearst, maybe half-clad," he recalled. "I couldn't tell because it was dark and there were lots of shadows. She possibly could have had her blouse torn off. It may have been a bathrobe but it was really hard to tell. . . ."

The action was so fast and confused he couldn't tell how many people rushed by toward the car.

"When I focused on her [Patty] what went through my mind was that possibly she was being raped. Then kidnap came to mind when I saw the trunk open. And in about that amount of time, they noticed us on the porch and they fired three warning shots.

"They went overhead. I didn't see any gun at all. . .These just went off immediately, very rapid-fire. We just freaked out immediately and ran back into the house."

Upstairs in the front bedroom of the same house, Ruth Reagan and her husband, Ed, were getting ready for bed. Their room overlooked Benvenue to the west, the driveway to the north.

Mrs. Reagan was 76, but her memory of that night was strong and clear.

"We heard the shots, and little Rocky had some boys, studying they were, going to have a test, so they were right there. When *they* heard the shots they

22

thought maybe they were Chinese firecrackers or something and then they heard this girl hollering. The boys heard the first shots. We heard the noise and the shots from the front. I jumped up and looked out the window. Oh, I saw the car, and I saw them put her in the car. You couldn't tell who it was because I have to wear glasses to see very good, and it was night. But I just saw them put her in the car, and slam the thing."

Back downstairs, one of Brown's friends was dialing 644-6161, the emergency telephone number of the Berkeley Police Department. The call was logged at 9:14 P.M. Seconds later the message went out on police radio: "Possible 207 kidnap at 2603 Benevue."

The message crackled through the receiver of Berkeley Officer Steven Engler's portable radio as he was out of his car checking on a burglary break in a few blocks away from Benvenue. He ran for his police cruiser. Lari Blumenfeld, alone in the city room of the Berkeley Gazette, heard the same message. She reached for the phone.

At the Reagan home, Brown dashed by his friend on the telephone toward the porch. "When I got to the door, the '63 [convertible] was leaving," he said. "So immediately we thought of getting the license number, and we tore off down the front and out into the street, and as the car turned the corner onto Parker, they fired three shots at us."

Across the street another neighbor thought she heard a total of at least six shots, possibly as many as twelve. "I ran to the window," she said. "I couldn't see anything. It was dark. But I heard a woman scream and cry, 'Please! Please! Not me!' Then I saw sparks and I hit the floor and I called the police." By that time several other calls were coming in at Police Headquarters. Her name was not logged.

One of the final fusillade of bullets missed Brown's head by a fraction of an inch, although later Berkeley police would say that all of the shots apparently were deliberately fired high.

"That got very close," Brown said. "It didn't graze my skin, but I felt a whisk go through my hair, and my

23

friend felt a lot of upshot from the cement. He just felt all sorts of little things shoot up at him."

One of the slugs shattered the front bay window of the Reagan house and buried itself in the paneling of the window frame.

Brown did not remember seeing the station wagon and the VW leave. But the '63 convertible "screeched around the corner, up Parker." Peter Benenson, bound and blindfolded, was in the back seat. Patty, also bound and blindfolded, was in the trunk.

Brown and his friends moved up Parker Street. Seconds later a slender figure stumbled toward them. It was Weed, who had made his way over fences and through backyards onto the sidewalk. He had knocked on the door of one house and told someone to call the police.

Brown, a premed student, assessed Weed's injuries in a glance. "He was bleeding but it wasn't really profuse," he said. "We took him in [to Apartment Number 4] and all he wanted to do was find out what happened to her, which to us implied that he didn't know they took her at that time. He was just saying, 'Where's Patty? Where's Patty? Where's Patty? I've got to find her.' "

In the months to come, Steven Weed would go to desperate lengths in seeking the answer to that question.

CHAPTER TWO

THE MEDIA RIPOFF BEGINS—
UNANSWERED QUESTIONS

Although the United States has been fortunate to escape the rash of political kidnapings that have shaken so much of the world in the past few years, we must not be beguiled into the feeling that "it can't happen here."

————Richard Ichord, Chairman House Committee on Internal Security. July 30, 1973.

I

When the flat, unemotional message came through on Officer Steven Engler's shoulder radio, he thought it was just another "routine" kidnap. Berkeley had been plagued during the preceeding months with a series of kidnapings, but they were spontaneous street-corner snatches. Almost invariably the motive was sexual greed—rape. Engler scrambled behind the wheel of his police cruiser, hit the switch for siren and redlight, and rolled toward Benvenue.

Engler pulled up in front of 2603 Benvenue at 9:17 P.M., just 120 seconds after the first telephoned report to headquarters. A large, excited crowd already was milling around in the street. Within seconds, from the confused, overlapping gabble of the crowd, it became clear that this was no routine street kidnaping.

Two, maybe three people had come out with this girl. She was half-naked, screaming. There were gunshots. The girl was stuffed into the trunk of this old car. There were two carloads of them, maybe three carloads. The cars zoomed up Parker, went north on Parker. There was a guy, young guy with a big moustache, all bloodied. He was back in the apartment house.

Engler radioed the best available descriptions of the getaway cars to headquarters. Other police cruisers and an ambulance were arriving at the scene.

Fifteen minutes later in Herrick Memorial Hospital, where Steven Weed and Steven Suenga were taken by ambulance, it became evident to Berkeley Police that this was a Big One. Two officers questioned Weed as doctors worked on his wounds in the emergency room. He could tell them little except that the victim's name was Hearst. Patty Hearst. Patricia Campbell Hearst. Her father was Randy Hearst, editor of the *San Francisco Examiner*.

Hearst: A VIP name in Berkeley, in California. Once it was one of the biggest names in the nation. It still was a name to be reckoned with. Here in Berkeley there was a Hearst Avenue edging the north side of the campus. On the campus itself there was the Hearst Greek Theatre, named after William Randolph Hearst; the Hearst Gymnasium, after Phoebe Apperson Hearst; the Hearst Memorial Mining Building, after United States Senator George Hearst, husband of Phoebe, father of William Randolph Hearst. Catherine Hearst currently was on the UC Board of Regents, governing body of the statewide university system. The *San Francisco Examiner* across the bay was part of the Hearst newspaper chain. There was the incredible Hearst Castle at San Simeon down the coast.

Hearst: The name was synonymous with wealth and power. This was a Big One.

The name was relayed to police headquarters. All

26

available resources of the Berkeley Police Department were thrown into the search for Patty Hearst. The FBI, technically unauthorized to enter a kidnap case for 24 hours, was notified by telephone. Agents swarmed "unofficially" into Berkeley.

Sergeant Robert Lawrence got the chore of notifying the Hearst family. The number was listed in the San Mateo County directory. The Hearst residence was in Hillsborough, a wealthy suburb 35 miles southwest of Berkeley. Victoria Hearst, at 17 the youngest of five daughters in the family, took the call. No, her father was not home. Could she take a message? There was no soft way for the sergeant to say it: Patricia Hearst had been kidnaped. The time was 9:34 P.M.

Shaken but in control, Victoria phoned Washington, D.C. Her parents were there for the twelfth annual U.S. Senate Youth Program, a scholarship plan sponsored by the Hearst Foundation. Victoria—Vicki in the family—broke the news. Six minutes later, Randolph A. Hearst was getting the sketchy details from Sergeant Lawrence by telephone. Hearst hung up, dialed again, and made reservations on the first plane leaving for San Francisco.

A few blocks away Charles Bates, special agent in charge of the San Francisco office of the FBI, was getting the same sketchy details a about the kidnaping from one of his agents by telephone. Bates also was in Washington on business. He dropped everything and arranged to fly back to San Francisco as quickly as possible. The Hearst case, the trickiest and most sensitive of his long career, now became his responsibility.

II

At about the same time Hearst and Bates were learning about the kidnaping, Berkeley police discovered Benenson's stolen convertible. It had been abandoned at 25 Tanglewood Court, only seven-tenths of a mile from the Benvenue apartment. The convertible's engine was still warm to the touch. No one was in it. Officers found a piece of nylon cord in the trunk and a woman's glove in the front.

Rocky Brown and his friends were taken to Tanglewood in a police cruiser. Yes, they agreed, that was the car the screaming young woman had been slammed into. "Did you open the trunk?" one of Brown's friends asked. "She may still be in there." He repeated the question several times and each time the officers ignored him. The trunk had been checked but the officers were too preoccupied to answer. Back at headquarters, Sergeant Lawrence also was too preoccupied to answer questions, and thus began the media ripoff—the use or misuse of the press, television and radio.

Lari Blumenfeld, a big, good-looking woman with long experience in crime reporting and excellent contacts in the Berkeley Police Department, became the first journalistic victim. The whole of the American news media would soon be ripped off too, by law enforcement agencies, by itself and by the kidnapers.

Lari was nearing the end of her shift at the Berkeley Gazette when she heard the 207 call on the office radio receiver. "I heard the kidnap-possible rape call within seconds after it happened," she recalled. "I called in and asked the cops what was going on and they 'covered.' Said they didn't know.

"I left my number and they said they would call back if there was anything to it. There had been six or seven kidnap-rapes in the two or three months before, and I figured what the hell—it isn't news anymore.

"I talked to Sergeant Bob Moore, the patrol sergeant. He said, 'I can't tell you anything now. I'll call you soon.' "

Lari waited, then decided to drive home to her place in the Oakland hills. On the way, listening to the police band radio receiver in her car, she heard the name Patricia Hearst. "But I'd never heard of her in my life," she said. "There are lots of Hearsts in Berkeley. And the name could have been Hurst. It just didn't ring my bell."

Lari had started her newspaper career on a Hearst

paper in 1942. She was hired as the first copygirl in the history of the *San Francisco Examiner*.

She finally got the word on Patricia Hearst's kidnaping from the *Examiner*. "Sam called me at home and told me about it, about an hour and a half after it happened," she said. "I said 'Jesus Christ! I'm going back.'"

Sam Blumenfeld, Lari's husband, also was a veteran reporter. He had been with the *Examiner* since its glory days in the late 1940s through the 1950s. Then, as a morning paper, it had dominated the field in northern California. It was probably the single most powerful institution in San Francisco.

Sam had survived the gradual decline of the *Examiner*, its merger with the old *San Francisco News-Call* in 1966, and its switch to the noncompetitive evening newspaper field. Now the dominant newspaper in San Francisco was the *Chronicle*, located next door to the *Examiner* on Fifth Street and printed on the same presses. The *Chronicle*'s publisher, Charles DeYoung Theriot, was a good friend of Randolph A. Hearst.

Tonight Sam was working the late shift in the *Examiner*'s city room on the third floor of the gray concrete building at 110 Fifth Street. The *Examiner* no longer maintained a Berkeley news bureau. It had been closed a few months before. The reasoning was that the campus had been too quiet to justify a full-time reporter; the "Berkeley beat" produced too few big stories these days, despite the undisputed fact that the university was the intellectual capital of the west coast.

So the news break on the kidnaping came not from an *Examiner* reporter, but from the newspaper's publisher Charles L. Gould who had received a call from Randolph Hearst in Washington.

The man sitting in the center chair behind the three desks known collectively as the city desk was Dave Deitz, a big tough-looking 32-year-old newspaperman with 11 years of experience. He had been tense when he began his shift at two o'clock in the afternoon. He had come to the *Examiner* the previous June and this was his first trick as night city editor. His appointment had been announced only the week before by the new city editor Larry Dum who also was 32.

Gould's phone call came at about 10:00 P.M. Deitz recognized the publisher's strained voice instantly. Deitz felt his inner tension snap up a notch. No newspaperman relishes a night call from his publisher, especially within a few hours of taking on a sensitive and demanding job like night city editor.

"Randy Hearst's daughter has been kidnaped," Gould said. "The youngest girl, Patty." Gould seemed calm but the mistake revealed that he too was under great pressure. He was an old friend of the family. Patty was not the youngest, but the middle daughter of the five Hearst girls.

"Jesus Christ!" Deitz said. Gould was not the kind of man you said *Jesus Christ* to. Deitz recovered quickly, took down what little information Gould could supply, and began organizing coverage of the story.

He worked quickly. He had only two reporters in the city room—Blumenfeld and Steve Cook, and another major story was developing. Mayor Joseph Alioto's wife had vanished 18 days before, angry at her husband because he neglected her for politics, and she had just returned. Deitz needed more bodies, fast. He called City Editor Dum at his home in San Francisco's Sunset District, then general assignment-rewriteman Jerry Belcher at his home in Oakland, then reporters Jim Wood and Carol Pogash, who lived but did not ordinarily work in Berkeley. He also called reporter Jay Bosworth in Berkeley, without thinking about Jay's intimate relationship with the family. Jay was married to Virginia Anne Hearst, one of Patty's sisters.

Wood was dispatched to Herrick Hospital, Pogash to the police headquarters. Belcher came into the city room to write the main running story. By the time he arrived Dum, Executive Editor Tom Eastham and his new assistant Ed Orloff already were there. Blumenfeld was on the phone talking to reporters in the field, taking notes.

Bosworth played a key role that night. He was 26 years old and had been working for the *Examiner* since

September 1972. As a member of the Hearst family, he was the only person police allowed to enter Steven Weed's hospital room—Wood had been rejected at Herrick by a polite but firm policeman. Weed was transferred later to UC's Cowell Hospital. It was there Bosworth talked to him.

Bosworth and Weed were not buddies—Jay considered Steve something of an intellectual snob—but they got along. Weed, as best he could, told Bosworth what had happened.

Bosworth later phoned the interview in to Blumenfeld. Bosworth scored one of the few major beats the *Examiner* would manage, to allow itself to manage, in this, one of the biggest running stories in the newspaper's history.

According to Bosworth, Weed was sure that robbery was not the motive, even though the kidnapers had taken his wallet and had asked if there was a safe in the apartment. "They acted very purposeful and intent," he told the reporter. The two men, both blacks, and the white woman operated in a precise, disciplined fashion that struck Weed as "commandolike."

Weed would give Bosworth—and police and FBI—only the most general descriptions of the kidnapers. He told Bosworth that on the previous Saturday night a black man and a white woman had come to the apartment and asked a number of "vague" questions about renting the place. "They were suspicious-looking," Weed said. "They looked like street people." He had not thought much of the strange callers at the time, but now he was sure they had been casing the apartment.

Weed also related how he had escaped from the apartment, out the back door, over the fences, but the details were sketchy.

Blumenfeld turned over the Bosworth notes to rewriteman Belcher. Wood and Ms. Pogash phoned Belcher further information but they were getting only what the Berkeley police wanted them to get. The FBI was not talking.

The Examiner's library had only bare-bones biographical information about Patricia Hearst, Steven

Weed, and even about Randolph and Catherine Hearst. The Hearst family had maintained a low public profile over the last few years.

About 4:00 A.M. Belcher began writing the main story. He tried to give the outward appearance of a professional calm but he could feel the tightness in his belly and his back. This was the biggest story he had handled in 20 years of newspapering. He typed the identifying slug in the upper left hand corner of the first sheet of copypaper: HAERST. He ripped the copy out of his IBM typewriter and started over: HEARST.

It was a long, complicated story, a sensitive story to handle. The writer, interupted by phone calls, quick conferences with editors and other reporters who just wanted to look over his shoulder, finished the story at 6:30 A.M. By then, however, the embargo was on. A "hold" had been placed on the story. Belcher, the other reporters, the editors, shared the sucked-out, empty feeling that afflicts all newsmen when they must put the lid on a big story. And this was the biggest.

The rationale for the news embargo was simple. First, the kidnapers might not know who they had. If not, perhaps their ransom demand would not be so exorbitant. Second, even if the kidnapers did know who they had, publicity would surely inspire the inevitable kooks to tie up the investigation with false leads and phony ransom demands. Officer Berger, the Berkeley Police Department's media man, had asked for a voluntary news blackout. Reporters from the newspapers, television and radio reluctantly agreed to sit on the story. They would continue to pursue the facts, but would not publish them. There was precedent for this sort of thing.

But there were serious doubts about the wisdom of the embargo, both on ethical and practical grounds.

"What do you think?" Eastham asked Belcher.

"Well, I can see the reasons for it, but I don't think it'll work," he replied. "It's too big a story. Too many people saw it and too many heard the shooting. I don't think it'll work."

"I'm inclined to agree," Eastham said. "But. . ." The

32

7:30 A.M. deadline for the *Examiner*'s first edition had come and gone. The first edition came up without a word on the kidnaping of the editor's daughter. The headline was: "Mayor's wife is home safe."

Belcher was asked to call some of the outlying newspapers to see if they were going along with the embargo. "We're sitting on one hell of a story here," he told the city editor of a suburban daily in nearby Marin County. "Everyone's agreeing to an embargo. The cops asked for it. Will you go along?"

"Well, what's the story?" the city editor wanted to know.

"Well, Randy Hearst's daughter has been kidnaped."

"Yeah? Is there any Marin County angle?"

"Not that I know of."

"Well then, we wouldn't be interested anyway."

III

By 10:00 A.M. scores of newsmen from all the major papers, radio and television stations were deployed in Berkeley, running down leads, interviewing witnesses. None knew if their work would be published or aired that day.

Then the *Examiner* city room got word that KGO radio was going with the story. KGO had heard the *Oakland Tribune*, the major East Bay daily run by former Senator William F. Knowland, was going to break the embargo in its next edition. Eastham decided the lid was off. The Hearst story started moving toward the presses. The Associated Press and United Press International wire services banged out bulletins. Within the hour the first installment of the Patricia Hearst kidnap story was flashing around the world.

At 10:30 A.M. reporter Gale Cook, recently succeeded as *Examiner* city editor by the younger Dum, came to Belcher's cluttered desk. "I hear a rumble that the SLA may be involved in this thing."

"The SL—*Who?*"

"Symbionese Liberation Army. You know. Might be worth a check with the Oakland cops."

Belcher called Don Martinez, the Examiner's East Bay news bureau chief. "Hey, Don, this sounds farout, but Gale Cook thinks the SLA might be in on the Hearst kidnap. Can you check it out?"

"Sure. Call you back."

Martinez called back just before the 11:15 A.M. deadline for the two-star edition, the main press run. "My source says he's very familiar with the SLA," Martinez reported. "He says Patty Hearst's name doesn't appear on any of the SLA's death lists—none of the Hearst names do. But my source does say he has reason to think—says he *fears*—that the SLA could be involved."

The rewriteman clattered out a fast insert for the main story. It was speculative, and the source could not be named, so he placed the insert well down in the body of the 78-paragraph story. The story carried the headline:

Randolph Hearst's daughter kidnaped

Patricia, 19, seized
In Berkeley raid

When the *Examiner*'s final edition rolled that day, the story had been told at length—66 inches of type in the main story, three sidebar stories, six photographs and a map. There were a few deliberate omissions. The fact that Patty and Weed were living together was missing. The fact that she was wearing only panties and a blue terry-cloth robe (a Christmas gift from her father) was excised. There were a couple of minor errors, but the report was as complete and accurate as any published that day. However, there were many unanswered questions.

Why Patty Hearst? Her family was well known and wealthy, but many better known and wealthier families lived in the Bay Area.

Why did the kidnapers make such a spectacular out

34

of their crime? Well-executed, conventional kidnappings are carried out by stealth, with as little commotion as possible. But these people had come out shooting, their victim screaming.

Why was Peter Benenson kidnaped, too? This, obviously, was a well-planned operation. Why would the kidnapers wait until the last moment before picking up a getaway car when they already had two cars? Why, as was learned by mid-morning on February 5, was Benenson left behind in his convertible on Tanglewood Road? Why, after he had freed himself of his bonds and torn off his blindfold, did he walk away without attempting to contact the police? Why, after the police contacted him, did he refuse to give more than the barest information?

Why was Steven Weed not shot to pieces as he broke and ran from the apartment? Weed had been a track man at Princeton but was he so fast that two "commando-like" gunmen could not drop him at such short range?

And the most important question of all: Where was Patricia Campbell Hearst? Who had her? Was she still alive?

Belcher, the rewriteman, was rerunning these questions through his mind when he returned to his Oakland home in late afternoon. He had not slept in 36 hours. Paranoia was creeping around the edges of his mind. He remembered that his byline was twinned with Jay Bosworth's at the top of the story.

He had a family, including a daughter two years younger than Patty Hearst. Before he fell into bed, he got a screwdriver and removed the nameplate from the mailbox in front of his home. Silly, probably. But Randy Hearst never thought his daughter would be kidnaped either. You never know.

CHAPTER THREE

THE HEARST ORIGINS

I

She bore a famous name. But until she was carried, struggling and screaming, from her apartment on the night of February 4, 1974, the name Patricia Campbell Hearst was unknown to the world outside her immediate circle of family and friends. She was an unknown, even in the San Francisco Bay Area, where her family had been a great power for more than a century.

In Berkeley, only a handful of people—her close friends, the old lady who lived next door, and a tiny clutch of then-anonymous radicals—knew she was a member of THE Hearst family.

On the crowded, busy campus which her family helped make one of the world's leading universities, she was just another attractive undergraduate, a little more "straight" and conservative in style and demeanor than most. Striped overalls, proletarian work shirts, redundantly patched, faded jeans were currently fashionable among women students. Patty wore simple but well-made dresses to her art history classes. Her golden brown shoulder-length hair was always neat and well groomed.

The name Patricia Campbell Hearst rarely appeared in print. In 1968 she was mentioned in passing as a bridesmaid in San Francisco society page stories about the wedding of her sister Virginia (Gina) to Jay Bosworth. In December 1973 there were photos of her and Steven Weed with brief stories announcing their engagement. Then, in January 1974, the feisty fortnightly *Bay Guardian,* a small-circulation publication which regularly sniped at the San Francisco establishment in general and the local establishment press in particular, there was a sharply critical article about her father's newspaper. It opened with a quote from Patty Hearst: "Dad, nobody under 80 reads the *Examiner* anymore. It has become irrelevant to the times."

Patricia Campbell Hearst was born February 20, 1954, in San Francisco's Mount Zion Hospital. Notice of her birth was not published in her father's newspaper until March 4, and then it was buried on page 23 along with all the other routine natal announcements. That alone said something about her father—and perhaps about the woman she was to become.

She was the child of inherited wealth and inherited fame. She was the third-born, middle daughter, of Randolph Apperson and Catherine Campbell Hearst's five girls.

But Patty's heritage of wealth and fame were third- and fourth-hand. The wealth came from her great-grandfather, old George Hearst. He was a Missouri farmer who preferred mining the earth of California and Nevada—gold and silver. He then invested his wealth to produce even greater bonanzas, in real estate.

The fame came from the only son of George and Phoebe Apperson Hearst. His name was William Randolph Hearst.

His wealth was fabulous, but it was not earned wealth. Willie, as he was known in his youth, was spoiled by his mother, indulged by his father. His father gave Willie his first newspaper (the then-faltering *San Francisco Examiner*) in 1887 when Willie was a rudderless young man of 24.

Willie Hearst—later and variously The Chief, WRH, "Imperial" Hearst—promptly began to earn his fame. Flamboyant, imaginative, heedless of cost, he invented a new form of journalism called "yellow journalism." He used his wealth, his undeniable talents and the talents of some of the most brilliant journalists of the time to build the biggest, most powerful newspaper and magazine empire in the nation. He used the empire to promote political causes,—at first liberal to radical, later conservative to reactionary. He used the empire to make or break politicians and movie stars, to muckrake giant corporate octopuses like Southern Pacific Railway, to crusade against vivisection of animals, to agitate for, and, some say, even start the Spanish-American War.

He used his wealth and his empire to cater to his every whim. And his whims were both trivial and grandiose. When he wanted fancy ice cream confections in the shape of Mickey Mouse for a party, he did not hesitate to call a city editor in the middle of the night and order him to drop everything to carry out the project. It was carried out. The staff of a San Francisco ice cream factory was roused from their beds, the goodies were created, and they were flown to his northern California retreat at Wyntoon the next morning. Damn the cost.

When his whim was to buy a monastery in Spain, he bought it, disassembled it and shipped it to San Francisco. When his whim was to live in a castle, he demanded construction of a 100-room architectural fantasy on the crest of a mountain overlooking the Pacific. Damn the cost. The cost was $20 million. Today the Hearst Castle at San Simeon is one of the California State Park system's most popular tourist attractions.

William Randolph Hearst, who died in 1951, was a quirky, romantic, ruthless, tenderhearted genius. He was admired as a great American patriot, execrated as a fascist, held in awe by admirerers and enemies alike. Even those who hated him were forced to admit that

William Randolph Hearst went his own way. In the phrase of his time, he was his own man. In current vernacular, he did his own thing.

II

Randolph Apperson Hearst, Patty's father, was quite a different sort. He was one of five sons of William Randolph and Millicent Willson Hearst. He and his fraternal twin David were born in New York on December 2, 1915.

He and David were only toddlers when their father separated permanently from their mother to live the rest of his life with movie star Marion Davies. The old man's love for Miss Davies was deep, abiding and never legitimitized because of his wife's steadfast refusal to divorce him.

Randolph and his twin were raised in the East, under the eye of their former showgirl mother. But, as with all the boys, their bond of affection for their father remained unbroken. They spent summers at San Simeon with their father, and at their grandmother Phoebe's in Pleasanton, near San Francisco.

Randy, as he was called from childhood, inherited little of his father's flamboyance and whimsicality, but he and his twin apparently were spirited kids.

When WRH, "Pop" to the boys, learned that the twins were not working as hard as they should at New York's "100 percent Christian" St. Bernard's School, he sent a telegram sharply upbraiding them. Then, in a letter to the boys' mother, he defended them.

"They have no particular bad habits, no evil tendencies," he wrote. "They are good boys. . .good thinking, well-behaved youngsters."

Randy and David were sent to different prep schools. Randy's was the conservative, strict Lawrenceville School in New Jersey. Lawrenceville's 1934 yearbook extolled Randy as a top-notch swimmer and a young man with a "cheerful smile and attractive personality."

At Harvard, Randy's career was brief. Like his father before him, according to gossipy historians, he was invited to leave Harvard. In Randy's case because he was discovered with a young woman in his room.

Soon afterward, the tall, handsome young man began his newspaper career at the Hearst-owned *Atlanta (Georgia) Georgian*. No one at the *Georgian* held the boss's son in awe. He was friendly, easygoing, frequently in need of a haircut and often out of pocket money. The staff called him Randy. But he was the boss's son, and he moved up quickly to assistant to the publisher.

It was in Atlanta that he met Catherine Campbell. She was the daughter of a telephone company executive, and she was a beauty with a soft, Southern voice, a debutante's respect for social convention, and deep devotion to the Roman Catholic Church.

Randy and Catherine were married in 1938, after he joined the Catholic Church. They were, and by all accounts, still are deeply in love. "He's quite a family man," said a long-time professional colleague. "No clowning around [with other women]. He's stayed close to the home fire."

By contrast his brothers (George and John are now dead) ran up a grand total of 13 marriages.

Randy, according to his older brother William Randolph Hearst Jr., was the smartest, coolest and most sedate of the Hearst boys.

Shortly before World War II, Randy, his wife and their first born daughter, Catherine, moved West permanently. Randy became the associate publisher of the *Oakland* (Calif.) *Post-Enquirer*. In 1942 he entered the Army Air Corps, ferried bombers overseas, wound up as a captain and flight instructor in Florida in 1945. He returned to the failing *Post-Enquirer* in 1946. The paper folded in 1950, leaving the Knowland-owned *Oakland Tribune* as the only daily newspaper in the city.

Randy moved across the Bay to become publisher of the doomed *San Francisco Call-Bulletin*. In 1966, seven years after its merger with the *San Francisco*

News, it vanished forever when it was re-merged into the *Examiner.*

He shifted through various top executive posts in the complex Hearst organization, but continued to live in the Bay Area. On February 23, 1973, he was named chairman of the executive committee of the board of the Hearst Corporation. He also was president of the *Examiner.* On June 5, 1973, a three-paragraph story in the newspaper announced that he had also assumed the title of editor of the *Examiner.* It was then a troubled newspaper; its staff demoralized, its circulation falling.

Randy was personally popular with the staff, at least those who knew him. Like staffers on the old, long since defunct *Georgian,* reporters, editors and copyboys alike called him Randy. He listened patiently to the endless gripes of reporters and editors. But if he moved to correct the paper's deficiencies or improve morale, the movement seemed glacial to the staff.

He was widely thought of as a dilettante who preferred to be with his family in Hillsborough, to golf, fish in Baja California, go duck hunting at his private club, ski in the Sierras.

A former top executive explained it this way: "He's very casual about most things. I'd have to say at the outset, in years past, the paper was a casual interest. I think his attitude changed when he nearly died of an ulcer. He was fishing in La Paz. He flew to Los Angles [to a hospital] in the nick of time. That was three or four years ago. After that, he became more serious, gave more time and attention to the paper."

One of the problems after the merger was a lack of youth and vigor on the staff—the old-timers had seniority and retained their jobs. "We listed them all," the former executive recalled, "and there were no kids in their twenties." There also were no minorities on the staff. The only black had been merged out of a job.

Randy threw his support behind a minority training program for young reporters, but it was not entirely successful. And, in the view of many, Randy remained out of the mainstream of the city room and was too slow to make decisions.

"He is low-key," said the onetime colleague. "And the last guy he talks to is the guy who wins the point. He never screams or rants. It is hard to see when he's angry. He listens to you intently and if you keep pressing, he says, 'Oh, screw it.' His political views have changed in the last five years to moderate to liberal. She [Catherine] is very conservative. He doesn't agree with Bill [William Randolph Hearst Jr.] He is definitely more liberal than Bill. I would say he is moderate to almost liberal."

III

If Randy was considered by many as too diffident, his wife was held to be of sterner stuff. Catherine Hearst, two years her husband's junior, once was described as "the iron magnolia." In middle age she was still a handsome and charming woman. She was, by all accounts, thoughtful and considerate of others. She also was deeply conservative politically and socially. She was, too, a devout Catholic, who often performed her devotions at St. Macrina Church, where the old-fashioned Byzantine rites were still used.

As a regent (member of the governing board) of the University of California, she carried on the Hearst family tradition of commitment to the state's premier educational institution. Appointed to the board by Republican Governor Goodwin J. Knight in 1956, she was aligned almost always with the more conservative regents. During the tumultous days of demonstrations, protests and sit-ins of the 1960s, Catherine Hearst was denounced by liberals and radicals alike as a reactionary. She became known as one of "Reagan's Raiders," the bloc which almost invariably supported the policies of California's hard-rock conservative Governor Ronald Reagan.

Apparently neither her husband nor, later, her daughter Patty entirely agreed with Catherine's positions as a regent. According to *San Francisco Chronicle* gossip columnist Herb Caen, Catherine had been "catching a little hell on the home front" for some widely reported remarks she made at a 1972 regents meeting. "She phoned newsman Ron Moscowitz . . . to say that Randy was angry . . . 'and [Randy] says the only time he wants to see my name in the paper again is in the obituary column.' "

She was a strong, independent woman. She was physically courageous as well. When an unknown gunman took a shot at her and narrowly missed, as she was being driven to a regents meeting in Los Angeles in June 1972, she was shaken. But she went on to take part in the meeting.

IV

This, then, was where Patricia Hearst came from. If her childhood was not entirely happy, neither was she ever in want for the material things of life, and love and warmth were there for her to accept. Friends, neighbors, servants and family agree that Patty always possessed a strong will and a quicksilver intelligence. She was sensitive, sometimes standoffish; she could be charming and she could be bratty. "Independent" and "unaffected" were the words most often used to describe her emotional set.

The 22-room white stucco, French provincial Hearst home in Hillsborough was a handsome, elegantly appointed place but by no means the most lavish or expensive in the fashionable Peninsula suburb. Its grounds were well kept, the swimming pool a fine place on hot summer days.

Dad was indulgent, quietly funny and generous. Patty got on well with her oldest sister, polio-crippled Catherine. She had her problems with the next oldest, Gina, and her younger sisters, Anne and Vicki. Mom was strict but loving. Patty shared her secrets with Emmy Brubach, the family cook, and Kathe Kellings, the housekeeper.

As a child, the church was important to Patty. As a teen-ager she defended the faith vehemently. In a letter to her then boyfriend, Stanley Dollar III, she wrote:

"I hate the way you always criticize the Church! Maybe you don't believe in god (capital "G" in some senses), but I do and things like your "Hail Mary" are uncalled for and really upset me. The Church can't be taxed, love, because it is a "non profit organization." Priests do earn salaries, all the money goes toward the upkeep of the building and its facilities and to the missions (i.e., there is no income to tax!) and you're jealous of that.

But church schools were another matter. Catherine Hearst decided that Patty would go to private, parochial schools appropriate to her class rather than public schools. At Santa Catalina School in Monterey, 100 miles south of Hillsborough, Patty was distinctly unhappy. She chafed under the tight discipline and petty chores imposed by the Dominican nuns. She earned a B average. After two years at Santa Catalina—there were rumors she was asked to leave and later reports, denied by friends, family and the school, that it was because she was caught smoking pot—she left the boarding school. She returned to Hillsborough and was enrolled in the small, exclusive Crystal Springs School.

There, at the age of 16, she first saw Steven Weed, the slender, good looking son of an upper-middle-class stockbroker from nearby Palo Alto. A recent Princeton graduate, a coolly intellectual philosopher, tall, blond, with a modish moustache. He was teaching math at Crystal Springs. To a teenage girl (not just Patty) he was a smooth item, and one of the few men on the campus. They knew each other casually, just to say hello. But Patty, among others at the all-girl school, apparently set her sights on him then.

She did well at Crystal Springs in everything except math. She got D's in math. She was not in Weed's class. In other subjects she earned A's and B's. She also involved herself in extracurricular activities—she sang in the chorus, took roles in several drama club productions. After school she worked now and again as a candy striper at Mills Hospital in Millbrae.

Always athletic and physically vigorous, she took part in ballet classes, rode horseback, swam, played tennis, went on long hikes with the outdoors club. She drove to and from school in an MG roadster, a birthday gift from her father.

Teachers and classmates, some of whom considered her snobbish or at least shy, thought of her as exceptionally mature for her years. She was "very superior" in terms of attitude and responsibility, according to Norma Fifer, academic dean at Crystal Springs.

Patty was graduated from Crystal Springs in 1971. In the fall she enrolled at Menlo College in Menlo Park, near Hillsborough. Steven Weed, still teaching at Crystal Springs, lived in a bachelor pad in Menlo Park.

Now she performed brilliantly—straight A's. She took an interest in photography and her work was displayed at school. And she became deeply involved with Steve Weed. She worked hard at school, relaxed with Weed. They fell in love.

Patty completed the academic year in June 1972, as the junior college's top scholar. She could take her pick of universities. Catherine Hearst's choice was Stanford University, close to home and traditionally California's most social school. Patty's choice was UC Berkeley. There was, according to Patty's friends, quite a battle between the strong-willed mother and her strong-willed daughter over their differing choices. It was less because Weed was studying for his Ph.D. at UC—although Catherine was never too happy about the romance—than because she felt Berkeley was too radical and dangerous.

Patty's determination won the day. After a summer touring Europe with a group of Menlo College art students (she was encouraged by both her family and Weed to make the trip), she returned ready to stage a small life-style rebellion. Steve Weed had already moved into the apartment on Benvenue. Patty moved in with him.

45

V

If there was any discord between the young lovers, they covered it over and kept it to themselves. They worked hard at UC, Steve preparing for his doctorate and teaching, Patty studying at first with the intention of going into biological sciences, later switching to art history when she found the going too tough in her old nemesis, math. They were rarely seen apart. At home in their apartment they were quiet, unpretentious and quite domestic.

"I met Steven when he first moved in over there, and she was abroad," neighbor Ruth Reagan recalled. "You couldn't think of anyone as nice as Patty, and as quiet, and as *everything*. . ."

She knew Patty and Steve were not married, but she had long since ceased to be shocked about matters like that. This was, after all, Berkeley, and this was a new generation. She also knew that her trim, neat young neighbor was a member of the Hearst publishing family, and that there was big money in her background. Patty herself, however, never mentioned her family connections or put on airs.

Mrs. Reagan remembered an anecdote: "The neighbor lady on the corner, Patty bought a fern from her. Mrs. Marion [the neighbor] said Patty asked how much money she wanted."

Mrs. Marion wanted five dollars. "And," Mrs. Reagan said with a smile, "Patty said it was a good thing she didn't want more than that because, 'I just have five dollars.' We both laughed about that the other day, Mrs. Marion and me, thinking of Patty's father with all the money he had, and she had only five dollars to pay for the fern."

Mrs. Reagan, although making no claim of intimacy with them, was genuinely fond of Patty and Steve. Patty once took the old lady's part in a neighborhood dispute over a dog's digging up the Reagan garden, even offered to go to court in her behalf if it came to that. She thought Patty was friendlier and more outgoing than Steve. "She was lovely," Mrs. Reagan said softly. "You never saw *them* living over there with a bunch of young people, making a bunch of noise. Or nothing. They were just themselves, and planting flowers and things like that. She had two cats. . .*they* never did come over in my yard."

Politically neither Patty nor Weed seemed to be a True Believer in any of the current causes. Those who knew them thought of them as loosely liberal. The conservative Hearst newspapers supported Nixon. Patty supported but did not campaign for McGovern. She did insist that Weed vote in the 1972 presidential election. Both cast ballots for the loser.

If there was tension between Patty and Steve it was over the strained relations with her family. According to Weed, Randy was not exactly pleased by the arrangement, but accepted it. Catherine was deeply disturbed. Gradually, though, they got used to the idea, and the slender young philosopher was drawn into the clannish family circle, especially after the engagement was announced on December 19, 1973.

Patty and Steven went skiing with her parents in the Sierras. Patty and her mother went on happy expeditions to shop for china. Patty told housekeeper Kathe Kellings she wanted a big wedding—not a church wedding, but perhaps a country club wedding.

Then, on a cold February night, Patty Hearst was torn out of her pleasant domestic world and thrust violently into a bizarre new experience that would change and distort forever her life and the lives of those who loved her.

CHAPTER FOUR

A NEW PLOT—A NEW PUZZLE

I

While the world agonized with Catherine and Randolph Hearst, awaiting some word of Patty's fate, another young woman about six years her senior, darker of hair and eyes and six inches shorter emerged to scramble the puzzle. Her legal name was Nancy Ling Perry. She preferred a more esoteric identification.

"My name was Nancy Ling Perry, but my true name is Fahizah. What that name means is one who is victorious," she wrote in a rambling letter she composed just 18 days before Patty was carried screaming from her apartment.

Nancy, a former cheerleader who had strayed into the Berkeley street life when she was about Patty's age, had taken some 3,800 words to explain an inexplicable, shadowy band of terrorists who fancied themselves as the Symbionese Liberation Army. Her meandering prose, in which she proclaimed herself part of its "information-intelligence unit," was an attempt to romanticize an organization she claimed was the military vanguard of an erupting revolution.

While radical movements and cells and actions had

been swirling out of Berkeley since the 1960s, the only thing anyone knew about this strange new organization was that three months before the kidnapping they had taken credit for the execution-style slaying of Oakland's black school superintendent, Marcus Foster. Within hours of Patty's disappearance, the FBI and the Oakland Police Department's intelligence unit began seeking a link between the SLA and her kidnap.

What Nancy dreamed of being victorious about was establishing a new social order, basing her goals on some special perceptions of life she said she had gained.

"I have discovered the truth about the military takeover and the police state dictatorship, not because I studied about it in college, but because I see it every day, and because truth is something that is honestly known, as easily as beauty is seen," she wrote.

Her truths spun out a bewildering splash of revolutionary rhetoric that only partially explained why she was now a fugitive, one of four people being sought in the Foster murder case. She had come so far from her beginnings her words glossed over the past.

She had grown up in Santa Rosa, a farm town in the midst of the wine country of northern Sonoma County just at the time it was feeling urban pressures from metropolitan San Francisco 58 miles to the south. A favored daughter of a well-to-do, but not wealthy furniture dealer, Hal Ling, she grew up in quiet, conservative family atmosphere. She had been a cheerleader in junior high school. By the time she reached Montgomery High School, she had moved into the more ladylike Girl's League.

"When I was in high school in 1963-64," she recalled in the polemic she entitled "Letter to the People," she said she "witnessed the first military coup against the people of this country. Here the coup was simply accomplished by assassinating the then President John Kennedy."

Nancy had been only 15 years old and apolitical when President Kennedy was murdered.

"The people I grew up around were so politically

49

naive that their conceptions of a military coup only recognized those that have occurred in South America and Africa."

Nancy's senior year was in 1964—the year Goldwater and Johnson held their raging debates over defoliation in Vietnam. A good conservative girl, she lent her smile and flashing legs to the Goldwater cause. She was fresh and decorative at a political rally.

"In 1964," she wrote in 1974, "I witnessed somewhat hidden beginnings of the military/corporate state in which we now live. And I heard my teachers and government-controlled media spread lies about what had happened. I saw the Civil Rights protests, the killings and the bombings of my black brothers and sisters and the conditioned reactions of extreme racism in school and home."

After high school graduation, Nancy followed the path of many other offspring of upper-middle-class parents. She entered Whittier College, the Southern California alma mater of President Nixon and many other conservative stalwarts. In her sophomore year, she transferred to a school closer to home—the University of California at Berkeley.

"When I questioned my teachers about how these occurrences related to the meaning of democracy and freedom that we were told existed to protect us all, the answer I got was that we were better off not knowing the truth about what was happening."

At Berkeley, she began studying English literature and had little to do with the political turmoil raging on campus, the turmoil movie actor Ronald Reagan was riding into the statehouse in Sacramento. She skipped school in 1967 to work at the California Department of Employment.

While working there, she met and fell in love with a lean, attractive young musician named Gilbert Scott Perry.

Perry was a pianist who also composed his own original works. He was also black. Their marriage in December 1967 shook the Ling household deeply, strained relations with Nancy, but did not sever them completely.

Almost compulsively explaining herself, Nancy attempted to outline "the evolution of my consciousness. Basically, I have three backgrounds: I have a work background, a love background and a prison background."

Love took only one sentence:

"What my love background taught me was a whole lot of what love is all about, and that the greater one's capacity for love is, the greater is one's longing for freedom."

Perry, who separated from his wife in February 1973, remembers her as a loving, humble person. Neighbors remembered other bits and pieces of her personality, some recalled "what incredible self-hatred she had." Others recalled her fling with dope and then as enthusiastically she dropped them all and went to health foods.

"What my work background taught me is that one of the things that every revolutionary does is to fight to get back the fruits of her or his own labor and the control of his or her own destiny."

This was the chief thread of her treatise—her revolutionary manifesto that tried to rationalize assassination of a popular black school official.

Foster had been killed in Oakland, just south of Berkeley outside school headquarters on Nov. 6, 1973 and his white assistant, Robert Blackburn, wounded. A SLA communiqué announced the slaying had been to halt a student identification tag program and the bringing of uniformed police on campus.

School board members who supported these proposals were warned they would be shot on sight. After the Oakland Board of Education dropped the two proposals formally, the execution was lifted in a document sent to area newspapers and radio stations entitled "Symbionese Liberation Army Western Regional Youth Unit Communiqué No. 2."

Foster, who had come to the troubled Oakland school system from Philadelphia, had been killed with

.38 caliber slugs laced with cyanide. The bullets were fired from ambush as he and his assistant, Blackburn, walked to their car outside district headquarters. Blackburn, who was hit by a dozen pellets from a shotgun, survived. His description of the assailants was as confused as other witnesses.

The executioners were variously described as teenagers and young men, or possibly as many as two women in a squad of three. Their complexions were thought to be brown, black or yellow. Until the letters arrived, there was troubled speculation the racial disputes in Oakland had reached a critical new stage. The SLA's swaggering rhetoric did little to ease this tension, making no sense to any responsible members of the political spectrum from conservative to radical.

The terrorists charged that Foster's crime had been that he had served on the the Philadelphia Crime Commission, that Blackburn had been a CIA man while working for the Peace Corps in East Africa and they had been trying to impose paramilitary measures in the schools.

Nancy's connection with this twisted logic was not to be uncovered for another three months after Foster's murder. The discovery was an accident.

II

Concord Police Sergeant David Duge's suspicions broke open the cover of the SLA.

Sergeant Duge was on patrol in an unmarked police car about 2:00 A.M. on Jan. 10, 1974 on the southern edge of Concord, a town east of Berkeley.

A red van had stirred his suspicions. He had never seen it in the neighborhood before, and it seemed to be cruising idly in circles around the residential neighborhood. Night-time patrols, which must always be on the lookout for burglars, keep close tabs on strange vehicles in quiet sections of town.

Duge put on his police cap, turned up his spotlight

and turned on the red flasher to halt the van. He first walked up to the driver's side of the van, a 1965 Dodge. When Duge asked if they were looking for someone, the passenger said they were looking for the DeVotos on Sutherland Court.

Duge's suspicions were further aroused, because the van had just passed the Sutherland Court intersection before he turned on his red signal. The driver's license listed his name as Robert James Scalise.

When Duge asked his dispatcher to check the vehicle and driver for any outstanding warrants, none were found. Neither could any DeVoto be found in the cross directory.

Upon returning to the van, Duge approached the passenger side and asked the other man to step out of the vehicle. The man did so without hesitation. As the man turned around to face the sergeant, a bulge was noticed at the man's waist. It looked like a gun and the man appeared to be swinging his arm back to draw.

Duge ducked behind the van and then ran behind his own patrol car before drawing his service revolver. The other man had not fired, but as Duge peered over the car, he said he saw two flashes of light and heard two shots fired in rapid succession.

As Duge returned the fire, the man ducked behind the van across in front of the driver, causing the sergeant to swing the gun that way as he squeezed the trigger. The man bent over and fled on foot as the van driver gunned the motor and sped away.

Duge had asked for a backup unit on his initial contact with his desk, but no help had arrived. The backup unit halted the red van a short distance away. The driver surrendered without any struggle. He was identified as Russell Little of Oakland and the driver's license discovered to have been obtained in the name of a boy who had died two years earlier.

The neighborhood was flooded with police units to search for the second man. As the minutes turned into hours and he was still not found, patrol units were posted at various points around the neighborhood. This had been done, because inside the red van had been found two more guns and a large packet of material headed "The Symbionese Liberation Army."

Officer Jim Alcorn's stakeout had been set up at Sutherland and Manchester Drives, a few blocks from the shootout. About 5:30 A.M., some three-and-a-half hours after the first shots were fired, Alcorn noticed a dog begin barking at one of the houses. When he investigated on foot, his gun in hand, a man stepped up from behind a car parked in the driveway where the dog was barking. The man held his hands in the air and tossed a revolver out in front of him.

The man was identified as Joseph Remiro, a 27-year-old Vietnam war veteran, who lived in Oakland. He had grown up in San Francisco, but after his discharge had become active in the Oakland chapter of the Vietnam Veterans Against the War.

Sergeant Duge spent the entire day completing all of his reports, rounding up all the loose ends and notifying the Oakland authorities, because of their interest in the Symbionese Liberation Army. Since he normally finished his shift at 7:00 A.M., he was exhausted by evening when a new alarm sounded from the same neighborhood.

Fire equipment was called to the 1500 block of Sutherland Court when neighbors saw black smoke emerging from 1560 Sutherland Court. Someone named George and Nancy DeVoto had lived there for some four months. The old directory the dispatcher had checked in the early morning hours had not shown them.

The fire was quickly extinguished, but what firemen found had brought a hurry-up call to bomb experts at the nearby naval station. Inside the house were a wide variety of explosive devices, dynamite and fire bombs that had to be carefully disarmed before any further work could be done.

Oakland police and Alameda County detectives were called to the scene early in the evening, because fireman reported seeing posters and books with the insignia of the Symbionese Liberation Army inside. But investigators were forced to cool their heels until about 3:00 A.M. while the bomb experts combed the debris to make sure none of the explosives had been over-looked.

Evidence found inside would take weeks to catalog. A device for drilling bullets, inserting cyanide and capping them with paraffin. Reams of documents from the SLA were strewn about the three-bedroom house.

Notebooks with names and numbers, some appearing to be the start of some code to match the names of Bayo, Faeza, Mwanga and others.

There was also a strange assortment of odds and ends. Combs and brushes like those used for the natural hair styles worn by blacks. A pair of pith helmets like those worn by the U.S. Postal Service employees in summer. A Berkeley library card made out to a Gary Atwood. Letters to a Nancy Ling Perry. A card in the name of William Lawton Wolfe. Several empty plum-wine bottles. A large collection of revolutionary literature that included Carlos Marighela's "Minimanual of the Urban Guerrilla" and others.

Tucked amongst the books and papers, there was a notebook that was to create terror for some Bay Area families. It contained a list of prominent citizens the SLA had marked as "kidnap and/or execution targets."

One was D.E. Stanberry of Oakland, a Colgate-Palmolive Co. executive, who was accused in the SLA documents of "murder, robbery and supporting and taking part in crimes against the people of Ireland, Brazil, Rhodesia and South Africa, the Philippines, Angola, Mozambique and Guinea-Bissau."

Charles W. Comer, head of a candy company that was a subsidiary of the ITT Corporation, was accused of crimes against "the people of Chile, Brazil, South Africa, Rhodesia, the Philippines and the American people."

The death warrants of both men announced they were "to serve notice on this corporation and its divisions, its subsidiaries and its executives that they have come to the attention of the SLA and the Court of the People, and have been found guilty of supporting the murder, oppression and robbery of the people of the world."

Although no public announcement of this list was made, the two men were warned. Stanberry moved his family from the area for several months as a precautionary measure.

III

The house at 1560 Sutherland Court had been rented by a woman who gave the name of Nancy DeVoto, who said her husband was an Army officer being transferred from the East to the Presidio at San Francisco. After Virginia Logan, the rental agent, showed the house, she paid $600 in cash, which included the first and last month's rent and $100 security deposit.

The description of Nancy DeVoto matched that of Nancy Ling Perry. The DeVoto name had been that of a Santa Rosa classmate, who was now married and living in Sonoma County.

Neighbors had seen her husband only once and never in uniform. He matched the description of Little and one neighbor later identified a photo of Little as being the man she had been introduced to as George DeVoto.

Neighbors had noticed no unusual activities at the home until November 7, some three days after the Foster slaying. They had called police when a young man angrily fired a shot in the air after arguing with Nancy at the front doorstep.

When police responded, a photographer for the local newspaper, who had been listening to the police radio, followed police cars. He took a picture of the lady of the house talking to police, telling officers she did not know who the strange-acting youth might be. The photo was identified later as being of Nancy Ling Perry.

The neighbor across the street told investigators she had called firemen quickly, because she had noticed a great deal of unusual activity at the house before smoke poured out of it. There seemed to be a lot of rushing around inside the house and the garage before a white Oldsmobile drove off in such a hurry it scraped bottom as it went from the driveway to the street.

The white Oldsmobile was found abandoned three miles away two days later. It was registered to William Lawton Wolfe.

IV

Remiro and Little were traced back by investigators after their arrest to what appeared to be a new branch of the prison movement. Both men had visited prison inmates regularly during the previous month. Visits to inmates were also traced through visitor registrations to both Nancy Ling Perry and William Wolfe, who usually signed his name, Willie.

Both of the men arrested in the van incident had been involved with a Maoist group that called itself "Venceremos."

At Vacaville Little and Wolfe had both attended meetings of a black culture and history study group approved by prison officials years earlier under the name of the Black Cultural Association. Some prison scuttlebutt suggested that radicals had taken over and most of the studies were of revolution. The name "Symbionese" had never been heard, investigators were told initially.

A link with the prison movement was also found with Nancy Ling Perry. Old friends and her parents said she was so dedicated to the prison movement she had given nearly all of her salary from Fruity Rudy's fruit juice stand to prison inmates.

She was a regular visitor with a Folsom inmate named Raymond Sparks. Sparks was a lifer from Los Angeles serving time for kidnaping, robbery and sex perversion. He was also believed to be a key figure in prison inmate radical organizing.

Until Nancy's letter arrived about a week after she

fled the Sutherland Court home, no one could confirm her reasons for this involvement. Her letter explained in revolutionary rhetoric.

My prison background means that I have close ties and feelings with our incarcerated brothers and sisters. What they have taught me is that if people on the outside do not understand the necessity of defending them through force of arms, then it is because these people on the outside do not yet realize that they are in immediate danger of being thrown into prison camps themselves, tortured, or shot down in the streets for expressing their beliefs.

Nancy also had some words for Remiro and Little.
"I would like to convey the word to my two captured compañeros: you have not been forgotten, and you will be defended because there has been no setback and all combat forces are intact."

She said that none of the people at the Sutherland Court home had been part of an SLA combat unit, nor were they offensively armed. Little and Remiro "are in a concentration camp now because none of us were offensively armed and because I was not aware that they were under attack."

Whether this note was meant to convey her power or merely an attempt to explain what happened to other units she could not contact directly, analysts were trying to discover.

V

The new name, Symbionese Liberation Army, had merely raised quizzical eyebrows after the Foster slaying. There had been so many "liberation" groups popping up since radicals began their shadowy activities a decade earlier that one more did not mean much. But Nancy's long, convoluted letter renewed inquiries.

Semanticists were asked its derivation. Experts in symbology were queried about the origin of the cobra's use in symbols—especially the seven-headed variety that appeared on the SLA material.

The key word in the title—Symbionese—sent researchers from biology to conservation to politics. Symbiosis was the root word. Since its primary application was to biology, some theorized a biologist might be the five-star general of the SLA. Conservationists had also adopted the word to describe what should happen in an ideal relationship between man and his environment.

Semanticist S.I. Hayakawa, an educator turned politician, was the first to trace the term to radical politics, noting that SLA communiqués referred again and again to "Black, Chicano, Asian and conscious White youth." He contended that using a symbiosis as the foundation for their grandiose title was based upon its dictionary definition, "the partnership of dissimilar groups for their mutual benefits."

The seven-headed cobra was just as tough to trace. First reports had linked it as a photocopy of a recording album cover of one of the late Jimi Hendrix's best sellers. An expert at UC thought the symbol might have originated in the Tantric mythology of India. An anthropologist said it had no meaning, dismissing it as an effort to create their own status through mythology of their own.

Origin of the SLA symbol was finally traced to a pseudo-scientist who was writing in the 1930s—Col. James Churchward, who recently was rediscovered by the young, when his books were reissued in paperback.

Originally a fish and game writer, Churchward spun a series of books around his version of the Garden of Eden. He called his land Mu and cited hieroglyphics, artifacts and folk tales to prove his theory that the land of Mu had been the foundation of all succeeding civilizations. He wrote that Mu was a lost continent in the South Pacific, midway between South America and Asia. His fanciful interpretations of others works, mostly established scientists, sold well to a young disenchanted generation eager to challenge old concepts and traditions.

The seven-headed serpent he called Naga, the symbol of the creator. The seven heads represented the seven commands of creation. He borrowed this name and symbol from real anthropologists who had explored the Khmer temple in Cambodia, Angkor Wat, where a group of glyphs has been translated:

"This temple is dedicated to Naga, the seven-headed serpent, who by his will created all things."

None of the researchers were able to establish, however, what dissimilar groups might be forming beneath this serpentine banner, nor precisely what philosophy lurked behind Nancy's romantic prose.

VI

Evidence taken in the van and at the Concord house January 10 slowly led to a wider field.

The van in which Little had been arrested was found to have a newer, hopped-up engine than originally installed in the 1965 Dodge model. Further investigation led to a 1969 Dodge van that had been stolen at gunpoint from a Berkeley man the previous October 12. The motor and transmission had been stripped from the newer van and its shell abandoned about a mile from the Sutherland Court home.

Donald Sullivan, owner of the 1969 van, identified the engine and other parts from the older van as having been from his. A man with a gun had walked up to Sullivan that evening as he returned from shopping.

The gunman said: "I'm in a hurry. Give me your keys."

The library card in Gary Atwood's name was traced to a former UC graduate student, who was located at the University of Indiana. He had been married to Angela de Angelis, but had separated from her the previous summer when she remained in the Bay Area. She had been living with former friends Emily and Bill Harris in Oakland.

Harris, it was noted, was a postman, who might have used the pith helmets.

Investigators arrived Jan. 28 at the Harrises' apartment, a neat fourplex at 434-41st Street, Oakland, just as the landlord was starting to comply with an unusual request from the Harrises. Mrs. Harris had called and asked him to sell their furnishings and send the money and personal belongings to her parents in Illinois. The Harris couple had been last seen at the apartment January 11.

Inside the apartment were signs that at least two women, Mrs. Atwood and Russ Little's ex-girlfriend, Robyn Steiner, had been staying there and were gone too.

The walls contained SLA posters and other revolutionary slogans. There were reference books on industrialists, news organizations and community leaders. There were revolutionary books and pamphlets, maps of various neighborhoods and notebooks.

Inside one of the notebooks, there was another list of SLA "targets" for kidnaping or execution. This list contained a dozen names, including one business executive who had died a year earlier. Warrants drawn by the self-styled Court of the People spelled out "crimes" similar to those charged against Stanberry and Comer.

Also found among the drawers and files was evidence that the Harrises had been regular visitors to prison inmates, some of whom Nancy Ling Perry had visited and others whom Remiro had visited.

The "dissimilar groups" appeared to be persons outside prison walls working with persons behind prison walls. But the "mutual benefits" being sought were not clear, because there seemed to be no benefit anyone inside prison could receive from Foster's death.

VII

There was another piece of evidence that remained hidden within the mass of books and pamphlets found in the two SLA homes. The scrawled notations would be overlooked for another week.

Inscribed in one of the notebooks was a telephone number to an apartment at 2603 Benvenue Avenue in Berkeley occupied by Steven Weed and Patty Hearst.

There were also some hastily scribbled words as if they had been written during a telephone conversation:

"At UC—daughter of Hearst."

"Junior. Art student."

"Patricia Campbell Hearst. On the night of the full moon of January 7."

Also noted were references to "action" and "teams" and the need to register some vans by February 1. The names of members of two teams were written in adjoining pages; "Yolanda and Camilla" and "David and Margarieta."

The importance of these notes was overlooked until after Patty was kidnaped.

As the hours grew into days of waiting for the kidnapers to announce their intentions, name their ransom or terms for Patty's release, the tension was squeezed tighter by the newly appointed U.S. Attorney General William Saxbe.

Saxbe, who had a reputation for spouting off without thinking, came fresh from a U.S. Department of Justice briefing to a press interview. He warned that there was reason to believe that the Symbionese Liberation Army was involved in Patty's kidnaping. He added that there was danger such terrorist activities could spread to the East Coast.

Saxbe made his statement in Washington, D.C. at about 10:00 A.M. EDT, about four hours before a message arrived at Berkeley radio station KPFA. The message contained more flamboyant prose from Nancy Ling Perry that left perfectly clear the political motivation behind Patty's kidnaping.

CHAPTER FIVE

SUBJECT: PRISONERS OF WAR

I

Paul Fischer, news director of radio station KPFA, was puzzled only an instant as the Mobil credit card slipped out of the envelope, the name "Randolph A. Hearst" rising through the plastic. He quickly pulled out the piece of paper with it.

It was headed "Symbionese Liberation Army Western Regional Adult Unit Communiqué No. 3" and was dated February 4, the date of Patty's kidnaping.

Subject: Prisoners of War.
Target: Patricia Campbell Hearst, daughter of Randolph A. Hearst, corporate enemy of the people.
Warrant Order: Arrest and protective custody; and if resistance execution.
Warrant issued by: The Court of the People.
On the afore stated date, combat elements of the United Federated Forces of the Symbionese Liberation Army armed with cyanide-loaded weapons served an arrest warrant upon Patricia Campbell Hearst.
It is the order of this court that the subject be ar-

rested by combat units and removed to a protective area of safety and only upon completion of this condition to notify Unit No. 4 to give communication of this action.

It is the directive of this court that during this action ONLY, no civilian elements to be harmed, if possible, and that warning shots be given.

However, if any citizens attempt to aid the authorities or interfere with the implementation of this order, they shall be executed immediately.

This court hereby notifies the public and directs all combat units in the future to shoot to kill any civilian who attempts to witness or interfere with any operation conducted by the people's forces against the fascist state.

Should any attempt be made by authorities to rescue the prisoner, or to arrest or harm any S.L.A. elements, the prisoner is to be executed.

The prisoner is be maintained in adequate physical and mental condition, and unharmed as long as these conditions are adhered to. Protective custody shall be composed of combat and medical units, to safeguard both prisoner and her health.

All communications from this court MUST be published in full in all newspapers and all other forms of the media. Failure to do so will endanger the safety of the prisoner.

Further communication will follow.

The communiqué was signed simply "S.L.A." with the slogan, "Death to the Fascist Insect That Preys Upon the Life of the People" typed in upper-case letters across the bottom.

Fischer immediately picked up his telephone and called the *San Francisco Examiner,* asking for Hearst's number. When the operator refused, but offered to connect him with the Hearst home in Hillsborough, Fischer hung up. He found the Hearst number for himself and notified Patty's father of what he had received in the mail.

Outside the Hearsts' two-story home a small army of newsmen had been encamped since Tuesday. Cars, vans and sound trucks were mixed with cameramen and reporters awaiting some word of the young heiress's fate.

After receiving word from Fischer, an announcement about the letter was sent out, but Hearst did not appear personally until the next day to make a statement.

"We'll do everything we can to get Patricia back. I hope they don't make demands that are impossible to meet," Hearst told reporters, towering above his wife and holding her hand.

Speculation had been growing that the SLA might want to exchange Patty for Little and Remiro, who were being held at San Quentin.

"Obviously that would be out of our hands," Hearst said. "If that happens, all we could do is try. That would have to be a decision by the governor and the attorney general, and that is not in our power.

"What bothers me a little is that if I were the target, they would kill me anytime they wanted to do it. The thing that really bothers me is that they took a 19-year-old girl and held her as hostage for something they think I may or may not have done.

"It's hard to interpret. The letter is well written, I think. It's probable, from the military wording, that some of them have been in the Vietnamese war or have been around military installations.

"I think they probably see themselves as a political group fighting injustice and some of the economic and social problems existing today. But I think it's self-defeating. I think they get whole communities in trouble."

Standing there in the glare of the television lights, his head bowed slightly, Hearst was the perfect picture of the embattled father trying to save his child. Catherine Hearst was dressed almost as if in mourning. She dabbed at her eyes with a handkerchief, but maintained her composure throughout. Both created strongly sympathetic images.

"I don't believe this is a group that is black oriented. It's probably Anglo-oriented, although I have no reason to know this. I just feel it," Hearst said, measuring his words slowly and carefully.

"I think minority groups today have a reason to be

65

frustrated. Education is not moving correctly, or as fast as it should move," he said, lifting his head briefly before bowing it again as if ruminating.

"Some of the programs that are supposed to aid people are being boondoggled to aid just a few.

"I think we have a lot of things wrong and I can understand people being tremendously frustrated and outraged."

Hearst looked up toward a television camera for the first time, a network camera that would be sending his image to millions of homes and undoubtedly the SLA hideout during the evening dinner hour.

"But I can't understand them taking it out on a young girl. I don't see that that does anything but discredit whatever legitimate cause they may have," he said calmly and reasonably.

The media battle was joined. It would reach an intensity usually reserved for international affairs and propaganda wars between nations.

Another new lead for news stories had already been handed out. An FBI artist had drawn his conception of the three who had carried Patty from her apartment.

One was a young black man in his early twenties who wore his hair in a closely cropped natural style, medium wide eyes, a broad nose and large, full lips. The other black man had a medium natural hair style, a thin moustache and a more triangular face with large eyes. The artist's drawing of the white woman showed blonde hair, medium Nordic features and a heart-shaped face, but the official description of her had said she had brown hair. One official dismissed the disparity as a flaw in the graphic process.

The drawings with a white woman between two black men seemed to argue with Hearst's analysis that the kidnapers were Anglo-oriented.

The SLA's one-page, typewritten communiqué No. 3 had ended simply:

"Further communication will follow."

Waiting for that communication became an excruciating pressure for Catherine and Randolph Hearst, their other four daughters, relatives and employees. The letter had been sent by mail from somewhere in Berkeley in an envelope with a return address in the affluent Piedmont section above Berkeley proper.

Investigators eliminated the possibility the people living there had was any connection and continued their work compiling lists of people who had been known to associate with the seven people they had linked to the SLA through evidence found in the Concord home and the Oakland apartment.

A list of some 25 people had been compiled, about a third of them from a radical group, Venceremos, that was formed in 1971 when factions of the college student-based Revolutionary Union split up over whether military or political action should come first in a revolution. The group began with a coalition of Stanford students and employees and Chicano youth from Redwood City, basing their revolutionary theories on the teachings of Mao Tse-tung. The links between SLA and Venceremos had been that some of the known SLA members had worked on the more controversial prison projects of Venceremos. Some of the members had lived at the same houses as well.

This work was feverishly and secretly carried out by an FBI task force of some 150 FBI officers, assisted by Alameda County and Oakland and Berkeley investigators. At the Hearst home, there were regular meetings between Randolph Hearst and FBI Special Agent in Charge Charles Bates. Little information was passed by Bates to ease the terrible pain of the family through the weekend.

Hearst's newspaper executives announced that none

of the *Examiner* reporters were to begin any investigation that might make the SLA nervous about reporters snooping around. He regularly called police agencies to see if there was any new information. He was told there was none.

Patty's fiancé Steven Weed was escorted to Hillsborough on Sunday, his head still bandaged, his eyes still swollen.

Steven told newsmen he hoped the lack of word did not mean Patty was no longer alive.

He assured the SLA he and Patty would take part in no trial to identify any of the kidnapers.

"I hope the leaders of the SLA believe that for the following reason—if we break our word or are forced to testify it would seriously jeopardize any future negotiations," he said.

The waiting continued through Monday with FBI Agent Bates the only hopeful one, predicting there would be a break soon.

III

Berkeley radio station KPFA's news director, Paul Fischer, received a bulky package in the mail on the morning of Tuesday February 12.

Inside the package was an eight-page letter, a declaration of war, a more elaborate diagram of the SLA's seven-headed cobra and a tape recording that held the message everyone wanted:

"Mom, Dad, I'm okay."

The voice was unmistakably Patty's but her message was sandwiched between two from black men who had a special message of a strange new plan they claimed would benefit "the people."

The words the first speaker used were as grandiose as Nancy's:

To those who would hear the hopes and future of our people that the voice of their guns express the

68

words of freedom: Greetings to the people, fellow comrades, brothers and sisters.

My name is Cinque, and to my comrades, I am know as Cin. I am a black man and representative of black people. I hold the rank of general field marshal in the United Federated Forces of the Symbionese Liberation Army.

Obviously reading a prepared statement, Cinque announced that Patty had been "arrested" for her parents' "crimes committed against we, the American people and the oppressed people of the world."

Before any negotiations would be considered for Patty's release, Cinque said the SLA would require "a good-faith gesture" in the form of food for the needy and unemployed. The letter accompanying the tape outlined in detail how the food was to be delivered.

Seventy dollars worth of food was to be distributed to anyone with welfare cards, social security pension cards, food stamp cards, disabled veteran cards, medical cards, parole or probation papers and jail or release slips. Top quality food was demanded. It was to be distributed Tuesdays, Thursday and Saturdays in the Mission District, Chinatown, Hunters Point and Fillmore sections of San Francisco, East and West Oakland, Richmond, East Palo Alto and Santa Rosa, all in the Bay Area, Delano in the San Joaquin Valley and the Watts, Compton and East Los Angeles areas of the Los Angeles basin.

Estimates of the cost of such a food program were set as high as $400 million, the highest ransom ever demanded for a private citizen in history.

The SLA launched its own media war challenge by demanding all of their documents be published in full by all newspapers and television. Television stations devoted special time for a reporter to read without emotion or inflection the eight pages of material. This included both their declaration of war and the goals of the SLA.

The SLA material smacked heavily of self-serving rhetoric calling for other radicals to join their cause. They had turned the establishment media into their recruiters, all of whom feared that to have refused would endanger Patty's life.

The SLA had appointed itself representative of many colors and creeds and had formed a federation of dissident groups. The SLA document stated that they "do now by the rights of our children and people and Force of Arms and with every drop of our blood, Declare Revolutionary War against the Fascist Capitalist Class and all their agents of murder, oppression and exploitation."

But it was Patty's words that caught everyone's heart. She spoke haltingly with an occasional sigh. Several stops and starts of the tape she explained were her own way of collecting her thoughts.

"I'm not being forced to say any of this. I think it's really important that you take their requests very seriously about not arresting any other SLA members and about following their good faith request to the letter," she said in the tone of a daughter patiently explaining to her parents about something they just would not accept or understand.

She said that she was being kept by a combat team armed with automatic weapons and was being attended by a medical team that had patched up her "few scrapes and stuff" suffered in the kidnaping.

"I just want to get out of here and see everyone again and be back with Steve," she said after a big sigh.

"These people aren't just a bunch of nuts. They've been perfectly honest with me, but they're perfectly willing to die for what they are doing," she said.

"The SLA has ideological ties with the IRA, the people's struggle in the Phillipines and the Socialist people in Puerto Rico in their struggle for independence, and they consider themselves to be soldiers who are fighting and aiding these people."

Her analysis of the SLA motives and goals showed she had empathy for them:

I am a prisoner of war and so are the two men in San Quentin. I am being treated in accordance with the Geneva Convention, one of the conditions being that I am not being tried for crimes which I'm not responsible for.

I am here because I am a member of a ruling-class family and I think you can begin to see the analogy. It's important that you understand that they know what they're doing and they understand what their actions mean; and that you realize that this is not considered by them to be just a simple kidnaping and that you don't treat it that way.

She closed her statement with an event in the news to show that she had been speaking on the previous Friday, February 8.

"Bye."

The second black man's voice was calm and intimate, addressing Hearst directly:

We wish to express to you and to the authorities and to the public that whatever happens to your daughter will be totally your responsibility and the responsibility of the authorities which you represent.

He suggested that there would be no telephone calls or regular communications "for security reasons and because of where we are at," adding that the good-faith gesture would have to be the first step toward hearing from them or Patty again.

The quality of the tape as played first by Fischer on KPFA and later repeated by other radio stations and television news programs made it impossible to determine immediately their surroundings at the time the tape was made. The delays in transmitting messages, sometimes four days, other times five made it seem they were in some remote area.

As Cinque signed off his message, he spoke in assured tones of a negotiator holding all the alternatives for himself.

"You can be sure and have our word, whatever that may be to you, that we will carry out our word to the letter, and," he paused for dramatic effect, emphasizing each word carefully, "we mean exactly what we say."

CHAPTER SIX

MILLIONS FOR FOOD

I

The kidnaping of Patricia Campbell Hearst was inspirational. It inspired hundreds of well-meaning amateur detectives, mystics, psychics and astrologers to offer instant solutions to the mystery. Astrology, especially, was very big in San Francisco at the time. Amateur and professional astrologers by the score phoned the *Examiner* and the *Chronicle* demanding the precise hour of Patty's birth (it was 4:30 P.M., February 20, 1954) so they could cast her horoscope and predict her fate. Psychics called begging for articles of Patty's clothing. They explained that they could "read" spiritual emanations from a blouse or pantyhose and determine where the kidnap victim was being held.

The kidnaping also inspired the less well-meaning—amateur and professional criminals. These Hearsts—they were rich and they were desperate, they'd be easy marks now. So went the reasoning.

The first ransom demand came from Washington, D.C., February 6, the day after news of the kidnaping broke.

Mary Sanchez, the blonde chief switchboard operator at the *Examiner*, took the call at 10:15 A.M. A man wanted to talk to Randy Hearst about something important. Mary, witty and quick thinking, tried to stall him long enough so tape recording equipment could be switched on. The caller got suspicious and hung up.

Fifteen minutes later he was back on the line. Again he got suspicious and hung up. At 10:45 A.M., a third call, and this time Mary switched him to the Hearst home in Hillsborough.

The San Francisco Police Department and the FBI, alerted after the first call, were tracing the call to Washington.

The caller took his time detailing his demands to the Hearsts, and he was specific in his instructions. The desired ransom was $100,000 in unmarked currency. It was to be placed in a suitcase and left in a taxicab which would be waiting behind the Giant Store, a market at 14th Avenue N.W., in Washington, at exactly 8:15 P.M.

FBI agents made the drop at the appointed hour. The suitcase was filled with blank paper cut to the specifications of U. S. currency. But no one showed up. There would be dozens of other fake ransoms and false leads in the case.

II

On the same day William Randolph Hearst III, Patty's first cousin, was giving up his bachelor apartment in the predominately black Fillmore district of San Francisco to move in temporarily at the Hearst home in Hillsborough. Like other members of the family living in the Bay Area, he had been put under police guard within an hour after the kidnaping. Now it had been decided all of the Hearsts should gather at Randy's place. They could provide mutual support and security arrangements would be simpler.

Like his grandfather at the same age (24), he was called Willie. He had been working at the *Examiner* since September 1972, first as a photographer, now as editor of the newspaper's Op Ed (opposite editorial) page. Although unschooled in journalism (he was a Harvard graduate in mathematics), Willie was bright, eager to learn and a quick study. Many *Examiner* staffers felt he was the last, brightest hope of the paper.

Willie was as mystified as anyone else by the kidnaping of his cousin, whom he liked and admired as a warm human being of exceptional intelligence. He saw Patty as "somebody with a very good sense of humor, and *bright*. . .people will say maybe she's stubborn or something like that, but I never really saw that side of her. I just saw somebody who had a lot to offer anybody."

He also liked the cop who had been assigned to protect him since the kidnaping, San Francisco Police Inspector Robert Martin. Now Martin was driving him to Hillsborough, and en route they talked about the kidnaping. Willie had done little else since the abduction.

"I remember this friend of mine, at the beginning, when he heard the cops talking the very first night about the possibility of its being political," Willie said. "He kind of scoffed and said, 'Jesus, everything's political, the Communist under the bed.' And that was kind of the way I felt, a little bit."

On the other hand, he had not ruled out political kidnaping. "I knew that we [the Hearsts] were targets in lots of way," he said. "I didn't think that we, specifically, Patty and I and the other cousins, were targets but that the Hearst family's reputation would set up some targets."

Martin, though, was certain that politics was at the heart of the kidnaping plot.

Willie was impressed by Martin's positiveness. "He told me three things," young Hearst recounted. "Before we knew anything, he said, 'The people who kidnaped her are the SLA, the same people who shot Marcus Foster.' He said, 'They will not call you on the phone; they will release something to the media; and they will ask, as ransom, for the release of Remiro and Little.' "

75

III

Martin was remarkably prescient. The SLA's first message about the kidnaping, "Communiqué No. 3," saying Patty was a prisoner of war, was delivered the day after Martin made his prediction to Willie. The SLA's first demand, along with a tape recording of Patricia's voice, was delivered February 12. Both were released through the media.

The demand for $70 worth of food for every needy person in California was stunning. Director David B. Swoop of the California State Department of Social Welfare at first said the cost of such a plan was "possibly incalculable," then guessed $133 million, and finally $400 million. That amount would cover the annual budget of the State of New Hampshire with some left over.

The size of the demand was unprecedented. The greatest previous demand in history was the Spanish Conquistador Francisco Pizarro in 1532. Pizarro captured King Atahualpa of the Incas, in what is now Peru. He decided the captive king was worth half the Inca nation's hoard of gold and silver. He got it: the equivalent of $170 million in current U.S. dollars. Burdened by loot but not by moral niceties, Pizarro then murdered Atahualpa.

The free food demand was not unprecedented. The People's Revolutionary Army, a Marxist guerrilla band in Argentina, commonly demanded "donations" of food, clothing, medicines to the poor in return for the relief of kidnaped American business executives.

The record ransom was paid by Esso Argentina, a subsidiary of Exxon Corporation, which put up $14.2 million for the freedom of 37-year-old Victor E. Samuelson, an American executive of the firm. Samuelson was kidnaped by the People's Revolutionary Army at a restaurant in the company's refinery at Campana, 60 miles north of Buenos Aires, on December 6, 1973.

The ransom was paid March 13, 1974. Samuelson was freed in Buenos Aires April 29.

The free food demand was unique in the United States—and the $400 million figure extrapolated from it was mind-boggling. And the free food plan was not the ransom itself, but merely the first step toward the release of Patty Hearst.

In his tape-recorded "Greetings to the people, fellow comrades, brothers and sisters" which accompanied the demand message, "General Field Marshal Cinque" delivered a verbal creed in which the United States was denounced as an "oppressive military dictatorship of the militarily armed corporate state." Randy Hearst was "the corporate chairman of the fascist media empire of the ultraright Hearst Corporation." Catherine Hearst, as a University of California regent, also was guilty of crimes against the people. "The UC Board of Regents, one of California's largest investors, supports through its investments the murder of thousands of Black men and women and children in Mozambique, Angola and Rhodesia. . ."

He went on: "For these acts and others, the court of the people finds the Hearst family accountable for their crimes and hold that they are enemies of the people."

And, in solemn quasi-judicial language and tone, he told Randy Hearst:

It is therefore the directive of this court that before any forms of negotiations for the release of the subject prisoner [Patty] be initiated, that an action of good faith be shown on the part of the Hearst family to allow the court and the oppressed people of this world and this nation to ascertain as to the real interests and cooperative attitude of the Hearst family and in so doing, show some form of repentence for the murder and suffering they have aided and profited from; and this good faith gesture is to be in the form of a token gesture to the oppressed people that aid the corporate state in robbing and removing their rights to freedom and liberty.

77

Then, on a personal and ominous note, Cinque told Randy Hearst:

Speaking as a father, I am quite willing to lose both my children if by that action I could save thousands of white, black, yellow and red children from a life of suffering, exploitation and murder, and I am therefore quite willing to carry out the execution of your daughter to save the life of starving men, women and children of every race; and I, along with the loyal men and women of many races who love the people, am quite willing to give our lives to free the people at any cost.

He concluded with words that would in part be a self-fulfilling prophecy:

And if, as you and others might so easily believe, that we will lose, let it be known that even in death we will win, for the very ashes of this fascist nation will mark our very grave." (Authors' italics).

IV

Randy Hearst was a wealthy man, his family a wealthy family, the Hearst Corporation a wealthy firm. But the SLA, which seemed to have a grandiose idea of itself and its mission, also had a grandiose idea of the riches of the Hearsts and the Hearst Corporation.

None of the Hearsts was in the same league with the Gettys, the Mellons, the Rockefellers or even the Kennedys. The name Hearst did not even appear in Ferdinand Lundberg's bulky best-selling exposé *The Rich and the Super-Rich.* (As is clearly evident from his book, Lundberg had no love for the rich or the super-rich. As is clearly evident from an earlier book, *Imperial Hearst,* published in 1936, Lundberg also had no love for the Hearsts or the Hearst empire.)

V

Old George Hearst was the founder of the family fortune. Genealogists have traced the family name to the Middle Ages in the Lowlands of Scotland, where it was originally spelled Hyrst, and later became Hurst. John Hurst emigrated to the colonies in 1608. By early in the next century, the name was fixed as Hearst.

George was born in 1820 in Franklin County, Missouri, the son of William G. and Elizabeth Collins Hearst. Their only other offspring, a daughter, died unmarried. When George's father died in 1846, he left his son with three small mortgaged farms, four slaves, a country store and several thousand dollars in debts. But George was interested not in farming or storekeeping, but in mining. At the time of his father's death, he owned a share in a Missouri lead mine. Indians in the neighborhood had their own name for George: "Boy That Earth Talked To."

On December 12, 1850, he joined the gold rush to California. George was not an educated man, but he was smart and he had taught himself a good deal about geology. He did not, however, strike it rich right away. It took him nearly nine years.

In 1859, George's geological expertise—and luck—paid off handsomely. Alvah Gould sold George Hearst his share in a mine near Virginia City, Nevada for $450. Gould felt pretty good about the deal—he figured he'd slickered George, because mining experts had said the mine was worthless. It *was* worthless—as a gold mine. But the blue-black stuff that got in the way of the gold seekers contained silver. The mine was part of the fabulously rich Comstock Lode, the richest silver deposit ever discovered.

George and his partners also bought a one-sixth interest in the Ophir Mine, the richest in the whole lode. That summer they mined 45 tons of silver-bearing ore—and it was worth $2,200 a ton.

The crafty Gould, who slickered George out of $450, literally wound up with peanuts—peddling goobers in a concession stand. George wound up a multimillionaire and a U. S. Senator.

Later George and his partners bought into the Homestake gold mine in South Dakota for $80,000, obtaining complete control within a year. Eventually he drew $4 million a year from Homestake. The Anaconda in Montana, then the world's richest copper deposit, came next. George owned 30 shares, the largest block. And he began buying enormous reaches of land, including the 48,000 acre Piedra Blanca ranch in California extending from San Simeon on the Pacific to the Santa Lucia mountains. The price was about 60 cents an acre.

George Hearst, a lifelong Democrat, was appointed to the United States Senate in 1886 to fill the vacancy created by the death of Senator John F. Miller. He was elected to the seat by the State Legislature the following year. In the same year, at the urging of his wife Phoebe (George called her "Puss") and their only son, the senator gave the struggling, second-rate *San Francisco Examiner* to Willie Hearst. George had acquired the newspaper seven years before in payment for a bad debt.

The senator was not above using his political position to advance his own interest—and his interest was primarily in land.

One Hearst chronicler wrote that the senator, as a member of the Indian Affairs Committee, learned before anyone else that the Apache Chief Geronimo had been captured by the U. S. Cavalry. The senator used the tip to buy up 200,000 acres of land in the chief's former domain in Northern Mexico for 20 cents an acre. Eventually, this parcel became part of the million-acre Babicroa Ranch.

But for his time, the earthy, rude, whiskey-drinking, poker-playing, acquisitive and exceptionally lucky George Hearst was generally considered honest and a decent sort.

Senator Hearst died in Washington, D. C., on February 28, 1891. There had been talk that he was worth $40 million, but he left an estate of only $18 million—and all of it went to his 48-year-old widow.

But young Willie had a way with his mother. He convinced her he needed another newspaper—the *New York Morning Journal*—and Phoebe sold the seven-sixteenth Hearst interest in the Anaconda Mine to finance the purchase, and other projects.

Phoebe, prim, cultured, sensitive and compulsively generous, a former schoolteacher, was not strapped by staking her son's enterprises. By 1900 Homestake was paying out $6 million a year. When she died in 1919—after having given away $21 million, much of it for education, and the largest share to the University of California—she left an estate of $11 million. Nearly all of it went to her son.

The life, times and spending habits of William Randolph Hearst are too well known to recount here. He made and spent money with greater flair than any one of his time. In 1935 *Fortune* magazine listed his assets as 28 newspapers, 13 magazines, 8 radio stations, 2 movie companies, $41 million in New York real estate, 14,000 shares of Homestake and two million acres of land in California and Mexico. *Fortune* estimated their combined worth at $220 million.

Other observers, however, called the *Fortune* article a piece of puffery to inflate the value of Hearst preferred stock. And it is known that the empire was at such a low point during the 1930's that WRH was forced to borrow $1 million from Marion Davies, the great love of his life.

William Randolph Hearst died at 9:50 A.M. August 14, 1951, in the bedroom of the house he shared with Marion Davies at 1007 North Beverly Drive, Beverly Hills. He was 88 years old. Miss Davies was immediately placed in limbo by the Hearst family and the Hearst empire. Delivery of the two local Hearst papers, the *Los Angeles Examiner* and the *Herald-Express*, was cut off the day after his death. She did not attend the funeral in San Francisco's soaring Grace Episcopal Cathedral. Millicent Hearst, estranged from her husband for decades, did. His body was committed to the enormous Hearst Mausoleum in Cypress Lawn at Colma, just outside the San Francisco city limits.

William Randolph Hearst's obituary in *The New York Times* ran to more than 20,000 words. His will ran to 125 pages.

He left a personal estate of $59.5 million. His will set up three trusts—$6 million in Hearst Corporation preferred stock for Mrs. Hearst; 100 shares of Hearst Corporation voting stock for each of the five Hearst sons, plus preferred stock to give each a minimum annual income of $150,000; and a residuary trust for charitable and educational purposes, which later was established as the William Randolph Hearst Foundation. The estate was not settled until nearly six years later.

The Hearst Foundation got the bulk of the estate—$43.7 million. The remainder went to Mrs. Hearst and the sons.

VI

The Hearst empire, much reduced in size at the time of The Chief's death (down from a peak of 31 newspapers to 18) was even more diminished by 1974—only nine newspapers remained. But the empire was still powerful and rich, and most of the newspapers and other enterprises that had been sold, merged or eliminated had been chronic money losers. In 1968, *Forbes* magazine predicted that the Hearst empire's assets would soon approach $1 billion and commented: "The major problem the [Hearst] corporation faces is what to do with its embarrassment of riches."

Exactly what Randy Hearst's share of this embarassment was at the time of the SLA's free food demand was not known, possibly not even by Randy himself. He had a large block of Hearst Corp. shares plus other investments and his salary as president and editor of the *Examiner* was in the neighborhood of $100,000 a year. Once Patty Hearst, in an uncharacteristic mood of family assessment, asked Steven Weed how much he thought her family was worth. He guessed between $10 million and $20 million. He said he learned later that his estimate was grossly above the mark.

"I had some idea of what his [Randy's] finances were," Willie said, "because I had some idea what my own father's [William Randolph Hearst Jr.] finances were. And I knew that he did not have $10 million, that he probably did not even have $5 million. [I knew] that he could easily have $1 million or less, and it wouldn't surprise me."

Randy Hearst *was* wealthy. But even billionaire J. Paul Getty, reputedly the richest man in the world, had trouble (or at least qualms about) coming up with $2.7 million ransom demand for his grandson in 1973. Clearly the $400 million "good-faith" gesture demanded by the SLA was beyond the means of a mere millionaire, even if his name was Hearst.

CHAPTER SEVEN

THE PEOPLE SPEAK

Sympathetic telegrams and letters and public pronouncements streamed into Hillsborough, expressing compassion for the Hearsts and Patty. The astronomical ransom demand of the Symbionese Liberation Army stirred emotions all over the world.

"I want to give you a dollar to help the poor people," second-grader Tracey Tozer of Edmonton, Alberta, Canada, wrote in a three-page, hand-printed note. "I will say a prayer for you every night until you come home to your own house and family and I hope you feel good again."

Donations came from the elderly and disabled veterans, too, all with declarations they would not accept aid obtained through extortion. A petition drive among welfare recipients announced they would not take the food either. Some sent money orders for $70, the amount specified by the SLA to be given the poor. There appeared to be a spontaneous rejection in store for any food handout that might be organized.

Another swift rejection came from radical groups and leaders who formerly had endorsed virtually any type of protest. The critics ranged from radical celebrity Jane Fonda to leaders of the Black Panthers.

"It's antirevolutionary. It sounds as if the self-styled revolutionary Symbionese Liberation Army is an arm of the most right-wing forces in this country," said David Dubois, Black Panther newspaper editor.

"The New Left does not kidnap. In fact, I have never heard the issue discussed. I don't agree that it is a useful tactic," said Miss Fonda.

Communist spokesmen of all degrees were sharply critical, calling SLA "pompous ultraleftists" whose "absurd action will not advance the antiimperialist struggle in America."

Dan Siegel, whom investigators had suspected of being linked with suspected SLA members, wrote in the national socialist newspaper, *The Guardian*:

"The SLA kidnaping is clearly giving the government and the monopoly press an opportunity to drive a wedge between the left and the people's movement."

Former Stanford English professor H. Bruce Franklin, whose defunct Maoist organization Venceremos, had been likewise connected by investigators to SLA, shaped his criticism with a word play on the SLA slogan:

"They are insects feeding on the life of the revolution."

Franklin also detected an alliance with the right by SLA, calling them a mixture of "crazies and agent provocateurs."

A barrage of SLA criticism came from former Franklin followers in press conference pronouncements, articles in the alternate press and letters to establishment media. Most troublesome of all SLA activities for these and other critics had been the slaying of Foster, a black administrator who had not been considered an enemy.

Only a communiqué from Bernardine Dohrn, long sought by authorities as a leader of the Weather Underground responsible for violent activities, could bridge this contradiction, suggesting that the Foster affair should not prevent other radicals from addressing the basic questions raised by SLA. She wrote:

> Committed political workers will be criticizing and discussing the Hearst kidnapping for a long time, but we must acknowledge that this audacious intervention has carried forward the basic public questions and starkly dramatized what many have come to understand through their own experience: It will be necessary to organize and destroy this racist and cruel system.

A group of revolutionaries, who announced they had separated from SLA after the Foster affair, were less charitable.

"It quickly became apparent to us that the Symbionese Federation was not fundamentally opposed to the errors of the New Left we had known, but was rather the culmination of all its defects. The process of the organization was totally top-down. The War Council made decisions in secret and the members were expected to obey orders without question, just as in a capitalist army," they wrote in an unsigned letter.

The general public was barraged in the media with an endless spectacle of revolutionary debate usually carried on by radicals in their endless talk-criticism fests or their house newspapers.

Although both the SLA and U.S. Attorney General William Saxbe had suggested there was an international conspiracy or at least a link with the new terrorists, speedy repudiations were issued from overseas.

SLA had claimed ties with the rebels in Northern Ireland, and movements in Puerto Rico and the Philippines. Spokesmen for each of these groups one by one denounced the kidnaping and denied any connection whatsoever with SLA.

Saxbe was forced to soften his alarms. Following the SLA analysis, he rattled more than sabers with tough talk about officers being derelict in their duty, if they did not immediately storm any SLA hideout they found. He drew bitter response from Hearst and some snide remarks from FBI officials before retreating the earlier FBI pronouncement that "we only have Patty's safety at stake."

Behind the scenes in law enforcement circles, however, there was growing tough talk. Only summary action was seen as the way to head off spreading use of kidnaping as a terrorist weapon in the United States. More and more officers in squadroom debates talked about the necessity for wiping out all the people connected with SLA when and if they were found. Police officials in key cities soon echoed their staffs' sentiments.

Intelligence officers and political analysts alike were tracing the parallels between the Symbionese Liberation Army and South American terrorists like the Uruguayan Tupamaros. Rumors were repeated that *State of Siege,* a motion picture patterned after the Tupamaros kidnaping of U.S. police official Dan Mitrione, had been required viewing for domestic revolutionaries. Newspaper and television editors quickly sought and published any feature that provided background on political terrorist activities from South America, the Middle East, Asia and Europe.

Analysts in the alternate press and radio were pursuing a different angle, one that had been growing more popular for the months since FBI offices were burglarized in Media, Pennsylvania. Memos from J. Edgar Hoover to FBI special agents starting in 1968 were found discussing a supersecret counterintelligence program to disrupt the New Left. This was being traced as the source for many of the more violent disruptions. Police agents were being blamed for much of the destruction and lawlessness.

Activist work-study groups that had been operating in enclaves all over the country rushed forward with evidence that the SLA must be part of a plot by the military and intelligence community to take over control of the country. Even Watergate's quasi-link to the CIA was cited to support their theories.

While readers and listeners were bombarded with

this vast guesswork, a major part of the puzzle remained untouched. The establishment editors were busy with their ethnic heroes, quoting Coretta King and Cesar Chavez on the one hand while the alternate press headlined the United Prisoners Union's Popeye Jackson.

The poor and hungry being courted by the SLA in their unique ransom demand were passed over or thought to be represented in the outraged letters being published daily. No one probed beneath the estimates of 4.5 million to 5.5 million said to be eligible for food under the SLA guidelines. If they had, it might have indicated that one-fourth of California's population did not have enough to eat. No one asked.

The SLA food demand had come at a key time—in February, when black and brown breadwinners are hit hardest by unemployment. Although the state unemployment rate was not far above the national average, it was as high as 25 and 30 percent in the ghetto areas designated for food handouts by the SLA. Seasonal slumps in service industries in the cities and agricultural jobs in the farm areas placed a lot of families on welfare during February.

State bureaucrats had already added to the problem, announcing a cutoff of food stamps to the elderly, blind and disabled just as inflation hit an all-time high. A demonstration called to protest this was canceled suddenly because its sponsors feared they would be tarred with the SLA brush in the public mind.

Almost overlooked was a statement by a black minister, Rev. G.L. Bedford of the Macedonia Baptist Church in San Francisco:

> I do not believe that Patricia Hearst was kidnapped with the intention of being harmed or for any personal gain on the part of her captors. But I pray it was for the purpose of getting together the heads of our country to take a good look at the many prevailing crises of our times.

Criticizing the undue emphasis on military and space programs, Rev. Bedford declared his hope that the tragedy of the kidnaping would cause a critical reappraisal of job priorities so that poor people could gain jobs to support themselves.

Most attention was being paid to a rediscovery of the ethnic diversity of the Bay Area, using image-conscious spokesmen like Rev. Cecil Williams.

Rev. Williams, whose flair for showmanship had attracted frequent television coverage of his Glide Memorial United Methodist Church services had been one of several groups named by SLA to monitor the food handout. No stranger to controversy, he had set himself up as Angela Davis's spiritual adviser during her lengthy trial two years earlier.

Rev. Williams called a press conference to announce he and the other five groups would be happy to help free Patty.

"We are concerned about the life of Patricia Hearst as we are about all human life. We are concerned about avoiding bloodshed in the case of both Patricia Hearst and the members of the SLA. Therefore, we are willing to appoint representatives from our organizations to serve as a liason between the Hearst family and the SLA," he announced.

His statement was joined by the American Indian Movement, whose leaders were about to go to trial for the Wounded Knee affair; Black Teachers Caucus; National Welfare Rights Organization, United Prisoners Union and Nairobi College, a young black college in East Palo Alto.

Their joint statement contained several references to the plight of their constituencies, but their meaning was lost in what had become a rhetoric of radical protest.

It is unfortunate that the needs and problems of the people—hunger, racism, unemployment, sexism, ill health, inadequate housing, injustice in our courts and prisons, the uneven distribution of wealth and other inequities which are really a reality, receive public attention only when critical situations like this arise. Unfortunately society does not look at the real problems of the people until confrontation occurs.

The coalition's statement, seemingly framed merely to please all of its political elements was soon swept aside in the rush of public and private emotion. Nearly everyone had a theory. Many had a solution, if only they could talk to Randolph Hearst about it. Others went to people they knew in the Hearst organization.

Mickey Cohen, a Southern California gangster now crippled and elderly, called Ed Montgomery, the *Examiner*'s Pulitzer Prize winner, who had worked with Cohen on some stories.

"Hey, Ed, I hear they got the boss's daughter. You want I should send up a couple of boys to help?" Cohen asked.

"No, Mickey, thanks anyway," said Montgomery, who had just returned from a fruitless three-day stake-out of a suspected SLA hideout.

"Who are they? They want money or something?" Cohen persisted.

"No, Mickey. This thing is political."

"Political? Some guy running for office? It's a funny way to run for office, kidnapin' the boss's daughter."

"No, this is a different kind of politics, Mickey."

"Well, if you need any muscle, just let me know," said Cohen.

Other people were more public about their attempts to help Patty.

A Salinas physician announced he would give up his $40,000-a-year medical practice and treat poverty-stricken people without a fee if the SLA would free Patty.

Russell Little's father, a labor relations specialist, told reporters as he boarded a plane in Florida bound for California that he wanted to offer himself as a substitute hostage.

Patty's father had seriously considered the same idea for some time, discussing it privately with a few people before deciding he might be misunderstood as trying to make a grandstand play.

CHAPTER EIGHT

OPENING THE PRISON DOORS

I

The tantalizing sounds on the tape recordings of Patty and Cinque had sent investigators scurrying in several directions. Sound specialists sought location clues with complex electronic instruments that dissected every pulse and tone. A trail already begun in the Foster case and reinforced by the artist's drawings of the kidnap suspects drew another team to interview prisoners, correctional officers and aides at Vacaville and Soledad. They sought the identity of Cinque.

The name was not new for prison authorities familiar with folklore of radical prisoners. Ruchell MaGee, the only convict to survive the August 7, 1970 shootout at Marin County courthouse when Jonathan Jackson tried to free his brother George, had taken the name early in his court fight. The radical National Lawyers Guild had published a history of the original Cinque in its newspaper, which often found its way into prisons.

The first Cinque was also a black man entangled in white men's laws. He had had the good fortune to have a former U.S. president, John Quincy Adams, as his defender. He had been charged with murder for leading a slave revolt aboard the *Amistad*, in which the captain and cook were killed in 1839. Bound from Havana to Port Principe's marketplace where Caribbean and U.S. bans against slave trade could not be enforced, the slave ship became lost in a storm, creating havoc on board.

Singbe, a young Mendi tribesman, led a revolt on the ship as the food ran out. They killed the captain, keeping the two owners of the ship to sail them back to Africa. Rather than sailing south and east, the whites ran a zigzag course that ended off Long Island in August 1839 where a Navy vessel placed the blacks under arrest. Former president Adams took the case, winning their freedom in an eight and one-half hour argument before the U.S. Supreme Court based on the theory that the blacks were free men and like all free men could employ whatever force was necessary to retain their freedom.

Singbe, whose African dialect was difficult for New Englanders to master, was renamed Joseph Cinque (and prounced sin-KAY), had his portrait painted by Nathaniel Jocelyn and was immortalized by the poet John Greenleaf Whittier before being returned to Sierra Leone in West Africa.

MaGee's adoption of the name of Cinque had been on the theory that his actions at the Marin County courthouse had resulted because he had been wrongfully "enslaved" at a Los Angeles trial that had originally sent him to prison by mistake.

When the Patty and Cinque tape was played, investigators knew immediately their earlier efforts had been in the right directions. The man's pronunucuation, "Sin-CUE", fit their theories that the entire affair was a new development in the alliance between ex-college radicals and prison inmates—an obscure historical figure like Cinque fed into the process by a student and spoken by a self-educated man, most likely.

In the FBI's electronic lab in Washington, D.C., the experts were having indifferent success with the tapes. They were able to establish that Patty and Cinque had recorded their first messages in separate locations. Cinque's were made in an urban setting. Patty seemed to have been in a rural or suburban area surrounded by foliage.

One tape from Cinque carried a telltale electronic hum, which experts said could come only from a computer made especially for station controls of the Bay Area Rapid Transit District (BART), the sophisticated new space-age commuter railway. This computer hum showed that Cinque was holed up somewhere within less than a mile of a BART station. But there were 32 BART stations, and they were located on both sides of the bay.

One of the tapes made by Patty had sounds of bird songs and wind rustling the leaves of trees. The birds were identified as being of a freshwater, inland variety. They decided she must be imprisoned in a wooded area not normally visited by sea birds. This could fit a wide area from the Oakland-Berkeley hills, bucolic Marin county, some pockets of San Francisco and even Patty's suburban hometown of Hillsborough on the peninsula.

Since lab work could not pin down precise locations, there was always hope a location might have been mentioned to some of the SLA's friends in prison. Interview teams were dispatched to Vacaville, Soledad and Folsom where some of the SLA suspects had visited regularly. Informants had already said five militant inmates had been top organizers of the SLA.

Three of the prisoners were still locked up. Clifford "Death Row Jeff" Jefferson was still at Folsom. Ray Sparks, a kidnap-rapist from Los Angeles, was said to be the SLA Chief of Staff. James "Doc" Holiday, a lifer from Los Angeles who headed the Black Guerrilla Family, was also on the select committee.

The other two prisoners named by informers had escaped the previous year from minimum security facilities. Both had been suspected of being SLA soldiers within hours of Patty's kidnaping.

One was Thero Wheeler, a 29-year-old San Franciscan, who had walked away from Vacaville on August 2, 1973 while working as a trusty gardener.

Two prison aides identified Wheeler as being Cinque

after hearing the voices on the tape, but a former inmate friend said he doubted it, because Wheeler's speech patterns were different.

Wheeler's broad, flat face did not closely match the drawing developed by the FBI artist. Only if one strained did there seem to be any similarity. Descriptions of the second man at Patty's kidnaping did match his wiry build and 6-foot-1-inch height.

A casual glance at his record did not show Wheeler with much leadership capability. Seeming hardly a cut above the average con, he had been unable to stay out of trouble since he started snatching purses as a teenager on the San Francisco streets.

Son of a laborer and brother of a county jailer, he first got into trouble just over the hill from where he lived on the outer edge of the blacker section of the Fillmore district. In 1961 he and a friend, Albert Swann, who lived around the corner from him on Bush, snatched a lady's purse. The lady turned out to be the VIP wife of British Vice Consul Reginald Gilbert. He was 16 and Albert was 19 that year. A year later, they were sent to prison for mugging a 57-year-old man just six blocks from their homes. Burglary, escape and other charges piled up over the years. He was doing 10 years to life when he disappeared from Vacaville.

Tracing his radical activities, it was discovered he had been studying Marx, Hegel and Marcuse since 1970, but many remembered him as a plodding scholar who had difficulty grasping abstract parts of Communist philosophy. He was also considered a Marxist in the Russian mold. When he joined the Maoist Venceremos group, insiders theorized he was merely using anyone he could to get out of prison.

Other prisoners left him alone, steering clear of him because of his reputation. He was called "Dragline" by the savvy cons, the nickname a reflection of his talent for seizing opportunities or riding someone else's coattails.

When Wheeler's membership in Venceremos was announced to the rest of the members in April 1972, he was described as being a militant and a writer dedicated to revolution. One of his poems was passed around, signed with both his Swahili and his given name.

My pathway lies through worse than death;
I meet the hours with bated breath,
my red blood boils, my pulse thrills,
I live life running up a hill. Ah no,
I need no paltry play of makeshift tilts
for holiday, for I was born against
the tide, I will conquer that denied.
I shun no hardship, fear no foe;
the future calls and I must go;
I charge the line and dare the spheres
as I go fighting down the years.
See you on the front line, comrades.
    Lasima Tushinda Mbilishaka
    (We will conquer without a doubt)
    Yours in Struggle,
        Thero

Wheeler had resisted the prison's stress program, a psychological testing program used by penal officials to see how prospective parolees react to stress. This had won him his Venceremos support in addition to their analysis that he would be a useful legal researcher on the outside.

"They recommended that I take the stress program at Vacaville, but now they want me to sign a paper reading to the effect that I will participate in the program and take any treatment that the docors feel is necessary," Wheeler wrote to his Venceremos comrades.

"I will not sign any papers whatsoever. They will never scramble these brains, not while I live."

Two members of Venceremos' Redwood City cadre, Janet and Sam Swift, organized a letter-writing campaign seeking a parole hearing for Wheeler. Janet's sister, Mary Alice Siem, began making regular visits to Vacaville to see him. Other regular visitors were the girlfriend of Russell Little, Robyn Steiner, and long-time Venceremos activist, Susan Flores.

A former cellmate of Wheeler told investigators that Wheeler had been an expert on revolution, able to quote extensively from Venceremos literature and thoroughly acquainted with tactics of guerrillas like the Tupamaros.

He had once shown his cellmate complicated organizational charts of a new group, whose name could not be recalled, and Wheeler had talked of escaping to learn karate, foreign languages and weapons use.

Both prisoners had attended a group started at Vacaville in 1968 called the Black Cultural Association, which had been formed by inmates to study black history and politics. They had won prison approval a year later when they obtained outside sponsorship from a University of California communications instructor named Colston Westbrook. The group was really a front for revolutionary studies, the inmate informant told investigators.

Westbrook, a stocky young black man who affected dazzling costumes, had spent time in Southeast Asia before coming to UC. He avoided answering directly any questions about his work in Vietnam, but some news organizations remembered he had tried to get work as a correspondent.

He took some of his UC students along to the BCA sessions including 20-year-old Willie Wolfe, the doctor's son from Pennsylvania being sought in connection with SLA activities at the Concord hideout.

Swahili lessons and black history rap sessions soon moved into full-fledged escape and guerrilla warfare planning, one prison inmate told investigators. Venceremos literature was used along with Carlos Marighella's *Minimanual of the Urban Guerrilla* and some material specially designed for inmates and aimed at destroying the prison system.

A check of the BCA visitors records showed a direct connection with the SLA group already tied to the Foster case. Visitors had included Little, Remiro and Robyn Steiner. Bill and Emily Harris had been on the approved list, but never attended. Nancy Ling Perry had sought and been denied permission. Prison officials were nervous about her, because she was already on the approved list for two lifers and they had to guard against any messenger service being set up between groups.

Two new names were also turned up. David Gunnell and Jean Chan, whose Chabot Road home had been a gathering place for radical talk, had also attended often.

Wheeler's resignation from Venceremos was cited by authorities as the basis for their having granted him trusty status. Yet a check of his visitor records showed that he continued to hear from Susan Flores and Mary Alice Siem. Mary Alice had seen him last on August 1, the day before he disappeared. His last visitor did not have to sign the visitor's log, because he was an investigator for Robin Yeamans, Wheeler's attorney: Robert McBriarty, her husband and investigator visited Wheeler that evening.

His disappearance the next day was discovered shortly before noon. Ms. Yeamans called the prison at 4:45 P.M., expressing surprise and concern at the escape.

The problem investigators had with the tape recording was the two distinct sounds and speaking styles before and after Patty spoke. First analysis had been that there were two men speaking, leading some to identify Wheeler as the second speaker.

Other inmates and prison aides were certain both voices belonged to one man, the other escapee investigators had already tied to the SLA, Donald David DeFreeze.

DeFreeze's escape on March 5, 1973 from Soledad had many of the same mysterious elements as Wheeler's disappearance from Vacaville. DeFreeze disappeared while working in a boiler room in a minimum security area of the prison. All he had to do was vault a low fence and walk to a waiting car.

DeFreeze's trusty status was more unusual than Wheeler's. He had been deeply involved in the BCA

98

activities when he was at Vacaville, trying once to take over its leadership. Having failed, he organized a subsection that took part in their meetings.

One inmate informant told investigators the escapes of Wheeler and DeFreeze had been planned during sessions of the BCA, that the BCA and the SLA were one and the same. Westbrook was questioned. While admitting that radicals had taken over the BCA, causing him to drop out, he did not believe they were one and the same. He noted that DeFreeze had dropped out of the BCA when he was transferred to Soledad in 1972.

DeFreeze's criminal record before he arrived at Vacaville showed little talent for revolution. Like Wheeler, he had been in and out of jails and prisons since he was a teen-ager.

One of eight children in a Glenville, Ohio family, DeFreeze had run away from home in 1957 when he was 14 years old. Dropping out of Empire Junior High School, he hitchhiked eastward along Lake Erie to Buffalo, New York. He became a ward of a fundamentalist minister, Rev. William Foster, but began running with a street gang.

Arrested for breaking into parking meters and stealing a car for a joyride when he was 16, DeFreeze was sent to a state reformatory for two years before he told authorities he had a family in Ohio and they sent him home in time for his father's funeral. His mother, registered nurse Mrs. Mary DeFreeze, could not quiet his restlessness and he moved soon to Newark, New Jersey.

When DeFreeze moved to Newark, he was part of a growing emigration of blacks that were forcing a new brand of politics on city officials. Irish political bosses were being displaced by a coalition of Italians and blacks, but the 18-year-old youth was not interested in politics.

When he was 20, he met Gloria Thomas, a bright-eyed woman he could talk to, who seemed to appreciate his bravado and ambition. She already had three children, but that seemed no obstacle to him and they were married. That was in 1963, when blacks all over the country were beginning to take more direct action in the wake of the Birmingham church murders, the slaying of Medgar Evers and the Mississippi civil rights lynchings. The year of the Watts riots, 1965, DeFreeze and Gloria, now with a child of their own to go with her three, moved to Los Angeles.

His first California arrest came in March 1965 while he was hitchhiking near West Covina. He was found to be carrying a sharpened butter knife, a tear-gas pencil and a sawed-off shotgun. Four months later, he was arrested 3,000 miles away in East Orange, New Jersey and charged with making a homemade bomb and firing a gun in the basement of a house there.

Two years later he was back in Los Angeles. Stopped for running a red light on his bicycle, DeFreeze was found to be carrying a homemade bomb in his pocket, and another bomb and a pistol in the bicycle basket. The gun was traced to a military supply house, where some 200 weapons had been stolen. He led police to the apartment of Ronald Coleman, another black, where they found all the weapons.

The first hint of DeFreeze's flair for the dramatic came at his trial, where he served as his own attorney. He read the Bible, wept and sang hymns to the jury in a flamboyant attempt that was wasted. He and Coleman suddenly pleaded guilty. In a letter to Superior Court Judge Willard Barrett, his wife reminded him that police had promised to help DeFreeze in return for recovery of the weapons.

He was freed on probation, only to be arrested less than two years later in Newark, New Jersey. On May 9, 1969, police charged him with kidnaping.

Claiming to be Black Panthers, he and another black man were said to have kidnapped Alfred Whiters, caretaker of the B'Nai Abraham synagogue. He was charged with threatening to hold him for $5,000 ransom. When his partner was cleared, the Essex County prosecutor's office dropped charges against DeFreeze, stating that more serious charges were pending in California.

On October 11, 1969, DeFreeze was found by

Cleveland police on the roof of a bank, armed with two pistols, a hand grenade and a burglar's tool kit. Freed on bail, he disappeared.

He turned up a month later in Los Angeles. Attempting to cash a stolen $1,000 check, DeFreeze tried to shoot his way out of a police confrontation. He was wounded and captured.

After his trial, in which he was found guilty of forgery, attempted robbery and assault on a police officer, DeFreeze gave the first insight into some of his personality conflicts:

"My wife, doctors for the last 15 years have spent the doggone time telling me I have got a problem. I'm sick. I'm this or that, but they never tell me why, what it is, what's wrong with me."

Superior Court Judge William L. Ritchie sentenced him to five years to life in prison and he was sent to Vacaville where psychiatrists found him to have a fascination with firearms and explosives so deep as to make him dangerous.

Informants inside the prisons told investigators that after his escape DeFreeze had gone first to the home of a tall, beautiful ash blonde, Amanda de Normanville, who had worked with him in the BCA. But a check at her home on Talbot Street in Berkeley failed to turn up DeFreeze or the woman.

Other leads given by informants proved as fruitless, a long list of names of women and former inmates now on parole were checked to no avail.

Involvement of the Foster slaying suspects and former members of the Black Cultural Association was the most substantial lead investigators had. The switch on the usual ransom demand, where money had to be picked up at a central point, had made it impossible for the routine FBI kidnap case methods to be used. The entire effort was turned into a slow, slogging through masses of names and addresses of friends and families and associates of the people turned up from the prison connections.

So many of the names were new to revolutionary and radical circles, a great deal of basic work had to be done. About the only things these new names and faces had in common were their upper-middle-class background, a college education and prison reform work. They seemed to fit the pattern of the protest movements of the late 1960s and early 1970s.

Like Nancy Ling Perry, most of them had been from the generation that erupted in disillusionment over the differences between image and reality in politics and morality.

Months of work by the Oakland Police Department and Alameda County District Attorney's office had provided a foundation, a central core from which federal officers began expanding. The 25 names gathered as associates of Remiro, Little, Wolfe and Nancy had simply come from the houses where the four had lived in the previous two years.

Tracing Remiro's connections had brought the largest bag of names, because he was more restless, more active. He had worked hardest on the Vietnam Veterans Against the War-Winter Soldier Organization. But he had also been involved in Venceremos efforts along with his roommates in a series of Oakland communes where he lived after he and his wife separated.

The 27-year-old Remiro had grown up in a Catholic family in San Francisco, his father a Chicano and his mother from the Balestreri family that had come from Italy some 60 years ago. After graduation from Sacred Heart High School, he had joined the Army and was sent to Vietnam while still 18 years of age.

An expert automatic rifleman, Remiro served two tours for a total of 18 months in a long-range reconnaisance platoon. His strong Italian features won him the nickname of "Pizza Joe" amongst his platoon buddies on search and destroy missions. He was back in the States before the impact of the Southeast Asia experience hit him. He withdrew from everything, refusing even to paint latrines before being discharged.

He lost himself along with hundreds of other Vietnam vets, who had fought the unpopular war, a conflict where guerrillas were so much a part of the populace, everything was ordered destroyed.

Using the GI Bill education benefit checks to buy dope, he remained stoned for long periods, marched in some peace demonstrations and coasted until after his son was born in 1971. He finally became active by joining the Vietnam Veterans Against the War, only to find himself one of two battle veterans in a chapter of 25. He could not speak their language, nor they his.

He tried Venceremos, where he added to his revolutionary education and reading of history. Here, too, he found only talk and more talk, none of which seemed relevant.

His meeting with Russ Little had come through women they had both met in Venceremos pads. And Little was involved with some people in the prison movement, who lived in Berkeley at 5939 Chabot Road. That's where he met Nancy Ling Perry.

Little's arrest the same day as Remiro also unfolded a long list of acquaintances being pursued by investigators in the kidnap case.

Little had been in Oakland less than two years when he was arrested and charged with the Foster murder. Born and raised a continent away in the military town of Pensacola, Florida, the 24-year-old had come from a typical Southern family and was aiming for an electrical engineering career when he became involved in his first civil disorder at the University of Florida. He joined demonstrations in 1971 protesting arrests of black students.

He and his girlfriend from Miami, 20-year-old Robyn Steiner, traveled across country to Oakland in the summer of 1972. They moved into the house on Chabot Road, which a friend of Robyn's from Coral Gables, Florida had suggested.

Robyn got a job as a checkout cashier in Lucky Supermarkets and they both immersed themselves in prison activities alongside most of the Chabot Road commune dwellers. During this time, she obtained a driver's license using the name of a dead girl, Joanne Renee Moser, giving an address at 1621 Seventh Avenue, Oakland, an apartment investigators identified as an SLA hideout after the Foster murder. Robyn also had lived at another apartment with Angela Atwood, Bill and Emily Harris just before she and Little parted company and she fled back to Florida.

Another interesting item from the public records was a driver's license obtained by Robyn with an address at 2933 Benvenue Avenue, Berkeley, just three blocks from Patty's apartment.

Nothing in this mountain of circumstantial evidence or tracing of radicals' associates brought investigators any closer to Patty. A new list was all that resulted—a compilation of people who had suddenly and inexplicably disappeared from their homes. They became more urgently sought for interrogation.

III

Some of the Chabot Road commune residents were still available for questioning, even though some of their answers were less than informative.

One of the puzzlers was Chris Thompson, a lanky ex-marine and former New York Black Panther who had come forward early in the Foster investigation, accompanied by an attorney. He had spent some loving hours with Nancy Ling Perry and knew well another mystery figure, Patricia Soltysik. Thompson was more concerned with guns than bedtime gossip.

While a part-time student at North Peralta Community College in 1973, Thompson had been president of the Malcolm Che Lumumba Society. Remiro had been cochairman at the same time. After Little and Remiro were arrested and charged with the Foster slaying, Thompson approached police.

He told them that he had sold Little a .38 Rossi with serial No. 96622 for $65 a few months earlier. He was concerned the gun might be traced to him as the original owner, if it was proved to be the murder weapon.

David Gunnell and Jean Chan, who played hosts at the Chabot Road commune, talked to investigators, admitting their role in the prison movement, but denying any involvement with the SLA.

Robyn Steiner was finally located in Miami. She refused to talk to investigators unless an attorney was present. No information was obtained from her.

IV

Patty's fiancé Steven Weed was another puzzle that worried federal officers. Partly because of his background and partly because his telephone number had been in the notebook found in the SLA hideout in Concord.

His background while a student at Princeton had included involvement with the Students for a Democratic Society, the group that spawned the more destructive Weather Underground. He insisted that his participation at Princeton had been only peripheral and far from revolutionary.

At a time in 1969 when radical students were running the ROTC program off most campuses, Weed had quarterbacked a Princeton SDS football team that played and beat an ROTC team. Former classmates confirmed this rather low-key and traditional confrontation had been about as radical as SDS could achieve then at Princeton.

Pressing him further, the FBI found answers to the other troublesome element, the unusually large stash of marijuana found in their apartment. A pound of grass was more than most people kept for their own use, even someone with Weed's affluent background. He admitted having sold marijuana in the past, contending he did as many students did, dealing stuff obtained in the

Haight Ashbury for extra pocket money while in school. He also admitted experimenting with LSD, the mind-expanding drug, mostly as an extension of his philosophical studies.

While there had been talk by tipsters of Weed's involvement with the Symbionese Federation, investigators could find no evidence to tie him to the revolutionaries.

The fact that his telephone number was in the SLA notebook considered important at the time, was not unusual especially since it contained many others of people vastly more important. Some of these, mostly corporate executives, had gathered up their families and shipped them off for extended vacations in Jamaica, Europe and other distant points they hoped would be out of the SLA reach.

V

Another of many bothersome puzzles was the identity of the female member of the kidnap team, the woman described as seeming to be the leader.

She had been described as being 5 feet 5 inches tall and weighing between 110 and 120 pounds and having long dark hair. The artist's drawing of her face showed her as a blonde with short hair.

This drawing bore a striking resemblance to a former neighbor and associate of Remiro's in the VVAW-WSO, Jeanie Dolly.

She and Robert Hood, 24, had lived in the house behind Remiro's at 4616 Bond Street. Remiro's telephone for the VVAW-WSO was located in her house.

Mrs. Dolly, 28, had moved from the West Bay to Oakland after years of involvement in Venceremos demonstrations and movements. Starting as an art teacher in a Menlo Park free university experiment, she had moved into the ROTC, antiwar, child care and prison work as radicals grew more popular.

No one could identify her as the kidnaper.

The description eliminated Cindy Garvey as too short and Amanda de Normanville as too tall.

News media linked the drawing to Mary Alice Siem after an all points bulletin was issued for her, because she had been one of Wheeler's last visitors. But no investigator seriously considered her as a prime suspect for the kidnap squad.

A friend of Patricia Soltysik named Camilla Hall had a description that could fit, except she was usually heavier. And available pictures showed such a funky round face and glasses necessary for seeing clearly, she did not seem too likely. She and her girlfriend were both among the missing who were being added to the special list of prime suspects.

CHAPTER NINE

SOME SOLID LEADS—WHO ARE THE MISSING RADICALS?

I

While some investigators chased down telephone tips, traced map routes left behind by the suspects in the Foster case and searched the underground tipster network for hot information, one part of the FBI hunt was being built around three intersecting leads.

The Foster murder investigation into SLA had developed two lists of suspects, one of some 25 people connected or acquainted or friendly with Joseph Remiro and Russ Little; the other a larger list created with the help of prison informants familiar with the Black Cultural Association and other prison radical groups. While several names appeared on both lists, there were two people who were of more interest because of something that happened in Chicago Feb. 8 less than 24 hours after Patty's kidnaping was tied to the SLA.

FBI Agent Vincent Inserra, head of the organized crime unit there, received a telephone call from a consulting engineer living in suburban Clarendon Hills, Frederick Schwartz.

Schwartz told Inserra that he had a "gut feeling" that his daughter was somehow involved in the kidnaping of the Hearst girl. He had no evidence, just a feeling he had gained from a letter his daughter had written him from Oakland, California a few days earlier. His daughter's name was Emily and she was married to a man she had met at Indiana University, William Harris.

He told Inserra the couple had become renegades, quitting their jobs and joining communal living with blacks in Oakland.

Such telephone calls from anguished parents no longer able to comprehend their children's violent reaction to the society they helped create were not new to FBI officers or local investigators dealing with radicals. What made Schwartz's call significant was the material already compiled in California. The Harrises' involvement in the Foster slaying and their disappearance the day Remiro and Little were arrested, and identification of Emily's glove, which had been found in the kidnap car, also made his call doubly important.

Schwartz agreed to show investigators the letter that had so disturbed him he felt duty-bound to call authorities.

Blonde, blue-eyed Emily, now 27 and long away from his control, was still Schwartz's only daughter. Her three brothers could never quite replace her. She had written a letter that was simply too shocking for him to take.

"Bill and I have changed our relationship so that it no longer confines us and I am enjoying relationships with other men. I am in love with the black man I referred to earlier and that love is very beautiful and fulfilling."

Her letter explained that this black man had taught her to dedicate her life "to eliminating the conditions that oppose people's being able to lead satisfying lives and replace these with conditions that make people truly free—so part of this process is to destroy and part is to rebuild."

This was not the child he had sent away to college

eight years earlier. Such behavior was no more comprehensible to him than had been Nancy Ling's decision to her parents, when she married Gil Perry. Such violent aberrations must be controlled for their own good.

II

Schwartz's daughter Emily and her husband Bill Harris also were included on a list seen as increasingly important, a smaller tally than the others, which contained names of radicals involved in prison affairs who had suddenly disappeared. Most had left so hurriedly they had failed to take their clothing and other possessions.

Investigators who visited the Harris apartment in North Oakland commented they might have arisen from an evening meal, washed the dishes, put on their coats and left. They simply never returned.

A few selected drawers had been emptied. But there remained a wealth of material linking them to the Symbionese Liberation Army. There were professionally drawn maps, lists of potential "targets" and gun receipts and some ammunition. Notes and letters indicated that a school chum of Emily's, Angela Atwood, had lived in one of the rooms of the immaculately kept apartment. Robyn Steiner, Russ Little's former girlfriend, may have shared the room with her, judging from some of the items found, but she had been located and was not on the special list.

Nancy Ling Perry naturally was on the list of the missing as was another native Californian from a small town near Santa Barbara, Patricia Soltysik, who was about Willie Wolfe's age. Wolfe had been on the list since the house in Concord was found burnt and his car abandoned a few miles away. The Soltysik girl led to a close friend of hers, Camilla Hall, who had left so quickly she had only taken her pet cat.

Other radicals were missing, too, but they did not appear to have any direct connection with Remiro or

Little. Investigators set out to find any common link between them. They found that besides their prison visits there were only general factors like upper-middle class backgrounds and higher education.

All were under 30 and covered a span from 23 to 29 years of age, members of the Disney fantasyland generation who grew up in front of the flickering tube, mesmerized by images on the phosphorescent screen. Emily had even worked in Disneyland one summer. All had been left to the tender mercies of television's version of the world until dinnertime daily while their achiever families pursued success in furniture, church, medicine or sales.

The entertainment was merry and bright. The big floppy ears of the Mouseketeers were fun until they wilted in the bathtub. Davy Crockett was a rouser for both boys and girls. Except mothers got funny looks on their faces when daughters asked for coonskin caps like Davy's. Too masculine. Identity problems crept in early for the girls because all of the fun heroes were male. The women either got clobbered or fainted or asked silly, stupid questions. But nice girls did not carry guns and shoot 'em up. They must be little ladies at all times.

Still there was a wide choice of fantasies growing up. Cowboys shooting Indians and ugly people. People who dressed oddly or had dark complexions being chased and shot by policemen. Or leopard-skin-clad heroes, always white, saving the poor dumb, crazily dressed black jungle natives, who genuflected a lot. Sometimes they had difficulty telling which was the fantasy and which was the reality.

When Jackie Kennedy clutched at her husband's head in the back seat of the car in Dallas, Texas, children from 12 to 18 could be forgiven if they had trouble distinguishing this violence from the make-believe. Many adults had the same trouble. When the president's accused assassin was shot live and in color for the television audience, the heroes and villains became still more confused. Followed closely by Robert Kennedy–Sirhan, Martin Luther King–Ray fantasizing became preferable.

And every night, right after the cartoons and cowboy and detective serials, there were the great war pictures from Southeast Asia. Bombs dropping on jungles, soldiers running past burned-out buildings and farm fields, children with broken legs and burned bodies. Confusing the real and the unreal was a simple trip.

When their parents began questioning some of their adolescent meanderings, the teen-agers had ready heroes who questioned the parents. The Beatles' riotous nonsense helped for a time, but that was ultimately traded in for a homely kid from Hibbing, Minnesota. He had changed his name to Bob Dylan and wrote songs the kids could dig, verses that cried that no one in the world understood or appreciated their unique dilemma. Dylan soon grew into the theme writer for a generation of protest.

Their heroes paid their dues. Sweet-voiced Joan Baez quit paying her income tax, if the money was to be used for war machinery. Janis Joplin put it down and dirty, the way the world was, the way she lived. They did not say one thing to the kids and live another.

Honesty became a badge of honor. Stark, cruel truth was wielded like a cudgel against their parents' easy euphemisms of love, courtship and relationships. Some simply announced their pastimes. Others fled to join their peers in more comfortable life styles when home life became too exacerbated by this flail.

Adopting the uniform of the poor, or what they believed to be their clothing, they wore old overalls and patched blue jeans, nondescript shirts and shifts. The affluence of their parents had become an embarrassment, a sign of their guilt and failure to share with others less fortunate.

Many went into studies of social science, psychology and other disciplines that could help save people, change the inequities that they perceived. They helped form welfare-rights groups, poor peoples' law services, neighborhood medical clinics and low-cost housing drives.

metropolitan miasmas.

All seven on the FBI's special list emerged from affluent neighborhoods on the edges of the nation's worst

Nancy Ling Perry had grown up on the fringe of the San Francisco-Oakland sprawl; Patricia Mizmoon Soltysik's formative years were on the windward side of Los Angeles's noxious smog basin; William Harris's childhood was spent in a fashionable enclave at the edge of Indianapolis; Emily Schwartz Harris came from the edge of Chicago; Angela Atwood had grown up surrounded by the clattering machinery of Paterson-Newark, New Jersey; Camilla Hall had come to puberty in ironclad Minneapolis; and Willie Wolfe's youth was spent in the quieter sections of the megalopolis that radiates, north, west and south from New York City.

All had been sent to colleges and universities for expensive educations, only to wind up greatly underemployed by the time they disappeared. Before dropping from sight, they had been working as a janitor, typists, waitresses, fruit juice vendor, mechanic and postman.

Another unique characteristic nearly all shared was their tardiness in joining the protest movement. Only Willie Wolfe seemed to have become involved at an early age, but his youth had helped him miss some of the storied confrontations and demonstrations of the late 1960s. They all seemed to be newcomers, a second generation eager to clean up the failures of their predecessors.

Seeking some clue to their motives and locations, investigators interviewed hundreds of relatives, friends, acquaintances and neighbors across the country.

The answers they received created images vastly different from people capable of murder, kidnaping, extortion or commencing any revolution.

III

The Harrises seemed to a lot of their old friends and former classmates beautiful people ready made for success, a handsome couple capable of being and doing anything they wanted.

113

William Taylor Harris had entertained people from the time he was the class cutup at Carmel (Indiana) High School, always ready with a quick, biting line. He had been an acolyte at St. Christopher's Church. Living at the edge of a golf course, he had learned young and made the high school team. He won a letter in track and field participating in cross-country runs. He was a natural to be rushed by Sigma Alpha Epsilon fraternity when he enrolled downstate in Bloomington at the University of Indiana in 1963.

His father earned a comfortable living selling commercial building equipment for an Indianapolis firm, enough for the family to live in a rambling ranch-style home in Carmel a northeast suburb of Indianapolis.

Bill's brash, gregarious nature aimed him early toward the stage and he once confided to his sister, Joann, that he wanted to become an actor. His courses the first couple of years were heavy in speech and drama. But his father died in 1965, turning the family upside down. Bill joined the U.S. Marines and was sent to Vietnam.

His military service was a radical new experience. Protected and sheltered from interracial strife in elementary and high schools in Carmel, he had first met a black man personally at the university, but that acquaintance had been only superficial.

The Marine Corps was a different world entirely. Thrust into a fighting mold from his first day of boot camp, he found the corps filled with hard cases such as he had never met around the golf course or university campus. The marines were accepting young men who frequently had their choice of jail or close probation or the service; their theory was that this restless dissatisfaction could be channeled into a fighting machine. Blacks, Chicanos and poor whites fed this bottomless meat grinder in a way that slowly grew apparent to Harris.

When he was sent to Vietnam along with thousands of others as President Johnson stepped up involvement in Southeast Asia, Harris was assigned to the supply base at Da Nang. The drug addiction and desertions had not grown to their ultimate level yet, but he saw the prelude. The blacks and Chicanos were shoved into the front-line meat grinders while his privileged college status kept him safe behind a desk. The military underground was slowly forming in the revolt of people of color refusing to fight against the Vietnamese, who were also people of color. Although early cases were dealt with harshly, the problem grew so severe that some of the rebels were stationed at Da Nang on the theory they could do less harm there than in the field.

Fragging incidents, where enlisted men assassinated harsh officers, became more and more frequent as the unpopular conflict dragged onward. By the time he returned home to Indiana in 1967, Harris was a changed man, some said so embittered he would not talk about it or have a gun around.

His mother had remarried by that time, Air Force Colonel Jerry Bunnell. Bill went back to Bloomington.

Bill met a blonde, blue-eyed girl from Illinois named Emily Schwartz the first month. She was a sophmore, an education major, a Chi Omega and a corn-fed beauty who would have eased any veteran's bitterness. Some could not understand what Emily saw in the rough, khaki-clad Bill and their friendship appeared casual off and on for nearly a year and a half. Both dated others. Emily spent her summers in California working one year at Disneyland hotel and the next waiting tables in a Newport Beach restaurant. Bill went to Europe one summer.

They moved in together Emily's senior year, sharing expenses and ideas and each others' needs and frustrations. After obtaining her bachelor's degree in English literature, Emily stayed another year to obtain teaching credentials. Bill was working toward a degree in speech education.

They were married in the campus chapel in 1970. Emily went to work teaching English and French at Binford Junior High School, while Bill remained at the university studying for his master's degree in urban education.

Their close friends in the mini-society of the graduate school were Gary and Angela Atwood. Angela was also teaching and working while Gary continued studying. But the Atwoods also had political views similar to those the Harrises were developing. And at times the politics became so intense, it drove other friends away.

"Bill became hostile toward people who were sort of middle-of-the-road. He was just so damned serious I began avoiding them. They became a little frightening," one fellow student recalled.

A friend of Atwood's told investigators he had stopped visiting the apartment "because there were times things got so heavy politically."

Gary was an Ohioan whose intellectualizing about revolution often grew vociferous and challenging, but few of their friends considered him more than a theorist, because he liked to talk so much. Angela came from North Haledon, New Jersey, where her father was a Teamsters Union official, a good Catholic girl brought up to honor her parents and respect other people's lives and opinions.

Angela and Emily were recalled as being more involved in their teaching and their students. Others remembered Emily liked to rap with the junior high schoolers about alternatives to the existing political system.

Angela, a former pep leader and high school thespian, had kept alive her interest in theater through college and going to work. Her dark, fine-boned face made her a natural for the stage and she used every opportunity to work in amateur theatricals. She once told a friend she believed theater could be most effective as a tool for social change.

The restless Atwoods left Bloomington first, driving to California in their Volkswagen van in late 1971. Their welcome to San Francisco was to have the van looted of its tape deck and tapes. They drove back across the bay to Berkeley and settled there.

The Harrises followed in October of 1972, renting an apartment in a fourplex on 41st Street in Oakland.

Jobs for teachers were diminishing with the end of the baby boom. Tenured teachers were being laid off.

Neither the Atwoods or Harrises found teaching positions, they had to settle for more menial jobs.

Gary decided that only a graduate degree would be enough to break the teaching job barrier and enrolled at UC, while they lived off Angela's salary and tips. The strain on their marriage was severe. When he finally obtained a job teaching in Chinatown across the bay, he was unable to persuade her to move to San Francisco.

She was involved in amateur theatricals, playing Thea in Ibsen's *Hedda Gabler,* and studying Marx, Mao and Lenin with a Venceremos cadre that was organizing support for Popeye Jackson's cause, a branch of the prison movement. They had several wild, shouting fights before she moved in with a girlfriend.

They relented long enough for them to both travel back to her family's home in North Haledon in June 1973 for her sister Elena's wedding. Gary stayed in the east and reenrolled at Bloomington, while Angela returned to California and moved into the Harrises' spare bedroom.

The apartment she and Gary had shared on Deleware Street in Berkeley was turned over to a friend—a tall, lanky youth with an incipient Fu Manchu moustache named Willie Wolfe.

IV

William Lawton Wolfe was 23 years of age when he disappeared, a restless young man who had gone to expensive private schools, attended UC and been involved in the Black Cultural Association.

His friends remembered him as a gregarious, active youth who was a varsity swimmer and sports editor for the school newspaper. He attended Mount Hermon School in Massachussets. He was politically active in high school, becoming embroiled in antiwar campaigns and other activities.

When he finished school at Mount Hermon, he told

his father, who had divorced his mother years before, that he did not want to continue the family tradition of attending Yale. Instead he moved out of his mother's house in Litchfield, Connecticut, and went to Harlem to live with a black friend, Michael Carreras. This was in 1969.

After a year in New York City, he told his father, an anesthesiologist in Allentown, Pennsylvania, that he wanted to travel. He went to Europe for nine months, wandering from the Arctic Circle to Greece before returning to the States and announcing he was ready to go to college.

He enrolled at UC upon his arrival in 1971, announcing a joint major of archaeology and astronomy. His attendance at the Berkeley campus was sporadic. Some quarters he would drop out to work. He was enrolled in March 1972 in a course taught by communications instructor Colston Westbrook.

Westbrook took him along on a class exercise to Vacaville Prison, where he participated and observed a prisoners' group studying black history and culture. On the next trip to Vacaville, Wolfe brought along a friend and former roommate, Russ Little, to explore the possibilities.

Westbrook told investigators that Wolfe eased a number of Maoists into the black study sessions and they gradually took over control, a control the instructor could not recover, he said, because prison officials ignored his warnings.

Wolfe's father visited him during the summer of 1971 and was impressed with his son's dedication to the prison cause. His son seemed genuinely moved at the prisoners' plight and convinced that they had been wrongly imprisoned. Dr. Wolfe presented Willie with a gift before he left, the keys to a white Oldsmobile—the same auto that was discovered abandoned after the Concord house was burned by the SLA.

At various times, Willie also lived in Berkeley in the commune owned by David Gunnell on Chabot Road, where he met Russ Little and Nancy Ling Perry, and in Oakland where he met the Harrises.

His father insisted his son was visiting him in Pennsylvania with the rest of the family when the Concord house burned. His older sister said she put him on a bus in Allentown on January 11, after he received two telephone calls from California. He disappeared from public view from that time.

V

Camilla Christine Hall was 29 when she and her Siamese cat disappeared on February 29 from her apartment at 1353 Francisco Avenue in Berkeley.

She had grown up in a religious family plagued with personal tragedy. Two brothers and a sister died at early ages, leaving her an only child. Her mother succumbed while Camilla was still a child. Her minister-missionary father kept a housekeeper to help bring her up, but she was a lonely child. She accompanied her father when he made missionary treks for the Lutheran Church to Africa and South America, where she found life stifling and oppressive. But they returned to Minneapolis in time for her to finish high school and enter the University of Minnesota, where her father served as one of three Lutheran chaplains.

The sprawling campus resting on both sides of the Mississippi River had not yet reached a radical heat when Camilla—her friends called her Candy—attended from 1963 through 1967. There were stories circulating around campus from those who had gone to Alabama and Mississippi on the freedom rides. Fund-raising efforts were held for more civil rights work and the antiwar effort was growing, but generally it was a quiet place to study. There were rumblings beneath the surface of the gay lib movement that was to take over student government in the 1970s, but most were still in the closet.

Camilla studied art and poetry and social science. She took classes in social science on the west bank of the river, then had to cross back across the cold, blus-

119

tery bridge in the years before a covered walkway was completed to shut out the northern winters.

Blonde Camilla, whose blue eyes required heavy glasses to overcome her nearsightedness, was a shy, sensitive girl who never fully entered a relationship with a man. She always had a bright smile, could always answer defensively with a lighthearted remark, but she kept her emotions locked inside. Her emotional attachments grew instead with other women until she made an announcement when she graduated in 1967. She considered herself a feminist and dedicated lesbian.

Upon receiving her humanities degree, Camilla obtained jobs as a social worker. She first went to Duluth and later returned to Minneapolis. The growing welfare caseload of unemployed Indians and other minorities swept her into a world of the underprivileged. The emotional level of radicalism was climbing in the Twin Cities during the two years Camilla was involved as a social worker. But she left in 1970, moving to the San Francisco Bay Area where she could pursue her first loves, painting and poetry.

Camilla made a place for herself swiftly in both branches of her work. Her poetry was read widely and her paintings were shown around the Bay Area.

Her jobs were varied. She had quit the social worker milieu entirely. By 1973 she was a gardener-groundskeeper in the East Bay Regional Park District that covers the hilltops between Alameda and Contra Costa counties. When park directors decided to lay off the women groundskeepers, she took part in a quiet protest that received only local attention.

Deeply involved in the feminist movement, Camilla had met several women with whom she formed fleeting attachments. One was a neighbor of hers when she lived on Channing Way in Berkeley and was working to try and support herself as an artist and sculptor.

The other woman was five years younger with an effusive, dynamic personality and a sharp, angular face that would challenge any sculptor. Her charismatic drive challenged Camilla's poetry, inspiring her to write several loving verses.

I will cradle you
In my woman hips
Kiss you
With my woman lips,
Fold you to my heart and sing:
Sister woman,
You are a joy to me.

At the height of their affair, Camilla wrote a glowing poem that so enchanted the woman, she took its title, "Mizmoon," as her legal name.

Patricia Soltysik became Mizmoon Soltysik.

VI

Patricia Soltysik, who had become Mizmoon and Monique and Zoya and Yolanda and several other names, had undergone many changes during her short 23 years.

Growing up in Goleta in Santa Barbara County, California, she was the daughter of a pharmacist among two older brothers and three younger sisters. She had caught the success fever early. She had been president of the Usherettes, the service organizaton at high school. Her top grades had won her an academic scholarship she hoped to ride to higher achievement.

Patricia—her family and friends called her Patty until well after she left for UC—had had trouble with only one man in her life. Her father, Louis Soltysik, had earned bitterness from his children when he moved out of the family home on Butte Drive. And she could never mention him dispassionately for years afterward.

She was a bright, eager and searching girl who was willing to experiment, willing to try new ideas and activities. The men she liked were doers, not talkers. One wrote her poetry, which caught her off guard and then touched her so deeply that a brief fling grew into an enduring friendship.

When she went to UC, she majored in French and Spanish. She and her mother and sister had spent several summers along the Baja California coast, where she had picked up some of the Spanish language. But despite her linguistic study she was not a verbalizer.

At Devereaux Beach, where the Santa Barbara crowd hung out, she did little talking. She had her symbols, the plain gold earrings and the brown bandanna she always wore as a tribute to her mother's Eastern European traditions. She listened mostly.

Her plunge into Berkeley changed her again as it had changed so many others before her. She had taken an apartment at 2430 Dwight Way and had a live-in boy friend very soon. Her emotional life was growing more intense until they finally separated.

The Berkeley experience in 1970 and 1971 was a restless, boiling one. Police were using tear gas on crowds of roving students and street people. Helicopters had become regular weapons for crowd control. There were some mornings students had to march to class between rows of fixed bayonets formed at Sather Gate.

Rape had become so endemic to the campus that coeds were being attacked in the daytime in stairwells and on the street. Women began enrolling in karate classes or seeking some other form of self-defense.

The attitude of policemen toward attacks on women drew another line between the establishment and young women. Patricia threw herself into the women's rights movement with the same ferocity she had always attacked her other goals.

The streets of Berkeley also brought her into her first contact with blacks. Black men made pleasant, flattering passes at her. One whom she found especially attractive was a tall, lanky man who wore round glasses and a skullcap. One evening Chris Thompson took her to a house on Chabot Road, where she met some fascinating people who were doing things.

The group at the house, which included several couples, had a food conspiracy going, a conspiracy to beat the food market ripoffs by buying in larger quantities at lower prices. They split the costs between the couples this way. She met another restless spirit there, Nancy Ling Perry, who seemed to be as intensely dedicated as she was to feminism.

She bounced in and out of a brief relationship with Thompson and into one with a neighbor of hers, Camilla Hall.

Camilla—she had asked her to call her Candy and she did—had helped her with an interest in photography. Candy's sense of design and composition had improved her picture taking until felt she could try a major project. She dropped out of school and set out interviewing elderly women in San Francisco, photographing them and asking them about their life styles 60 and 70 years ago. An exhibit was planned.

Patricia inspired Candy, too. Her lean, angular face was a challenge to the sculptress. Her brisk, forceful manner brought deeply erotic verse from the poet in Candy/Camilla.

The poetry caught at Patricia. One poem calling her Mizmoon, so moved her, that she followed an impulse and changed her name legally to reflect this touching tribute. Their affair grew rapidly from soulmates to physical expressions of love.

Friends watching the two felt Mizmoon was the more forceful of the two, that the blonde, bubbly Candy/Camilla simply followed wherever Mizmoon led. The older woman had vaguely liberal ideas, but Mizmoon called her a "goody-goody liberal" who was afraid to do something directly revolutionary.

The two of them separated, moved to opposite ends of Berkeley about the time Mizmoon quit school and took a job as a janitress at the UC library. Talk around the library janitorial staff became increasingly militant, leading one elderly librarian to confide once that "we have criminals working here."

Patricia Mizmoon's life changed completely, when two of her feminist friends brought a black man to her

123

apartment and asked her to hide him for them. The man's name was Donald DeFreeze and he considered himself a revolutionary/visionary.

VII

As investigators pieced together every strand possible from the suspected SLA soldiers' past lives, they found numerous ties to the prison movement and key inmates considered to be radical leaders. Visits and letters to Clifford "Death Row Jeff" Jefferson had come at times crucial to the planning of both the Foster slaying and the Patty kidnaping. Others had kept in close touch with Albert Taylor, Raymond Sparks, James "Doc" Holiday and others believed to be leaders in the Black Guerrilla Family.

But the puzzle was whether this group was leading or following the blacks. Underground informants told investigator after investigator that the escapee, De-Freeze, who now called himself Cinque, had begun organizing the SLA while still behind bars, that the escapes of DeFreeze and Wheeler had been planned with the help of the outsiders.

Studying DeFreeze's history and background placed a lot of question on the man's ability to suddenly emerge as a leader.

When he had entered prison, his writings and court statements lacked any of the flair evident on the tapes.

Whether prison revolutionaries had developed some hidden talent, could only be guessed. He had been deeply involved in the Black Cultural Association at Vacaville, but his attempt to take over leadership of the group had failed. After he complained to prison authorities that the BCA was not properly set up, he was allowed to form his own group, Unisight, which acted as an independent cell within the BCA.

In the hands of highly educated people like the other

seven suspects, a DeFreeze could be made to feel he was the leader, but not everyone else was convinced. One bit of the past that weakened the picture of the new Cinque as a leader was found in the public record of the court case that sent him to prison for robbery, kidnaping and assault.

His letter in 1970 to Superior Judge William L. Ritzi could either be considered a supreme effort of a black's shuck and jive of a white jurist or a revealing insight into the man who was to become General Field Marshal Cinque.

Dear Sir

I know you may think I am trying to be funny or smart because I sent you a Motion for a recall of a sentence And Commitment and you denied it, I am sending you another one with this letter.

What I want to do is just talk to you, "Thats all," I want you to hear the truth of everything, you never give me a chance to talk or anything, I am in Jail, but I still want to let you know what really happened and Why.

I am going to talk to you truthfully and like I am talking to God. I will tell you things that no one has ever before know.

To Start a story of a mans life you can't start at the end, but at the start, this start will begain at the age of Sixteen.

At that age, I had Just gotten out of a boys school in New York after doing 2½ years for braking into a Parking Meter and for stealing a car, I remember the Judge said that he was sending me to the Jail for boys because he said it was the best place for me, I was sixteen at the time and didn't have a home, life in the little prison as we called it, was nothing but fear and hate, day in and day out, the hate was madening, the only safe place was your cell that you went to at the end of the day, I only had two frights, if you can call them frights, I never did win, it was funny but the frights were over the fact that I would not be a part of any of the gangs, black or white. I wanted to be friends with everyone, this the other inmates would not allow, they would try to make me

125

fright, but I always got around them somehow, they even tried to make a homosexual out of me, I got around this to, after two½ years I found myself hated by many of the boys there.

When I got out of jail, people just could not believe I had ever been to Jail, I worked hard, I didn't drink or any pills nor did I curse, I didn't hang out at night in the Street and I believed in God and really tried to live a good life.

But I was still lonely, I didn't love anyone or did any one love, I had a few girl friends but as soon as there Mother found out I had been to Jail, that was the end.

Then one day, I met my wife Glory, she was nice and lovely, I feel in love with her, I think, I believe I was just glad and happy that anyone would have me the way I was, I was Eighteen and in love and life really became real to me, I asked Glory to Marry me and she said yes, we had just met one month before we were married. My wife had three kids already when I met her.

We were Married and things were lovely all the way up to a few months, then Seven months later I came home sooner than I do most of the time from work and she and a old boy friend had just had relations, I was very very mad and very hurt, but I told the boy he could have her and she him before I killed someone, the boy said he didn't want her at all, she was just another girl to him, we tried it again, as time went on we started to be a family, then one day I found out that none of my kids had the same father and that she had never been married.

I really put faith in her, but somehow little storys kept coming to me, one was that my boss had come to my home looking for me and that my wife had come to the door in the nude, I closed my eyes to it all, I loved her and her kids and I did everything to be a father and husband, I worked hard to give them a home and the things she wanted, but somehow they would never be enough for her.

I thought that if we had kids or a baby we would be closer, but as soon as the baby was born it was the same thing I had began to drink very deeply, but I was trying to put up with her and hope she would change.

But as the years went by they never did and she told me that she had been to see her boy friend and that she wanted a divorce because I was not taking care of her and the kids good enough, I was never so mad in my life as I was then after all I had tried and forgiven. I could have killed her, but I didn't, I through her out of the house and I got drunk I got a saw and hammer and completely destroyed everything I ever brought her and I mean everything, all of it when she came back, there was nothing to come back to!

For months later she came and begged me to take her back she said she had made a mistake and that she really loved me, I was weak again, I took her back and started making another home for her and our kids But I couldn't face anyone any more, I started drinking more and more and staying at my job late and all the people that lived around us would be asleep, I started playing with guns and firer works and dogs and cars, Just anything to get away from life and I how happy I was I finely got into trouble with the Police for shoting off a rifle in my basement and for a bomb I had made out of about 30 firer works from fourth of July.

I made up my mind to lieve New Jersey and my wife made all kinds of promises to me and begged and begged me to take her.

I moved to California, I put my age up so no one would think about me having so many kids I looked like I was nineteen. I told my wife I would forget all that she had did to me and everything as if it never happened, I treated her like a man should his wife.

But I was wrong again, because more and more I was happy with everything, I started playing with guns, drinking, pills but this time more than I had ever before did. I was arrested again and again for guns or bombs. I don't really understand what I was doing, she wanted nice things and I was working and buying and selling guns and the next thing I knew I had become a thief.

127

I thought that if I made her a lovely home here in California she would finely wake up and be a wife.

I worked two Jobs and was a trief [thief] in between, she has all she wanted, TV's in every room, her home looks like or better than a movie stars, I tried to hind my weakness and unhappiness in work, I worked 22 hours a day and still I had no peace and she wanted more.

You sent me to Chino and I lied to them and didn't tell them all the truth. I think they think I am nuts.

God has told me to go home if I believed in him and changed my life and forgave everyone that had did me wong and I did, my wife also I forgave I kept my promise. But you should have never sent me back to her.

The day after I got home she told me she had had Six relations with some man she meant on the street when I was in Chino. she said she wanted nothing between us and thats why she had to tell me, I said that I forgave her and I can in some way understand why she did it But I never did, if I love someone I don't want anyone but her no matter what, anyway I thought to myself that God and you had forgiven me, so I must forgive to No Matter how bad it is, and try to make a Marriage.

Sir that didn't last long.

I wanted to get away from her somehow, I said to myself that I would go with them, my wife and kids to New Jersey and help them get things fixed up in there nice home and then come back to California.

My wife started geting on me for more money for this and that and really making me feel like I was crazy, one day I went and took $100.00 from them. I took that money home and gave it to my wife, I through it in her face, I was that mad, she said I was a fool! I could have Stole all of the money which was $1500.00 but I only took $100.00 of it. Sir what she said really did something to me, it opened my eyes to what she was and what she had made me became, that night I got into my car and I drove for two days

128

and nights and came back to Calif. to go to Jail and do whatever time I have to start my life over. I never got a chance to give myself up I was arrested.

Sir Don't send me to prison again, I am not a crook or a thief nor am I crazy, I hope you will believe me, I am foolish. Honest and Truthful, but I was very proud and very weak when it came to my wife. But that's over and gone.

Sir even if you don't ever call me back or want to see me againm Thank you for all you have done and all I can say is God Bless you,

Yours truly,

Donald DeFreeze

Investigators could only guess at whether the man who wrote that letter could educate himself in three and a half years to a leadership position in a terrorist band.

They had just as little success in obtaining a lead that would enable them to find the terrorists and Patty.

After having traced the bank accounts, past addresses, drivers licenses, automobile registrations, passport applications and endorsements and other vital statistics, they were no closer than they had been the morning of February 5.

They even muffed one bright opportunity across the street from their Berkeley FBI office. Bank accounts were there in the names of Nancy Ling Perry and Camilla Hall. Bank officials were put on alert.

Camilla walked into the bank four days after the discovery, withdrew $1,565 in cash and left after commenting that it made her nervous to carry so much cash around the streets of Berkeley. The teller who knew her by sight had not been notified that Camilla was being sought by the FBI.

A locksmith was found in Palo Alto who sold a dead-bolt lock to Camilla Hall and two black men. Her father had said the last he had heard his daughter was moving from Berkeley to Palo Alto to take care of someone's estate while they were in Europe, but he did not know the address. Nor did the investigators.

CHAPTER TEN

THE MEDIA IS THE MESSENGER

I

"The strange part of this story is that usually the
press refuses to be used by anybody for any reason.
The minute we feel we are being used, we pack up and
leave. But this time we all want to help the Hearsts get
that girl back, so we're saying, "Here we are, use us."
————Ron Eveslage, NBC cameraman. February 17,
1974.

Almost from the beginning the media was the messenger. With two exceptions, all of the communiqués
and tape recordings from the SLA to the Hearst family
were delivered directly to a news media outlet and
relayed (often within minutes) to the public at the same
time the family of the kidnap victim got the messages
in Hillsborough.

The media in all its forms—newspapers, magazines,
radio and television—became an errand boy, initially
for the terrorists, but soon thereafter for the Hearst
family as well.

Ron Eveslage was being naïve or disingenuous when
he said that the media "usually refuses" to be used. It

usually balks a bit, but frequently *does* allow itself to be used if the circumstances require it or if the user is clever or powerful enough. For good or ill, with or without its knowledge, the media is used by politicians, by big businesses, by pressure groups, by celebrities, even by cranks and kooks to carry their messages to the public.

There is, after all, a multimillion-dollar pseudo-profession (it calls itself public relations, the media calls it flackery) devoted to creating favorable images of its clients, to bandwagoning social and political causes, personalities and products.

In theory, conscientious reporters despise the thought of being used. But as a practical matter, they also know there are many occasions when, unavoidably, they must allow themselves to be used in order to get the story. Sources do not often spill secrets, officials do not often leak information because they believe the public has a right to know, but because they feel spilling and leaking will serve their own purposes. Newsmen try to avoid the implicit ethical dilemmas by "getting both sides of the story," by digesting and interpreting raw information, by constantly checking asserted "facts," before presenting them to the public. One of the newsman's most vital roles is to put self-serving rhetoric into fair and balanced perspective for the public.

But the SLA, as one reporter put it, was a different kettle of cobras. Never before, at least in the United States, had the media been used quite like this. Never before had it been manipulated by the threat of violence. Never before had it been so blatantly blackmailed.

Someone in the SLA was a "media freak," a close and shrewd student not only of news and propaganda techniques, but also of the psychology of the communications industry. Any kind of spectacular event magnetizes the media. Stage an event that is simultaneously spectacular and mysterious—one that involves an attractive young woman, a famous name, wealth, violence, bizarre symbols, melodramatic devices—and the media is supermagnetized, instantly and irretrievably drawn to and stuck on the story.

Someone in the SLA knew that, however competitive and hard-boiled the media might seem to the public, it also is clannish and sentimentally protective of its own. Patty Hearst was not chosen as the SLA's first kidnap victim because she was the child of wealth, although that certainly was a factor. She was chosen because she was a media princess. In kidnaping Patty Hearst, the SLA knew it was capturing the Hearst empire—and with it, threatening all other communications empires in the country.

II

News manipulation began within minutes after the kidnaping. First, reporter Lari Blumenfeld's policeman friend failed to call back to tip her to the importance of the case; then came the short-lived embargo imposed by the Berkeley Police Department. But the master manipulation did not begin until February 7, with the delivery of the SLA's "Communiqué No. 3" to radio KPFA in Berkeley. The penultimate paragraph of the brief "arrest warrant" for Patty Hearst stated:

> All communications from this court MUST be published in full in all newspapers, and all other forms of the media. Failure to do so will endanger the safety of the prisoner.

At least in this instance, the SLA's blunt injunction was redundant. No editor or news director could resist using the letter in full because it was sensational news. Virtually every newspaper, radio and television station in the country—plus hundreds overseas—carried the story as its lead, printing or airing every word of the communiqué, including a slogan that soon became all too familiar:

133

"DEATH TO THE FASCIST INSECT THAT PREYS UPON THE LIFE OF THE PEOPLE."

But with delivery on February 12 of "Communiqué No. 4" and the tapes of Cinque and Patty Hearst (the free food demand), editorial soul-searching began in earnest.

The questions were both ethical and practical. Was the media's primary responsibility to inform the public and put the story into rational perspective, or to protect the life of a single individual? If the victim were a ditch-digger's daughter instead of a media princess would editors and news directors accede to the SLA's demand that its long, rambling revolutionary tracts be printed and broadcast in full? And was it technically (not to mention economically) feasible to devote great blocs of newspaper space and air time to SLA propaganda?

At the *Examiner,* executive editor Tom Eastham gave passing thought to merely excerpting key passages of the communiqué and the tape transcriptions. Then he considered using full texts but printing them in space-saving agate type. But Randy Hearst was the editor, the prisoner was his daughter, and there was no question in his mind about what should be done: print it all, print it in regular type-size.

At the neighboring *Chronicle,* the big morning paper which styles itself "The Voice of the West" and is published by Randy's old friend Charles DeYoung Theriot, managing editor Gordon Pates also decided to abide by the dictates of the SLA.

"Suppose you don't," said Pates, "and the girl or somebody else gets killed, what do you do—argue freedom of the press?"

The *Examiner* and the *Chronicle* (separate entities editorially, but printed on the same presses and distributed by the same delivery system) obediently printed unedited, complete texts of the SLA message and tapes, plus long news stories. If the SLA had bought the space at regular advertising rates, the cost would have been close to $16,000. Other Bay Area news media, including the staunchly conservative *Oakland Tribune*, also went along. The Associated Press and United Press carried complete texts on their wires, too, and many news outlets across the country published them in full or part. A "request" from Randy Hearst went to all Hearst-owned newspapers, radio and television stations that they publish the SLA material in its entirety. It was.

A few San Francisco newsmen—notably *Chronicle* reporter Tim Findley—agonized over the wisdom and ethics of going along with the terrorist demands on the media. Most, though, agreed there was no other way. "What the hell," commented one veteran who had rewritten hundreds of handouts publicizing commercial and political events, "it's just another front office 'must go' story."

Another reporter speculated that the next SLA demand would be that the traditional "Hearst Eagle" on the *Examiner*'s masthead be replaced by a seven-headed cobra. Other *Examiner* staffers were less cynical. Reporter Bill Boldenweck posted a note on the union bulletin board in the city room. "We are of your family and the pain of your home is our pain," it began. Before the day was done, more than 250 persons—reporters, copy-readers, editors, printers, pressmen, truck drivers—had signed the note.

During a discussion of the SLA's news—space blackmail, one rewriteman commented seriously, "I'm with Randy. If the SLA had my daughter, I'd give 'em the whole goddamn paper."

The *Examiner* and the *Chronicle* continued printing the full texts of tapes and communiqués from the SLA (there were six more) until April 3. The *Oakland Tribune*, which had broken the embargo on the day after the kidnaping, again chose to go its own way.

Joseph W. Knowland, Jr., who took over as the *Tribune*'s editor-publisher after the suicide of his father, former U.S. Senator William F. Knowland, on February 23, announced the decision in a page-one editorial on March 10. He wrote, in part:

As editor, I have issued a policy directive to the *Tribune* nullifying the SLA demand to the *Tribune* and other media to publish SLA communications in their 'exact form, not omitting any area.'... The SLA's extortion, placing tyrannical demands on the Hearst family, the public and the media alike, seeks to enslave us all, the public as well as the press.

He wished God's blessings on Patty Hearst and her family, then addressed his journalistic colleagues directly:

... I say: NOW is the time to protect our country's freedoms, not "tomorrow"; for if not "now" there will be no "free tomorrows."

The *Berkeley Gazette*, along with several other papers and electronic news outlets in the Bay Area, immediately followed the *Tribune*'s lead.

III

February 20, 1974, was Patty Hearst's twentieth birthday. It also was the day of the Big Hunch in Hillsborough. For the past several days an atmosphere of tense, electric expectation had been building among the family sequestered inside the big Hearst home on West Santa Ynez Avenue and the newsmen in semipermanent encampment on the once-quiet tree-lined street outside. Not everyone shared it, but generally there was a gut feeling inside and outside the house that the SLA just might release Patty Hearst on her birthday. Even the hard-nosed Charles Bates, the FBI agent in charge of the case, had cautious hopes she might be freed.

There was some basis for the speculation. The SLA was given to bold, melodramatic gestures. Four days before Patty's birthday, the SLA had sent a message by way of Rev. Cecil Williams of the Glide Memorial Methodist Church indicating that it would accept a "reasonable" food distribution plan as the first step toward freeing their captive. Then, on the day before Patty's birthday, Randy Hearst announced the $2 million People in Need free food program, which struck at least the public at large as a more than reasonable gesture of good faith.

By February 20 a kind of symbiotic relationship had developed between the newsmen and the Hearst family. The Hearsts needed the newsmen to transmit their replies to the SLA; the newsmen needed the Hearsts as central characters in one of the most dramatic news stories of all time. There was, however, more to the relationship. A genuine mutual affection and respect had developed. The consensus among newsmen was that Randy was a nice guy and Catherine was a gracious lady.

Soon after the first platoons of newsmen arrived at Hillsborough, the Hearsts opened up the unused two-room chauffeur's quarters next door to the house as a "warming room" for chilled reporters and photographers. Emmy Brubach, the family's pert, *gemütlich* German cook, brewed great urns of coffee, set out cookies, cooked huge pots of soup, all for the newsmen.

Three days after the journalistic encampment was established at Hillsborough, newsmen took up a collection, bought a large bouquet of flowers and presented it to Catherine Hearst. "We are so terribly moved," she told them. "Oh, this is such an awfully nice thing to do." Not long afterward, she asked a member of the press corps to collect the names and addresses of all the reporters and photographers regularly working outside her home. It was a future guest list. "Catherine said that when Patty comes home, she's going to throw us the biggest party we've ever seen," the list-maker explained.

In their brief but frequent appearances before the press during the first weeks after the kidnaping, Randy and Catherine came through to both reporters at the scene and millions of Americans who watched them on the nightly TV news as quiet, unpretentious people showing enormous presence and control under tremendous stress. Randy, handsome and looking younger than his years, always spoke in measured tones. Catherine, blonde and still pretty, wore dark glasses, dark clothes. Sometimes her voice faltered, sometimes there were tears in her eyes, but she never broke down on camera. Consciously or unconsciously, the image they presented—serious, deeply concerned about their daughter, affectionate and supportive of one another—was precisely the right one for the eyes of Middle America.

Photographers jostled one another to get poignant pictures of Randy and Catherine standing before the microphones and holding hands behind their backs.

Reporters were uncharacteristically deferential toward the Hearsts. Seldom did they ask tough questions. In fact, questions of any kind were infrequently asked and almost invariably couched in sympathetic terms.

With few exceptions, the newsmen agreed that the behavior of Randy and Catherine fit Hemingway's definition of courage—grace under pressure. News reports, especially on television, reflected their attitude.

More than once in broadcasting live reports from Hillsborough, KGO-TV reporter John Lester's voice broke and tears appeared in his eyes. Lester, 38, good-looking, mannerly and well-bred, had been one of the first reporters regularly assigned to cover the Hearst home. By unspoken agreement, he quickly became the pool reporter, liason man between the Hearsts and the media. When Randy and Catherine were too busy or too preoccupied to appear at a press conference, Lester acted as their unofficial spokesman. When a question arose that newsmen thought required an immediate answer, Lester knocked on the door, went inside, discussed the matter with the family, and returned with their reaction. Some reporters resented his intimacy with the family, but most agreed he did a good job. He never violated his trust by using his rapport with the family to develop exclusive stories for himself.

Lester also advised Randy and Catherine on media techniques, especially on how to "get through" on television. Once Randy asked Lester if there was any particular thing he should avoid doing when on camera.

"Just don't do this," said Lester, imitating a country rube picking his nose.

Randy, who liked an earthy joke, thereafter used the nose-picking gesture himself as a signal to Lester that he was ready to step outside to face the cameras.

Lester eventually resigned his reporter's job and was hired by the Hearst Corporation as Randy's official spokesmen. He also began writing an "authorized" day-by-day diary of the Hearst family's long ordeal.

IV

Al Bullock, a bouncy, outgoing photographer, was Lester's KGO-TV teammate when the Hearst case broke. He had been the first newsman on the scene at the Hearst home, arriving minutes before Randy and Catherine got back from Washington, D.C., shortly before noon on February 5. He made the initial contact with the Hearsts and provided Lester with the entrée which led to the reporter's liaison role and in the end, his position as Randy's paid spokesman.

Of all the newsmen in Hillsborough on February 20, Bullock was perhaps the most convinced that Patty would be given a birthday gift of freedom. When he arrived that day, Bullock carried a large, professionally lettered poster under his arm. He Scotch-taped it over the doors of the big double garage next to the Hearst home. It read:

HAPPY BIRTHDAY PATTY
Al Bullock and News People

Several of the more than 80 reporters, cameramen and technicians stationed in Hillsborough complained to Bullock about the sign; they said they understood his feelings, but the poster looked gimmicky, like a stage setting. Besides it made them appear unobjective, too involved in the story.

Bullock removed the sign from the garage, but a few

minutes later mounted it on the street side of the wall in front of the Hearst home. "The garage is the Hearsts'," he explained. "The wall, it's kind of *ours*." Bullock had never met Patty Hearst, but over the past two weeks he had come to feel that he did know her. He wanted to welcome her home in his own way.

Throughout the day, newsmen were jumpy and anxious, half expecting that Patty might step out of the next car that stopped on West Santa Ynez Avenue. Inside the house, the same hopeful anxiety prevailed.

To Willie Hearst, still staying with Randy and Catherine at that time, February 20 was possibly the high point of expectation for the family. "Yeah, everything seemed to be tied to that," he said. "It seemed, like the perfect opportunity for them (the SLA) to do something humanistic ... defy what people were saying about them. You have to remember that at that time the communiqué had come down where Patty had said anything you do will be all right, and where Cinque had said we will accept a good-faith gesture on your part ..."

The mutual media massage between newsmen and the Hearsts had lulled both into a mood of undue optimism. Patty Hearst was not freed. Instead, late that night, another SLA tape was delivered to Rev. Cecil Williams. Cinque, in a tough, no-nonsense tone, called the $2 million food program "a few crumbs," demanded that Randy add $4 million to the plan within 24 hours and said his daughter's status as a prisoner of war would not change until the status of the imprisoned SLA soldiers Joe Remiro and Russell Little also changed.

The next day the mood of the news crew in Hillsborough was one of deep depression; it was even deeper inside the house.

V

There was no investigative reporting at the Hillsborough estate except at the most trivial level. One reporter wangled his way into Emmy Brubach's big, old-fashioned kitchen and learned exclusively that one of the two live-in FBI agents liked Alpha-Bits cereal for breakfast, while Randy preferred poached eggs and was served in bed. This scoop was offered to the reporter's editor and turned down.

Day after day, messengers arrived with boxfuls of mail for the Hearsts, and television cameramen scrambled to film the event. Once there was an even greater scramble to film the messenger as he sneaked out the back door with a mysterious package in his arms. Reporters finally discovered that the package contained the FBI agents' dirty underwear.

Other journalists, though, were engaged in serious investigative efforts. Ed Montgomery and Carol Pogash of the *Examiner,* Tim Findley of the *Chronicle* and Marilyn Baker of the "Newsroom" staff of KQED, the San Francisco educational television station, devoted most of their working days running down possible news leads in the case.

Montgomery, a 1950 Pulitzer Prize winner, had wide-ranging, buddy-buddy contacts with law enforcement officers in California and Washington, D. C. A political conservative, his exposés of Communist and radical activities had made him a popular villain to both Old and New Left in the Bay Area.

Montgomery's sources put him onto dozens of leads, some false, some legitimate. Early in the case, a false lead sent him to the scene of an FBI stakeout of a cabin deep in the Santa Cruz Mountains, 80 miles south of San Francisco. Montgomery, a young reporter named C.P. McCarthy, and an old pro photographer named Bob Bryant, spent three tense uncomfortable days and nights waiting for the FBI task force to make their move on the cabin where they believed Patty Hearst was being held.

That lead fizzled when an agent crawled on his belly a half mile in pitch darkness, scrunched under the cabin and listened for hours with an electronic device for any sign of life inside. There was none.

Montgomery also learned of another FBI stakeout near the city of Redding, 200 miles northeast of San Francisco. This time a U-2 spy plane was borrowed to make an over-flight of another cabin, also suspected as a holding point for the kidnap victim. The U-2's sophisticated heat sensors showed there was a fire in the cabin's fireplace, that the engine of one car parked outside was still warm, the other cars cold, and that three persons were holed up in the place. A telephone lineman then went in on foot to make a "routine" inquiry about service to the cabin. Patty was not there. The three occupants were in no way connected with the SLA. Another dead end.

But many of Montgomery's leads did work out. Within four days after the kidnaping, Montgomery had learned the names and backgrounds of several members of the SLA, including Donald David DeFreeze and Thero Wheeler. Here was a major news beat and Montgomery ached to print it. But the word had come down from Randy Hearst: nothing was to be published that might conceivably endanger Patty's life. There was the chance that the story would provoke DeFreeze. The *Examiner* did not print it.

Examiner reporters Carol Pogash, Steve Cook and Don Martinez were the first Bay Area journalists to probe deeply into the SLA. They were on the story almost immediately after the murder of Oakland Schools Superintendent Marcus Foster. The burned-out SLA hideout in Concord, discovered after the arrests of Remiro and Little, was a gold mine of leads. Ms. Pogash rummaged through the place like a terrier. Using leads she found there, Ms. Pogash, Cook and Martinez cooperated in putting together an exclusive story connecting Nancy Ling Perry to the SLA, reported in depth on

142

her middle-class background, and discovered her alias of Nancy DeVoto.

From that takeoff point, the 28-year-old Ms. Pogash, who lived in Berkeley and had excellent confidential sources there, began piecing together a sketchy outline of the terrorist organization. She developed one valuable source who was intimate with several members of the SLA. The source promised to set up key interviews when the time was right.

But when Ms. Pogash came up with a story connecting the Vietnam Veterans Against the War with the SLA, City Editor Larry Dum killed the story. It was, he said, possibly libelous.

Ms. Pogash fought the decision, but lost the argument. She later conceded that Dum probably was correct in his decision. But she was so discouraged that for the time being she stopped pursuing the SLA story.

After the kidnaping, Ms. Pogash suggested that she renew her contact with the Berkeley source who had offered to set up interviews with SLA members. The suggestion was turned down on the same grounds Montgomery's DeFreeze-Wheeler exclusive was killed. "We were told not to pursue it," Ms. Pogash recalled, "definitely not to go back to that source. I was told by Larry Dum that Randy said not to investigate."

Frustrated and disappointed, the usually self-starting Ms. Pogash again backed away from pursuit of the SLA story. "I felt shitty, just terrible," said the blunt Ms. Pogash. "I was sympathetic to Randy, but I was absolutely frustrated. I felt I knew more about the SLA than any other reporter at the time." Realistically, though, she knew the *Examiner* was in a uniquely untenable position so far as pressing the investigation of the SLA was concerned.

"I realized that Randy was a father first and a [newspaper] businessman second," she said. "If I were working for the *Chronicle,* I might have felt really ripped off. I don't think the *Chronicle* had to be so overly protective."

Chronicle reporter Tim Findley *did* feel ripped off. He too had been digging into the SLA before the kidnaping, but his editors weren't much interested. After the kidnaping, the *Chronicle*'s policy was nearly as cautious as the *Examiner*'s, and for the same reasons.

Findley, whose reputation as a reporter with strong New Left sources had been established long before, claimed he knew the identity of DeFreeze before the abduction of Patty Hearst but sat on the story because he had not been able to check it out entirely.

Findley claimed that three days after the kidnaping he was ready to go with the DeFreeze-Cinque story— but *Chronicle* city editor Abe Mellinkoff was not. It was spiked for two weeks.

When it was finally published on February 15, Findley's long, rambling account struck many readers as more of a New Left apology for the excesses and revolutionary romanticism of the SLA than a news story. Findley also made much of Cinque's strong taste for plum wine.

At least in journalistic circles, Findley's story was assessed as something less than a major coup, especially since basically the same story had been broken the night before by Marilyn Baker on KQED's "Newsroom" television show. Mrs. Baker, a reporter who had developed several good police and FBI sources over the years, was considerably more aggressive than most television journalists in the Bay Area. She also had been working the SLA story since shortly after the Foster assassination. Unfettered by most of the restraints placed on *Examiner* and *Chronicle* staffers, she came up with a number of scoops. Newspaper rivals somewhat sourly derided them as exclusives by default.

Mrs. Baker, a tough-talking middle-aged blonde, was one of the few reporters to come out of the long-running story with even a shred of glory, and that was bestowed upon her largely by the mass circulation *TV Guide* magazine. In an admiring cover story by Bill Davidson, she was made out to be a combination of Superfly, Lois Lane and John Peter Zenger. Davidson went so far as to nominate her, unofficially, for the Emmy and Peabody awards for outstanding television reporting.

By contrast, Findley—who had quit the *Chronicle*

several years before to work for *Rolling Stone* and then returned to "The Voice of the West"—quit once again when editors changed the lead sentence of a story he had written about SLA members Mizmoon and Camilla Hall. He hit the lecture and interview circuit to claim that he had risked his life to dig up stories about the SLA, only to have them suppressed or censored by journalistically irresponsible, timid, old-fogy *Chronicle* editors.

Chronicle City Editor Abe Mellinkoff shrugged off the Findley diatribes with a slightly cynical (and inaccurate) comment: "In all my years as city editor, only two reporters have quit in a huff—and both of 'em were Tim Findley."

Montgomery, the *Examiner*'s star investigative reporter since the late 1940s, was disillusioned not only with the treatment of his stories but with the paper's overall policies as well. "I've had it with the *Examiner*," he confided to city-room friends. "I'm going to retire as soon as I can."

Ms. Pogash and a number of other *Examiner* staffers also were disenchanted, partly because of the way their Hearst stories were handled, partly because of the confusion and lack of leadership at the paper, which were aggravated by the tensions and frustrations generated by the kidnaping of the editor's daughter.

Of the scores of reporters who worked the Hearst case, the one who pulled the biggest coup was not from the Bay Area but a carpetbagger from Chicago.

Thirty-nine-year-old Ron Koziol of the *Chicago Tribune* was a tough, hard-digging investigative reporter who had begun developing police sources in the Bay Area in 1968 when he drew an assignment to cover antiwar demonstrations in Berkeley. Cops like the burly, cigar-chomping Koziol—he had worked the police beat in Chicago and he talked their language. He kept in touch with his Bay Area sources over the years. In June 1974 it paid off.

In the June 30 editions of the *Chicago Tribune,* the page one banner line was:

FBI bungled a chance
to find Patty Hearst

Koziol related how, on February 25, the FBI had learned that Camilla Hall/Gabi and Nancy Ling Perry were still maintaining active accounts in the Central Bank in Berkeley. The bank was directly across the street from the FBI's Berkeley office.

In blunt, Old Journalism style, Koziol told how, on March 1, Camilla Hall walked into the bank, withdrew her money, walked out and vanished.

If the FBI had staked out the bank—a basic investigative technique—she could have been tailed and possibly led the FBI to the SLA's hideout. And Patty Hearst.

The FBI would not comment on Koziol's story.

The next day Koziol broke another big one. He reported that, on the day after the kidnaping, the FBI had discovered a box of cyanide-tipped bullets under the bookshelf in the Benvenue apartment of Steve Weed and Patty Hearst.

Both of Koziol's stories came from police sources in the Bay Area. Hearst's *Examiner,* following up on Koziol's scoops, not only confirmed both stories but learned that some local cops were decidedly disturbed by the way the FBI had handled the whole Hearst case. Some of their remarks about FBI Agent in Charge Bates were unprintable.

"We share our information but the FBI doesn't share theirs," was one of the milder comments from an investigator. "The Berkeley police didn't even know about this bank thing until the whole thing was cold. The time they should have been told was on February 25, when the trail was hot."

Unlike Marilyn Baker, Koziol did not get a glowing write-up in *TV Guide.* But then he wasn't a blonde with long eyelashes. Koziol was content with his page-one by-lines.

VI

Examiner executive editor Tom Eastham, a journal-istic technician rather than an ethical theoretician, shared some of the staff's feeling of frustration but felt that the paper did its job reasonably well under the circumstances. He admitted there was censorship and suppression of stories, minor and major.

On Eastham's orders, no mention was made in the *Examiner* of the fact, quickly reported elsewhere, that Patty and her fiancé Steven Weed were living together. "I asked," he said, "that there be no reference to Patty sharing the apartment with Weed. I personally was not (at the time) aware of the circumstances."

A reference to Patty being carried from the apartment "half-naked" was cut out of the *Examiner*'s first-day story.

"We had to think about the effect on the family," Eastham said.

Like his colleagues on the *Chronicle,* Eastham was convinced that investigative reporting by his staff might endanger the victim's life. "I thought, hell, I wouldn't want to be responsible for the death of that girl . . . None of us liked it (the suppression). We participated in the biggest ripoff of the press in history."

Eastham could offer no surefire safeguards against future terrorist blackmail of the media. "I'm not ashamed of the *Examiner*'s performance, but like most people in the business I am very concerned that a small group like the SLA can have a very profound effect on all the media," he commented. "I've tried to figure out what could be done if it should happen again.

"Nobody should have the power to do the things Randy Hearst was able to do in response to his daughter's kidnaping. There should be something—a law—to sort of intervene, neutralize the power of a man who is operating under great stress.

"I think it might be necessary (if it happened again)

for Randy to resign his position. Suppose Nixon's daughter was kidnaped, and that's entirely possible, what does he do? Turn the country over to 'em? Turn over the atomic arsenal? Where does it stop? The country should be discussing where it stops in times of terrorism."

Some Americans were discussing these questions. But others, including publications such as *Newsweek,* also were discussing such titillating questions as whether Patty really had been expelled from Santa Catalina School for smoking pot.

And, in private, some policemen, newsmen and eventually ordinary citizens were raising more sinister questions: Was Steve Weed, the boyfriend with the funny moustache, in on the abduction? Was Patty Hearst a conspirator in her own kidnaping?

CHAPTER ELEVEN

THE MOVEMENT—FROM THERE TO HERE

When Marge and Hal Ling attended the University of California at Berkeley, they knew it fondly as "Cal." Its less fond nickname was "the factory." This was the name bestowed out of idle resentment at not being able to discern the features of one's professor. Most were far away from the students, elevated on a podium above an auditorium more appropriate for assembly lines than individual learning experiences. Dynamics of the 20,-000-plus student body had begun to reduce each student to a mere cog in the machinery. By the time the Lings enrolled their daughter Nancy in their alma mater in 1966, the distortions had become heightened.

There were new nicknames, new life styles and new perceptions emerging from a student body that had grown past 30,000. The "factory" had become a conscious symbol, representative of all of society. All of its shams and hypocrisies were targets of the students' resentment and disillusionment. A growing number decided there was no longer any point in following the traditional studies. They saw this as merely becoming another of a long line of carbon-copy grads programmed for financial success. This revolt fueled the start of a protest movement that was to spread for a decade.

"Jumping off the conveyors, we have become a community of furiously talking, feeling and thinking human beings," wrote one protester.

Parental dismay fed upon by politicians' demagoguery drowned out any understanding of the protesters. The gap was widened further by the youthful urge to shock their elders by kicking over old language taboos.

Four-letter words became the bait and then the title of the revolt. The students dubbed their drive the Free Speech Movement, while university administrators and editorialists insisted it was the Filthy Speech Movement.

Instant celebrities like Mario Savio and Jerry Rubin had first used the words as rallying cries, crowd pleasers. But upon seeing the response of the media, who could find no way to report directly the words being spoken, they escalated the words to colorful signs and slogans. Because the newspapers, magazines and television seen by adults could not report the text of their protest, the students were pushed further and further into extremes.

Newspapers for years had used the pleasant sounding "intimate with" to hint at "had intercourse with" and "assault" had always been substituted for "rape." When students began trumpeting "Fuck the Draft" and "Fuck the Cops" and "Fuck Reagan," the culture shock was so strong that the Movement became instantly isolated. Aims of the protest and its reasons were obscured beneath a welter of words that only more vividly demonstrated for the students the obvious paradoxes of the society they were entering.

Most had heard their parents and other older people use such language with impunity. Their responses to their children using the same words became a challenge to the Movement's inventiveness. The Vietnam war was a ready target:

"Why is it more heinous for an American soldier to FUCK an eighteen-year-old unmarried American girl than to KILL an eighteen-year-old unmarried Vietnamese girl?"

UC was filled with students forced into school to avoid participating in the unpopular Southeast Asian conflict. A mixture of guilt and resentment fed the protest. Some felt guilt that their parents' affluence had enabled them to avoid military service that others who were black or brown or poor could not dodge. Others merely resented their being forced to become professional students.

Besides the Vietnamese war, draft and war-industry protests, events in neighboring cities around Berkeley had created other pressures that drew some of the activists off campus. Conflicts between police and blacks in Berkeley, Oakland and Richmond created a new black protest movement.

A UC law grad, Donald Warden, had formed an Afro-American Association that had drawn young blacks from these areas as well as San Francisco. In 1966 he lost a large segment of his more militant members who split in several directions, dissatisfied with his cultural studies and consciousness-raising talk as too slow. Roy Ballard organized a San Francisco faction under the name of Black Panther Party of Northern California. Ron Everett drifted south to Watts, changed his name to Ron Karenga and formed the United Slaves party. Two Merritt College students, Huey Newton and Bobby Seale, quit to organize their young street-wise friends into the Black Panther Party for Self-Defense; they won recruits by arming themselves with guns and establishing a citizens' patrol to help police officers work in the ghetto.

After her first year at UC, hearing the revolutionary talk echoing through Berkeley's coffeehouses, communes and campus, Nancy dropped out to spend a year working. She first entered the volatile black community by falling in love with a slim, strikingly handsome black composer, Gil Perry.

By the time she returned to the university in 1968, Nancy had a new perspective, one in which she felt both isolated and unique—being married to a black

151

man. The assassination of Martin Luther King, the slaying by police of Panther Bobby Hutton, and imprisonment of Eldridge Cleaver the previous April, all had a special, personal meaning for her. Her husband was not politically involved at the time, but Nancy took upon herself the guilt for which she blamed white people for those tragedies.

Patty Hearst's view of the world was shifting too that same year. She had been forced to return to a strict, sometimes harsh private school for well-behaved daughters of the affluent, Santa Catalina School in Monterey. Uniformly-clad nuns set and administered uniform rules that were to be followed uniformly and without deviation by their young charges. Patty had tried to avoid a second year at the plodding, uninteresting routine, but her mother had insisted the discipline would be good for her.

Mrs. Hearst was embroiled that year in a raging controversy at UC involving blacks. Eldridge Cleaver had been hired to teach a class at Berkeley. Free on appeal while lawyers argued over his parole status in the April incident, Cleaver had become the outraged target of conservatives on the UC Board of Regents. Max Rafferty, then state superintendent of schools and a candidate for U.S. senator, had rallied the support of Governor Reagan, Mrs. Hearst and others on the board in an attempt to block Cleaver's teaching. They failed and Cleaver taught two classes before jumping bail and fleeing to Algiers.

Hardly noticed in all the acrimony over Black Panthers, the Vietnam War and the draft, a small group from UC's law school Boalt Hall, had been sending delegations to prisons, working on several prison reform measures. They were to work this way for some three years before any radicals became interested.

Conspiracy theorists on the right, who had fallen from favor with the late Senator Joe McCarthy's demise only to rise with Ronald Reagan, blamed the Movement on a renewed alliance between liberals and Communists. The Students for a Democratic Society, which established liberals helped form in 1962, became the target of the right in these accusations. Young Communists did participate in the Berkeley upheavals, but their theories demonstrated another type of generation gap. Where their parents had favored Communist Party-USA with Russian ties, these new ultraleftists were cheering modern figures like Fidel Castro, Che Guevara and Mao Tse-tung.

Berkeley's SDS was different from the quiet, symbolic organization Steven Weed experienced at Princeton. Other campuses had still different forms. Around the Bay Area more violent versions emerged. Politics grew like barnacles, fed by tidal shifts of racial struggles in Richmond, disillusionment at Stanford, disenchantment in San Francisco. Groups were spawned with colorful names like the Revolutionary Action Movement, White Panthers, Grass Roots, Young Partisans and Revolutionary Union. All fed into a group that hoped to become a multiracial band of revolutionaries with the Spanish name, Venceremos.

Roots of the organization that was to play a key role in the prison revolt that led to Patty's kidnaping came from all of the factions. But the largest share came from the Revolutionary Union that was set up by an Alameda County Superior Court judge's son, Robert Avakian.

Capitalizing on a controversy that erupted over a policeman's slaying of a black youth in Richmond, Avakian set up several groups that ultimately became the RU. He worked for a time with the fledgling Black Panthers before expanding around the bay into an organization built largely around white students at universities and colleges.

On the San Francisco peninsula, Avakian teamed with a Stanford professor, H. Bruce Franklin, and a former editor of the campus newspaper Barry Greenberg. With their help, RU carried out a coup that swept up a Menlo Park free university experiment and edged out its loose-knit leadership of theoretical anarchists.

The Midpeninsula Free University, which RU took over, had attracted flower children and idealists like biology research worker John Dolly and his wife, Jean.

They moved into a psychodrama commune where they lived while both taught classes, John took care of the research animals at his regular job, and Jean became an expert in graphic arts, macramé and collage. Before long, they left the commune in a faction fight over whether they could keep guns for self-defense.

Franklin was emerging as a charismatic leader. An associate professor of English who taught his students the working-class themes of Herman Melville's works, his academic writings showed more and more of his Maoist theories.

Franklin portrayed himself as a disillusioned Democrat who had done precinct work for the election of President Lyndon Johnson. He had been an intelligence officer in the U.S. Air Force, working at a lower level of the Strategic Air Command before entering college. He graduated from Stanford after a short scholarship stint at Amherst. As one of the RU leaders, he was involved in demonstrations against Dow Chemical's constructing a napalm plant in Redwood City, the move to ban ROTC from campus and drives against Department of Defense research.

Less than two years later, Franklin was leading a large share of the RU membership into a group that teamed with a Redwood City Chicano group that had chosen the Cuban victory cry for its name, Venceremos.

Fidel Castro used the word to close his impassioned speeches as he neared the end of his revolution. He would raise both arms aloft and shout: *"Patria o muerte. Venceremos,"* meaning literally: "Fatherland or death. We will win."

Insiders said Franklin split with Avakian over Maoist doctrine. Franklin was supposed to have favored immediate military action in their revolution, while Avakian favored a slower approach. But Franklin insisted that the position paper he wrote on military strategy was written in haste, manipulated by Avakian to make him look bad.

Franklin took RU members from Stanford, Redwood City, San Francisco, Richmond and Hayward including Jean Hobson, John and Jean Dolly and a fellow Stanfordite from Coral Gables, Florida, Janet Cooper Weiss. Janet and Mrs. Hobson were on the first Venceremos central committee along with four Chicanos and Franklin.

Avakian soothed his wounds by a trip to the People's Republic of China with Mrs. Greenberg and another RU leader. They met with Chou En Lai and other leaders of China before returning to the United States to make a series of talks about the success of the revolution. Avakian then took up residence in Chicago, leaving the field to Franklin and his group.

Venceremos' projects ranged from Stanford antiwar demonstrations to a medical clinic in Redwood City to agitation in favor of a group of young Chicanos called Los Siete, who were on trial for murdering a San Francisco policeman. The campus at Stanford took on the air of an embattled city with pockmarked walls, broken windows, bombed out offices and arson-caused fires. But their members were never arrested for anything more than throwing rocks, sitting in or resisting arrest during a demonstration.

Venceremos' rein on Stanford campus ended directly from a bit of guerrilla theater. Franklin and a group of his followers attempted to indict Henry Cabot Lodge, former ambassador to Vietnam, as a war criminal.

Lodge had been invited to the staid Hoover Institution for War, Peace and Revolution as the keynote speaker of the 1971 UN Day observance. Lodge was unable to make his speech in public, because of hecklers in the audience. Franklin was charged by the university administration with having participated, opening a year-long controversy that also included accusations he incited students to riot. After court fights, academic hearings and demonstrations—some punctuated with gunshots, gang fights between students and police and bombings—Franklin was fired. He became the first tenured professor in 70 years to be dismissed for radical activities.

His charismatic leadership was spiced with an almost

demagogic ability to stir crowds. Franklin could play society's strait laces like banjo strings, always finding the off-key one to puncture pomposities. He was able to take advantage of the unpopular Vietnam War for crowd-drawing issues, attracting followers from both conservative and liberal backgrounds. One of the active members was Chris Katzenbach, son of the liberal former U.S. attorney general. Another was the daughter of a retired Navy commander who had invented several war tools. Kathy Barkley, who left Venceremos to marry Pentagon Papers codefendant Anthony Russo, was even more vocal and violent than Chris.

Attractions were many and varied for student participation. Aside from peer pressure to kick over the traces, there was an excitement and thrill of the carnival atmosphere, the excitement that anything could happen and often did.

A wild, disorganized decathlon of running, throwing, swinging would stir the most lethargic supply of adrenalin. Pitting themselves against shielded, helmeted automatons that were the police tactical squads became a valiant deed right out of mythology.

There was the new sexual freedom, too. Experiments in communal living where a boy or girl could try several partners without ties or responsibilities. All that was a light-year ahead of the coed dorms, where everyone was like their own brothers and sisters back home. The interracial experimentation could be done without the pressures they might suffer in other surroundings.

Some of the young faculty wives, who had missed their flings because they had to work to put their husbands through graduate school, leaped into the new morality with glee. Those who had lived sheltered lives as teen-agers or as freshmen fell into a world they had only read about in *Playboy* and *Penthouse,* never believing it had been anything more than fantasy.

Some of the radical experiments by these inexperienced revolutionaries naively strayed into dangerous territory. One of Franklin's group once tried to organize two of the motorcycle outlaw gangs near Stanford, hoping to use them as fighters in confrontations with police. Bikers listened to the revolutionary ideas inattentively, preferring to fondle the female members and edge them toward a handy mattress. They were less interested in fighting police, and the experiment lasted only through one case of beer and three lids of grass. A few more sensitive radicals were turned off entirely by the bikers' heavy male superiority attitudes.

While Venceremos members' attitudes toward sex were open and experimental, they prohibited heavy drugs and alcohol. Only marijuana was allowed, but never when there was danger of arrest for its use.

Another group that attracted the more monastic, those who preferred neither sexual nor mind-bending drug experiments was the Weathermen, who ultimately changed their name to the Weather Underground. After an explosion wiped out one of their bomb factories in New York City, the organization became completely secret, issuing directives only occasionally over the signature of Bernardine Dorhn, a Midwest doctor's daughter who many believe is using a new identity in Berkeley.

Franklin's firing and banishment from Stanford came as the Vietnam war was being wound down. Pressures were greatly reduced on campus for joining groups like Venceremos. Revolutionaries had already shifted their emphasis elsewhere, leaving only a small core on campus for labor organizing. Janet Cooper Weiss, who had been banned from campus with Franklin, had gone into white-collar clerical labor work. Jean Hobson was visiting prison inmates at Tehachapi and Vacaville in search of radical converts.

Switching into prison organizing was barely noticed because they had backed earlier prisoners' movements in their newspaper and backing some of their fund-raising efforts. A rhetoric had already developed that the entire capitalist system was a prison. It was an easy step to the theory that prison inmates were only the most oppressed within this general prison.

The prison movement was an almost inevitable step for activists, exposed as they had been from the first to the degradations of jails and prisons.

Idealistic young people had trekked to the Deep South during the early 1960s civil rights drives. In doing what they believed to be legal, they had become intimately familiar with jails. Registering blacks to vote often ended with the activists imprisoned. The paradox of power and law was not lost on them.

Draft resistance and antiwar demonstrations added still more young people to the nation's cells. This was a new brand of prisoner who came to sit alongside those already imprisoned for drug violations. Emotionally enacted drug restrictions had flooded prisons with educated young men and women, who saw themselves as the victims of their parents' hypocrisy. Imprisonment of ethnic leaders like Newton and Cleaver and continued controversies with inmates like George Jackson only dramatized the brotherhood between prisoners inside and outside the jails and penitentiaries.

Burglars, stickup artists and other ordinary, old-fashioned criminals readily took to the new prisoners' rhetoric, because few had accepted responsibility for their own misdeeds. And it helped their self images to reverse the label of loser and cheap crook for that of revolutionary. Studies in rebellion like Algeria, where a few rebels took over a country of 12 million, began a new prison movement. New parolees quickly went in search of the movement upon their release, becoming gun runners and bank burglars like DeFreeze in what the romantically believed to be a budding revolution.

Few noticed Venceremos's swing to prison organizing. Campuses had been cooled. The prisoners of war were coming home. Attention was being drawn to noises about Republican leadership complicity in espionage and burglary at a place called Watergate. Franklin, who had taken up the study of horticulture while compiling a couple of books on revolution, attempted to make public statements on public affairs from time to time. But most editors had decided the Movement was dead, and yesterday's radicals no longer good copy.

This was after Nancy Ling Perry had returned to

Berkeley after working in a San Francisco nightclub as a topless blackjack dealer. She was still a few months away from discovering the prison movement.

Patty Hearst was in the midst of her biggest rebellion to date, asserting her independence at age 18 by setting up housekeeping with Steven Weed on a quiet street in Berkeley.

CHAPTER TWELVE

YOU CAN'T TELL THE DRAGONS FROM THE KNIGHTS

I

Planning for the prison revolution was no secret. Not from Federal Bureau of Investigation Director J. Edgar Hoover, his successor or California Attorney General Evelle Younger. They received regular intelligence reports from spies in the midst of the planning as early as July 1970.

Hoover had inaugurated a top-secret counterintelligence project in 1967 that had infiltrated all of the radical student and black movements. Younger's Criminal Identification and Investigation division had been nearly as thorough. Before any of the violence erupted, both state and federal authorities had received full details and had posted officers at key trouble spots.

In the summer of 1970 there were two action spots the revolutionaries believed were safe and free from infiltration. One was a 120-acre plot of scrub land at the 3,500-foot level of Loma Prieta's southern slope south of San Francisco. The other was a frame house surrounded by eucalyptus and redwoods on Day Valley Road in the foothills southeast of Santa Cruz. But police agents reporting to both agencies freely came and went at both sites.

The mountaintop hideout had a checkered history. Purchased by two young men from Los Altos and Palo Alto, it had been used first as a crash pad for draft resisters. They could camp out for days while awaiting arrangements to go to Canada or Europe. The property, known in the underground as "The Land," was a mile from the nearest road.

Anyone laboring up the steep trail could be spotted easily by anyone hiding out there. The remote, rocky scrub land was not apt to attract anyone, because it was so worthless the Resistance had been able to buy it cheaply.

Use of the land by the Resistance had dwindled by the end of 1968. Word got around it was vacant and the Black Panthers made some trips there for target practice and other maneuvers through most of 1969. One of the few whites dealing with the Panthers at the time went along on several of the jaunts. Tom Mosher, a former Stanford University student, had been underground since being arrested by Palo Alto police for assault on a police officer and possession of illegal weapons. He did a lot of gun running and transportation of explosives for the Panthers.

Tom Mosher was also an informant for the FBI.

One of Mosher's friends from Stanford came to him in early 1970 asking help in finding a hideout. Jimmie Johnson, a history student from Harlem, had kicked a sheriff's deputy in the butt during a student demonstration and he had been identified. He was afraid deputies would make other charges once he was in custody because he had been suspected of participating in bombing and arson at the university.

Mosher took him to "The Land," where he brought him food and supplies on several occasions. Johnson built a small cabin among the trees and scouted the mountains for alternate escape routes. He was convinced that a revolution was about to ignite and he planned to be part of its wilderness support.

Another regular visitor to the mountaintop was partially responsible for Johnson's fixation that revolution was imminent.

The visitor was James Edward Carr, a muscular holdup man from Los Angeles, who had just been released from Soledad Prison. Carr was living in the frame house on Day Valley Road.

II

Soledad Prison's long history of interracial violence had exploded in three deaths on January 13, 1970. Enmities between blacks and whites, blacks and browns, browns and whites had occasionally ended in fatal fights, but never had it ended so violently as that day. The death weapon was a rifle in the hands of a white guard. All of the fatalities were black inmates.

Soledad Prison, just off Highway 101, some 140 miles south of San Francisco, had halted integrated exercise periods in 1968 after a black inmate was killed. Killings had continued over racial conflicts until 1969 when black inmate W.L. Nolen filed civil litigation accusing prison guards and other officials of fomenting the strife.

On the morning of January 13, the first integrated exercise period in months was set up in a 40-by 150-foot concrete yard off O-wing with fifteen inmates participating: seven blacks, five whites and two Chicanos and a Samoan who sided with the whites.

In a newly constructed gun tower above the exercise yard, a retired army sergeant from Woden, Texas named Opie G. Miller watched the inmates with a .30 caliber rifle cradled in his arms.

When a fight started between Nolen and the Samoan, Miller shot Nolen in the chest, then shot two other black inmates, Cleveland Edwards and Alvin Miller, who came to his aid. Black inmates Earl Satcher and Tom Meneweather, who were also in the ward, said Miller refused to allow any hospital aid until the three were dead.

Three days after the deaths of the inmates, the Monterey District Attorney told a television reporter that Miller's killings were "justifiable homicide." Within an hour of the broadcast, white guard John Mills, had been beaten and thrown from a third story cell tier, the first guard to be killed in the history of Soledad. Charged with his murder were Fleeta Drumgo, John Cluchette and George Jackson.

The three had their case transferred from the county seat at Salinas to San Francisco in a controversial change of venue as they became known in radical circles as the Soledad Brothers. Jackson's attorney John Thorne joined with several other of Jackson's friends on the outside to commence a fund-raising effort called the Soledad Brothers Defense Fund. Joan Hammer, a tall, slender patrician daughter of a pioneer San Jose family, was one of the fund's officers. So was a University of California at Santa Cruz sociology professor, J. Herman Blake. Blake had met Jackson when he worked as a counselor at Soledad.

III

James Edward Carr considered George Jackson one of his best friends and mentors. Jackson had spurred him to get an education, something he had lacked when he entered prison seven years earlier at age 20. Carr had studied until finally receiving his high school diploma and then enrolling in junior college math. He won straight A's in mathematics and then studied anthropology and human relations. He credited Jackson with all his success.

"George was a different type of fellow, you know. Like in the early days, you had no Panthers or nationalists that we knew of," Carr once told a friend.

Carr was granted a parole July 31, 1970 and entered the University of California at Santa Cruz. Blake obtained a place for him to stay, the house on Day Valley Road, and a job assisting a mathematics professor at the university.

163

As soon as Carr arrived in Santa Cruz, he was visited by his younger sister Gwendolyn and her husband Louis Tackwood. Tackwood's presence was more than a friendly family visit, because he had been assigned to Carr by his superiors in the Los Angeles Police Department Criminal Conspiracy Section. He was a police spy.

His intelligence bosses had loaned him to Younger's CI & I Division. His reports were filed as Agent T-14.

Agent T-14 reported that plans were in progress to free Jackson and the other defendants in a scheme to take over complete control of the Marin Country courthouse. The courthouse was in the city of San Rafael and was the location of many trials for inmates from San Quentin prison. Several alternate plans were in the works. Most would use inmates freed by a force of armed revolutionaries who would invade the courthouse. Some of the defense funds—at least $10,000—had been diverted as bail money for the release of one of Carr's cousin's Tommy Lee Walker, who was supposed to participate.

A list of lawyers, academics and radicals was furnished by Agent T-14 as the plotters for the courthouse takeover. One of the more impatient was George Jackson's 17-year-old brother Jonathan, who visited the house on Day Valley Road several times while gathering guns for the assault.

Young Jackson one day took along a celebrity of the Communist Party-USA, Angela Davis. She had been invited to speak at UCSC. She thought Jonathan's gun purchase was just another black self-defense effort.

Carr had been out of prison only a week when young Jackson kicked over all the planning. Agent T-14 informed his contacts that Carr had sawed off the barrel of a shotgun Jackson had purchased on August 5, but that the teen-ager had gone ahead on his own.

On August 7, while one police officer watched outside the Hammer home and another outside the Marin County courthouse, young Jackson walked into the courthouse and into the courtroom of Marin Superior Judge Harold Haley. Haley was hearing a complaint of

California prison authorities against Quentin, inmates James McClain and William Christmas. Inmate Ruchell MaGee was in a holding cell just off the courtroom when Jackson sat down.

When the tall, slender youth stood up, a gun in his hand, he took over the courtroom, freed the inmates and began a long walk back to his waiting van. Tackwood later told friends that the plan had called for someone to be at the wheel of the van, but the van was empty. When Jackson could not start it, McClain got behind the wheel. They drove only a short way before gunfire exploded.

Judge Haley, around whose neck the sawed-off shot gun had been tied, died along with Christmas and McClain. Two other hostages and MaGee were wounded. Jackson was killed by rifle bullets.

Agents trailed Angela Davis around the country for weeks before finally arresting her in New York City. A long, costly trial ended with her acquittal on all charges. Tackwood told friends she had been duped by the plotters.

Also tried was MaGee, who commenced a marathon barrage of court petitions and motions, basing his defense on the contention that like the original Cinque he had been a slave and justified in using force to free himself.

In none of the trials for MaGee or Miss Davis was any of the intelligence material mentioned. None of the plotters were indicted or accused. The files remained locked under a security cover.

Carr spent eight months in San Francisco city jail after a small tussle in one of George Jackson's hearings, but Agent T-14 reported that his direction of planning continued from inside, using his many visitors for couriers.

On August 18, 1971, Carr was visited in jail by Jackson's mother, a friend and her attorney.

On August 21, during a wild melee inside the walls of San Quentin, three white guards, two white inmates and Jackson were slain in what prison authorities charged was another attempt to free Jackson.

Versions of what happened vary between prison administrators and prison inmates. The official version is that a gun was smuggled to Jackson by visiting attorney Stephen Bingham and that Jackson got the drop on his guards, freeing several prisoners who killed their guards and two white inmates.

Bingham had also been active in the Soledad Brothers Defense Fund drive. He was like a growing number of young attorneys who are more involved in radical causes than building a lucrative law practice. He had no need to be concerned with monetary matters anyway, coming from an affluent family so well established that one of the oldest cities in New York State was named after them. A former governor and a congressman from that state are in his immediate family.

Bingham hid his affluence under a self-effacing manner and denims. He disappeared without a trace the day Jackson was killed.

Prison officials said that Bingham had brought the gun into Jackson hidden inside a tape recorder. A woman with him, who signed the register as Vanita Anderson, handed Bingham the machine, which Correctional Officer B.M. Betts took apart without finding anything hidden inside. He said he could see all of the insides of the machine except for three inches.

Prison officials' refusal to allow any outside, impartial investigation of the bloody affair contributed to creating a martyr myth around Jackson. Already made a public figure by a book he wrote from prison and a compilation of his letters, Jackson swiftly became a violent hero to challenge the nonviolence of Martin Luther King. Huey Newton, who met Jackson in prison, helped the canonization with a gradiose funeral memorial that was echoed in black communities across the country.

Agent T-14 reported that Carr had decided he should take over Jackson's embryonic army of prison rebels. He planned to make sure his friend was killed in any escape attempt, so he would become a martyr and a movement could be built upon his martyrdom.

Agent T-14 named the outside hit man who was to have executed Jackson if he had escaped.

Tackwood later told friends that Bingham had been duped into carrying the gun inside the prison. The woman identified as Vanita Anderson had been someone else and planted by the plotters, he said.

Bingham's disappearance left behind many rumors, stories of his murder, others of his being spirited away to Canada and then to Africa.

Carr was released from jail in December 1971. His parole officer chose not to revoke his parole and allowed the time served for the courtroom tussle to be punishment for that crime.

Before being jailed, Carr had worked himself into a handy position at UCSC, obtaining a job as a teaching assistant and marrying one of a string of girls attracted to him as a revolutionary visionary. He married Joan Hammer's daughter, Betsy, and they had a daughter they christened Gea Jackson Carr. Using his mother-in-law's address in San Jose, they had applied for and obtained welfare assistance two weeks before he was arrested at the hearing for Jackson.

Upon his release, Carr made several trips to Los Angeles, where he was seen once in the company of Black Panther strong-arm man Lamarr Lloyd Mims.

Angela Davis's trial was resuming in San Jose when FBI undercover agent Tom Mosher came in out of the cold just in time to tell several stories. One was that Carr had been working as a hit man for the Panthers.

He told FBI officials and a special congressional committee that Carr had executed a former Panther captain, Amon Fred Bennett. His witness was his friend Jimmie Johnson, who had told him of helping Carr set fire to the body after Carr shot him. The bones were then crushed into bits and strewn around the mountaintop that had been Johnson's hideout. Mosher told of helping Johnson flee the country to Canada.

Bone pieces found on the mountaintop were sent to be studied by an anthropologist at the University of Arizona, who reported back they were human bones and

167

might belong to Bennett. A ring and a button at the site were identified as belonging to Bennett.

No charges were ever filed against Carr in the Bennett case.

Rumors began circulating during the Angela Davis trial that Carr would be called as a witness for the prosecution. Local authorities who had state connections said it was to be about having sawed off the shotgun for young Jackson, the report that had come from Agent T-14. The prosecution refused to confirm or deny their intent to call Carr.

Carr had just obtained a construction job at a new motel the first week of April 1972. He had arisen early April 6, eaten a light breakfast, kissed Betsy and Gea and walked out the back door.

As he opened the door to his jeep, gunfire exploded from the side of the garage. He fell dead, killed instantly by bullet wounds in the head and body.

Just 23 minutes later, police 21 miles away in Morgan Hill stopped a car containing Richard Rodriguez, 24, and Lamarr Lloyd Mims, 21, both of Los Angeles. Their car carried a bucket of fire bombs plus a rifle and handgun that were ultimately linked ballistically to Carr's execution.

Records were found in their possession showing they had spent $540 during a week's surveillance of the victim. The two men refused to make any statement about the case to investigators.

During a preliminary hearing, Assistant District Attorney William Hoffman attempted to question Carr's wife and mother-in-law about connections with the Marin County courthouse case, but they denied any knowledge of that incident or any other reason anyone would want to kill Carr. The two hired executioners pleaded guilty and were sent to prison.

Agent T-14 was out of the business by that time and could provide no information on who had ordered Carr's execution.

He had already furnished Younger's intelligence network the background on what many considered to be only a fantasy army. His dry, straightforward reports failed to reflect the bitterness and frustration still left over from the O-wing exercise yard at Soledad.

The memories of embittered inmates like Earl Satcher and Tom Meneweather, as they were freed on parole, were not easily cooled. Nor were the seeds planted by George Jackson and Carr.

Hidden away in the secret files and overlooked by investigators was one of the final reports by Agent T-14 on another seed.

Carr had many alternatives in mind, if the timing never worked properly to free his friends inside prison walls:

"One was to kidnap the children of influential people. Not the people themselves. He believed that if you kidnaped their children, you could get a lot more out of them."

CHAPTER THIRTEEN

THE CHINO ESCAPE CASE—ANOTHER LINK TO REVOLT

I

Andrea Holman had the apple-pie good looks of Patty Hearst. Her face was rounder and softer, while Patty's was angular and sleek. Both grew up on the San Francisco peninsula, just 13 miles apart in space, but worlds apart in interests, education and acquaintance with the street—until they came face to face with the prison revolution.

The daughter of Dr. Halstead Holman, Guggenheim professor of medicine at the Stanford Medical School and former dean of the school, Andrea leaped into the protest movement shortly after entering Gunn High School in Palo Alto. Her older brother Michael had become active in Revolutionary Union and then Venceremos demonstrations. She began following her brother around. Protest was a family tradition the Holmans had exercised for years in New York, where he had been on the staff at the Rockefeller Institute before moving to Stanford in 1960. Where the parents' politics had been Old Left, their children were attracted to the heroes of the 1970s, Mao and Fidel.

In 1971, the year before Patty took a Menlo College study tour of Greece and the Greek Islands, Andrea investigated an island in the Carribean—Cuba. She cut sugar cane with a Venceremos brigade and studied Communist law, socialism and penal practices there.

She dropped out of high school her senior year, increasing her participation in Venceremos activities. Most of her time she and Venceremos central committee member Jean Hobson worked on a growing new interest in prisons and prison inmates.

Jean Hobson, then 44, was the wife of an electronics engineer and had brought three of her five children into Venceremos. Active in low-cost housing fights in Palo Alto, she participated in the Poor Peoples' March on Washington; once ran for the Palo Alto City Council before moving to neighboring Mountain View and had been Venceremos's representative to the Women's Conference with the Indochinese the same year Andrea went to Cuba.

Andrea and Mrs. Hobson and a few of their friends and neighbors quietly moved their organization into the prison movement while other radical groups marched and demonstrated in support of Angela Davis. Venceremos had been conspicuously absent in the Angela protests and the Soledad Brothers demonstrations, This small cadre began visiting prisons, writing letters to inmates and sending literature.

They uncovered immediate interest and inmates well versed in the Maoist doctrine. Inmates without much to occupy their time were increasingly involved in radical literature. Some inmates were drawn into it only because prison officials had banned such material—possession of such books became a badge of honor. Others found the writings of Mao, Ho Chi Minh and other leftist revolutionary heroes fascinating. Some even fantasized and rationalized themselves as crusaders.

At Tehachapi, Chino, Tracy, wherever they visited, inmates were flattered and attracted to Andrea. One especially handsome and charming Chino inmate was Benton Douglas Burt, a thirty-year-old who had also grown up on the peninsula. He had been in prison for

171

10 years, but was due to be released soon. Andrea and Doug fell in love. When he was released, they moved into an apartment in Hayward across the bay from Stanford.

Burt made an ideal Venceremos recruit, because of his intimate knowledge of prison routines and procedures. He and Andrea and their friends accelerated their visiting of prisoners. Their success in finding kindred spirits behind prison walls had been most exhilarating. It provided a symbolic link with revolutionary folk heroes who had spent considerable time behind bars. Ho Chi Minh. Fidel Castro. Regis Debray. Little notice was paid to the difference between their circumstances and Burt's.

Burt had been sent to prison as a petty burglar. Unable to adjust readily to the unique society within the prison walls, he had gotten into fights that extended his prison term to the full 10 years.

None of the Venceremos leaders made any conscious distinction between revolutionaries and petty crooks or criminals whose psychological makeup led them inevitably to satisfy their own personal drives first. The doctrines of Venceremos sought leadership from the so-called Third World of the black, Chicano, women and poor whites. The large black and brown population inside prisons seemed a natural place to seek this leadership. Imprisonment of more and more young ethnic rebels added to the incentive.

The California Department of Corrections, which had historically been staffed with low-paid and poorly educated officers, found itself unable to cope with a growing militancy imported with this new type of prisoner. They reacted predictably with their ancient tools of solitary confinement, brutal responses to simple-minded provocations and extended prison terms in their disciplinary hearings that were no more than ill disguised secret kangaroo courts. Prisoners less disposed to become involved soon found themselves pushed into the radical stream to survive.

While Venceremos worked among Third World

172

prisoners, their first priority was aimed at a white friend of Doug Burt.

A former cellmate of Doug's, Ron Beaty, had made deep impressions upon the Venceremos contingent. Andrea and Mrs. Hobson both corresponded with him regularly, recruiting him into the organization. Beaty's membership was hailed in the party newspaper, *Pamojas Venceremos,* as an example of the growing awareness of prisoners. With his poor white background in Missouri, born in the midst of the depression 35 years earlier and victim of a broken home, Beaty's status as a prison inmate rated him a special place in the organization.

His membership was soon followed by the recruitment of Thero Wheeler at Vacaville and several other prison members.

The slender, muscular Beaty became subject of special attention, some members said, because of Mrs. Hobson's particular attraction to him.

II

Ron Beaty was being transported from Chino to San Bernardino Superior Court on the afternoon of October 6, 1972 for a hearing that had already been canceled. He was riding in an unmarked state car with two unarmed guards, Jesus Sanchez and George Fitzgerald.

Two old cars forced the prison car off the road enroute. Three men and a young woman carrying guns freed Beaty. They removed his handcuffs with bolt cutters, then handcuffed the two guards. One of the gunmen shot the two guards at close range before the attackers fled. Sanchez died. Fitzgerald survived his wounds.

Left behind in the state car was a folder containing letters to Beaty from Andrea and Mrs. Hobson.

Six days later Cheryl Hockin, a neighbor of Andrea and Doug, was arrested. The next day David Strain, a neighbor of Mrs. Hobson, was arrested. After both were taken to San Bernardino for questioning, they were released for lack of evidence.

Twelve days after the escape, warrants were issued for Andrea Holman and Doug Burt, charging them with murder and lynching. They surrendered three days later.

Just two months after his escape, Beaty was spotted in a car crossing the San Francisco-Oakland Bay Bridge from east to west. When police halted the car after a high-speed chase, they found Mrs. Hobson was at the wheel with Beaty as her passenger.

The next few days were to be some of the most educational ever experienced by Venceremos in the ways of the con. Beaty began singing loudly and long.

Not only did he implicate Mrs. Hobson, her son Bruce and several neighbors, he said Bruce Franklin had been the brains in the background. Franklin was said to have emerged only rarely. His name was dropped occasionally for its ability to impress, he told investigators.

Franklin was arrested. So, too, were a physician, Dr. Harry Bishara, and his wife, Lorraine, and an attorney, Michael Goldstein. Their homes at Fort Defiance, Arizona on the Navajo Indian Reservation was said to have been a hideout. A Los Altos Hills couple, Laura and Milton Taulbee, were also said to have hidden Beaty in their home.

Beaty also lead officers to a cache of explosives near Bakersfield, which he first identified as Venceremos material, but later admitted belonged to another Chino inmate.

Beaty began changing other stories, too, when he was placed under oath before the San Francisco Federal Grand Jury. His tales about Franklin were shifted to what "someone" had told him about Franklin, and a voice on a telephone who said he was Franklin, and so on. Charges against Franklin were dropped.

Charges remained against Andrea Holman, Mrs. Hobson, Doug Burt, Bruce Hobson and a neighbor of the Hobsons, Bob Seabock. The 22-year-old Seabock, a longshoreman who had been in Venceremos for two years, was accused of being the triggerman.

Venceremos girded for what they estimated would be a $200,000 court battle and began shifting the official line on Beaty.

Where his escape had been celebrated in their official newspaper, Beaty was now labeled a police informer.

"Some people wonder how people who are trying to live revolutionary lives could one day celebrate someone's escape from prison and the next day learn he has turned his back on the people," a scribe wrote in *Pamojas Venceremos*.

"Beaty is the type who would like to have his cake and eat it too. His is the most dangerous kind of informer, because he comes from the working class and has experienced real oppression. Somewhere inside him he may desire to be part of revolutionary change, but when the chips are down, he puts his own skin above everything else," members and other readers were told as revolutionaries first probed beneath a previous myth about the purity of all prison inmates.

But in the midst of this new interpretation, Beaty's full responsibility was shoved aside in favor of suspicions he might have been planted by police as an agent to entrap them.

III

A shock wave hit even the radical community when Andrea Holman was charged with murder and assisting in the escape of Beaty. Talk about "offing the pig" and "tearing down the pig system" had been common for years. This talk had become so automatic, the rhetoric so easy and flowing that the words were hardly noticed by those who spoke them or those who heard them. But the idea of taking such violent action was shocking, especially when Andrea's tender age was considered.

She was 18 and it seemed a matter of only weeks before that she had been one of the ragtag gang of kids at

Lytton Plaza's rock concerts. She had grown noisy and strident at some of the demonstrations at Stanford, but this was winked at as merely the impetuousness of youth. Older members of the campus community had whispered to each other that the Holmans were in danger of raising a couple of young terrors in Andrea and Michael. But murder? Never.

She was accused of having driven one of the ambush cars and of having bought the bolt cutters she used to remove Beaty's handcuffs.

Some blamed Bruce Franklin and his wife Jane for Andrea's predicament even more than her parents. The Franklins had encouraged their own children to take part in demonstrations and to organize fellow high school students into political cadres. Their influence on the other youngsters among campus radicals was broad.

Such sympathy boosted an immediate and urgent Chino Defense Fund drive into high gear. Operating out of the Holmans' sprawling campus home, the organizing work began. First efforts were aimed at trying to equalize some of the screaming headlines that had greeted the arrests.

Information summaries were typed, mimeographed and rushed to friends and acquaintances among media representatives, both alternative and establishment. As donations were gathered, there followed a 24-page broadside entitled "The Chino Escape Case; An Analysis of a Government Frameup." This came with pictures of the accused, their radical backgrounds and listed seven outlets for organizing defense committees.

One was the Holman house and another at Venceremos headquarters where the party newspaper was published in East Palo Alto. Three were at communes where members lived including one in Palo Alto, another in Redwood City and in San Bernardino, where the trial would be held. The East Bay headquarters was set up in Oakland at 2842 Montana Street, where some of Venceremos had moved to do labor work. In San Francisco, the defense fund was coordinated at the United Prisoners Union office at 3077 24th Street.

176

The prisoners union had been set up originally by Wilbert "Popeye" Jackson as an attempt to win prison inmates wages beyond their token payment of 30 cents a day. Jackson, who had been released in 1970 after spending 19 years imprisoned for burglary and robbery offenses, became something of a local celebrity speaker at colleges and high schools, telling young people the horrors of prison life. Some felt his organization had been taken over by Venceremos and was virtually a front organization within months of their alliance.

The defense-fund drive had a two-fold benefit for an organization like Venceremos. Its 24-page analysis of the case not only sought money support, but active participation in an expanded prison reform movement. New members were attracted by the emotional issues involved.

Many new members were drawn into defense-fund work. A skeleton crew in the East Bay called upon old friends to help out. Jean Dolly had moved into the Vietnam Veterans Against the War and was able to recruit several from there including Joseph Remiro and a postman named Bill Harris. Harris's wife Emily was helpful because she had access to office machinery where she worked, which could be used to reproduce the reams of news releases and broadsides to be published. Emily Harris brought a friend of hers, Angela Atwood.

New Venceremos recruits were brought into the organization by slow careful stages. If their only interest happened to be the defense-fund effort, they usually progressed no further. More frequently they took part in political awareness sessions, weekly education meetings where Mao, Marx and Lenin would be dissected, discussed and argued. New members soon found themselves assigned to take some philosophical or doctrinal thesis to study and bring back for discussion at a subsequent meeting.

Talk in these sessions often strayed to practical methods of putting theories into practice. Favorite themes that most often shocked newcomers were bombings and forays to "off the pig." One such newcomer was a young San Francisco policeman, Al Jason, who had been assigned by his department's intelligence division to infiltrate Venceremos. His first talkfest was so filled with this loose theorizing, he feared he might be forced into a plot to kill a fellow policeman his first night undercover. But in ten months inside the group, all he heard was talk, talk, talk. It was apparent Venceremos had two levels, one public and the other secret.

Venceremos cofounder Franklin freely admitted this split between secret and public divisions, but insisted he did not know the secret band.

It was understood that only the most trusted members ever qualified for this elite squad. How they reached this stage was still a mystery, except to a few intelligence officers, legislators and State Attorney General Evelle Younger, who had been listening to a new expert on revolution.

IV

Ron Beaty had made his peace with state authorities by pleading guilty to murder and turning state's evidence against Venceremos members accused in his escape. He offered state officials some additional benefits, asserting that he had participated in the innermost circles of the revolutionary organization.

His expertise became so popular that he was called before legislative committees studying the radical movement at both the federal and state levels. The State Senate Subcommittee on Civil Disorder headed by ex-FBI agent Dennis Carpenter, now a Republican state senator from Orange County, found Beaty especially helpful and called him back several times.

Beaty proudly described himself as the best-read convict on revolutionary literature, which he said he had obtained from members of the radical National Lawyers Guild, members of Venceremos and from fellow inmates.

Beaty charged that his escape had been the first step

in a general prison revolt that was to free prisoners by ambushing prison transportation details.

"We would have a training camp where we would take these people and train them in illegal activities: sabotage, assasination, kidnap and robbery," said Beaty.

He outlined a plan for spreading this band throughout the nation.

Details were said to be contained in an operations manual Beaty claimed he helped draft. No copies were ever found. A timetable had been established to train a ten-member squad of men like himself within 90 days, he said. Part of the graduation ceremonies would be a major burglary or robbery to obtain funds to extend the project. The ten-member squad would then divide into five sections of two persons each. These teams would spread to five different sections of the country to repeat the process again and again until a small army of terror squads had been formed.

His own escape was portrayed as a textbook exercise in underground terror squad work. The squad was limited to six members for security reasons. None of the squad knew all of the details of the plan, he said.

He knew only that he had to obtain an excuse to be transported outside the prison walls and that his main contact would be on the ambush team. His hideout was another team member's responsibility, but its location was not known by the others. Each team member took part in only one aspect of the planning so that he could truthfully answer any interrogation he did not know other details.

The Venceremos central committee was said to have been all-powerful in his escape and other projects, giving detailed directions at several stages. Beaty also linked the group to bombing of a U.S. Army recruiting office. He said that Mrs. Hobson's son Bruce had bombed the recruiting station in Mountain View under orders from the central committee.

"Everyone is submissive to the central committee. Whatever you are told to do, you must do without question," Beaty said.

V

Before the trial of Andrea and Doug was completed, changes appeared to be taking place in Venceremos. Andrea and Doug had married in jail just as the trial was opening, but a tough judge in San Bernardino took the session behind tight security barriers reminiscent of the Angela Davis trial, shutting off any publicity gain for the two lovers.

In October 1973, Venceremos central committee members announced they were disbanding the organization, because they had failed to rally revolutionaries behind a multi-ethnic organization. Some of the early workers in the defense-fund effort had dropped out. Most of these were from radical groups who felt only emotional sympathy for Andrea and her family, but disliked Franklin's style of leadership. Many called Franklin too sexist and elitist. The dissolution was dissected and analyzed by radical watchers, editorialists and opposing radical leaders for weeks and then forgotten.

Experts listening to Beaty's testimony behind closed doors doubted the authenticity of the move, suspecting that members had only moved underground or sprouted new organizational names. Prison officials noticed that the same people seemed to be visiting prison inmates around the state.

A lot of these visitors seemed to be visiting prisoners linked to radical prison organizations like the Black Guerrilla Family, the Black Liberation Army, the Mexican Mafia, the United Prisoners Union, the Aryan Brothers, the Polar Bear Party. All of these groups had been set up along racial lines, but prison authorities had received word radicals were trying to redirect the racial animosities toward the prison administration.

Three of the more interesting visitors had been regulars chatting with a San Quentin lifer from Los Angeles named James Harold Holiday, whose friends called him "Doc." These regular visitors were Bill and Emily Harris. A check of Holiday's visitor register showed the other name that had not yet shown any link with Venceremos—Robyn Sue Steiner.

Robyn Steiner had visited Holiday nine times in 1972 and six times in 1973. She lived at 5939 Chabot Road, Berkeley, and was a regular participant in a prison organization authorities had granted official sanction in 1969, the Black Cultural Association.

Beaty had identified "Doc" Holiday as the second inmate scheduled to be freed by Venceremos after himself. State investigators have not yet disclosed how deeply they traced Beaty's leads into the various inmate organizations. Their reports remain locked inside security files in Sacramento. But California Department of Corrections Director Raymond Procunier claimed that Black Cultural Association link to the Symbionese Liberation Army came as a shock and surprise to him personally.

Investigators did admit they traced Beaty's charges of Venceremos involvement in bank robberies. State Senator Carpenter's subcommittee was told in a secret session that the robbery division of Venceremos had helped finance the Chino Defense Fund.

A January 1974 Bank of America holdup in Berkeley was linked to Venceremos with the arrest of Earl Lemar Satcher. This was the same Satcher who was present in the Soledad exercise yard when the three black inmates were killed by a guard in January 1970. He had been paroled to a Long Beach veterinarian, Allen Ross, who had given him a job and helped him buy a van.

Ross had met Satcher during visits to Tehachapi Prison, where the inmate had been transferred after the Soledad turmoil. Satcher had also been visited regularly by Mrs. Hobson.

The $16,000 taken in the Berkeley robbery was to have been for the Venceremos organization, not for Satcher personally, Carpenter's subcommittee was told. Satcher had been driving his van and carrying a credit card belonging to Ross at the time of the robbery, an investigator said.

Venceremos's dissolution was said to have been only a cover for this kind of new enterprise.

Both Andrea Holman Burt and Benton Douglas Burt were found guilty of second-degree murder in the Beaty escape, the verdict being handed down a few days after Patty was kidnaped.

Patty's spectacular kidnaping that swept the SLA to a new prominence pushed Beaty and the Chino Defense organization into the background everywhere except for Carpenter's group. Called before the subcommittee, Beaty announced that the SLA and Venceremos were one and the same organization.

Beaty said he knew people from Venceremos involved in the SLA escapades, but declined to name them, hinting that he could not because he was cooperating with the investigation.

"The events since their action with Patty Hearst are practically out of the manual that we wrote. They are just six months behind schedule," Beaty testified.

CHAPTER FOURTEEN

THE $2,000,000 GOOD-FAITH GESTURE

I

On February 13 Randy Hearst stepped before the television cameras ranked in front of his doorstep in Hillsborough and said what everyone knew he must say. The $400 million "good-will gesture" free-food demand was impossible. But he told the SLA he would come up with a counter proposal within 48 hours.

Then, as if she were somewhere in the mob of reporters and cameramen before him, he leaned toward the microphones and spoke to his daughter. "Rest assured your mother and I will do everything we can to get you out," he said. "Tell them [the SLA] not to worry; nobody's going to bust in on them."

Catherine Hearst, her eyes hidden behind dark glasses, her voice strained, also spoke directly to her daughter. "We love you Patty. I'm sorry I'm crying. I know God will bring you back."

But even to work out a valid counter proposal within 48 hours was impossible. On February 16, in a tape delivered to Rev. Cecil Williams of Glide Memorial Methodist Church, Patty Hearst spoke to her parents.

First, about the good-faith gesture. There was some misunderstanding about that and you should do what you can and they will understand that you want to meet their demands and that ... they have every intention that you should be able to meet their demands.

They weren't trying to present an unreasonable request. It was never intended that you feed the whole state.

So whatever you come up with basically is okay.

Then the voice of Cinque: "You may rest assured that we are quite able to assess the extent of your sincerity in this matter, and we will accept a sincere effort on your part."

II

But what was good faith; how would sincere effort be demonstrated? What would be basically okay with revolutionaries out to destroy the system which had created men like Randolph Apperson Hearst?

Within the Hillsborough home, the Hearsts devoted themselves almost exclusively to developing the counterproposal. Willie Hearst, cousin of the kidnap victim, took part in the marathon discussions.

"One of the things I'll never forget about Randy," he said in his rapid-fire delivery, "is when we were talking and saying, 'Now what should this good-faith gesture be?' I mean there just wasn't four hundred million *anywhere* we were going to get our hands on. And we thought the communiqué took cognizance of the fact that it wasn't practical. That they were kind of saying, 'Now that's what we'd like, now what will you offer?' I thought we should offer something that protects us against them saying, 'That ain't shit.' We should have a sort of fall-back position."

He paused to light a cigarette, then went on.

"I said to Randy I thought something like $250,000—or at one point, even less than that ... Randy sort of held back in the conversation, and the others came out and said about the same thing I did.

"And he said, 'No, no. I'm not going to do that. I think the right figure is $2 million.' And my mouth fell open."

Willie argued against the figure. "He wasn't even listening," Willie remembered. "He wanted to be able to take a lie detector test ... know in his heart that he had not tried to save money ... that he had looked at his personal resources and said, 'This is a good-faith gesture. There it is.' We all looked at each other and said, 'Well, Randy, whatever you want to do, we're behind you. We don't think it's tactically wise, but if that's the way you want to do it, that's the way it'll be.'"

III

That's the way it was.

On February 19 Randy Hearst was before the cameras again, announcing a $2 million gesture of good faith. "This is not a ransom," he said, "They asked me to make a gesture of good will, to make a gesture of sincerity, and that's what we've done. I expect them to make a gesture of sincerity themselves. Naturally in my position and in Mrs. Hearst's position, the gesture they could make would be the release of our daughter."

The program had been thrashed out the day before at the Airport Hilton between the Hearsts, representatives of the Community Food Coalition and A. Ludlow Kramer and Peggy Maze of the State of Washington. The program was named People in Need, a free food distribution scheme modeled after the Neighbors in Need program Mrs. Maze headed in Washington. Kramer, Washington's Secretary of State, was a supporter and promoter of the program in his home state. He was named acting director-administrator of People in Need, which was promptly given the headline acronym of PIN.

185

Randy Hearst introduced Kramer and Mrs. Maze to the nation at the televised news conference that day. Kramer looked fine on the screen. Handsome, dark-haired, mod but not too mod. Sincerity in every word.

He called for a thousand volunteers and for free use of warehouses and for donations of food. Speaking into microphones that would carry his words to millions, he said, "We are not looking for news stories or publicity. We want to get food out so Patty Hearst can come back home."

A cameraman from a suburban paper whispered to an Associated Press reporter, "He seems like a nice guy." The AP man countered, "He is a politician."

The money for PIN came from Randy Hearst and the William Randolph Hearst Foundation—$500,000 from the editor, $1.5 million from the charitable foundation established under terms of his father's will. Randy, in reply to a reporter's question, said his contribution represented one-fourth of his personal wealth.

PIN sounded simple: rich man, rich foundation, pump cash in one end, poor people get free food at the other end. To make the simple concept work, though, was enormously complex.

An instant bureaucracy had to be created. A work force had to be recruited overnight, then motivated, encouraged, supervised. Equipment—from giant refrigerator trucks to paper clips—had to be rented, borrowed, begged, purchased. Office space, warehouse space, distribution centers had to be acquired.

Thousands of details had to be worked out—from such obvious ones as the kind and amount of food to be handed out to such obscure matters as the type and size of paper bags in which groceries would be put to the quantity and quality of toilet paper needed in the warehouse restrooms.

The circumstances were not the best—and the pressure was beyond measure. Forceful leadership, clear channels of communication, an unimpeded flow of power and responsibility, were absolute requirements if the program was to work. Trust and credibility—on the part of the SLA, on the part of those in PIN—had to be firmly cemented.

Leadership, communication, power and responsibility, trust and credibility—all were to break down at one point or another during the brief life of PIN, which originally was envisioned as a program that might be an ongoing social program for years to come.

And yet PIN *did* work—in a chaotic fashion. People who were in need of food did get food.

"We did feed 155,000 people," Lud Kramer reported when it was all over. That's what went out of the warehouse."

Kramer's legion of critics disputed his figures, as they disputed virtually every one of his statements. But none disputed that many thousands of hungry people in the Bay Area did get needed food. But the critics also argue that this was not because of Kramer's efforts, but despite his ineptitude.

IV

There was almost instantaneous and broad public support for PIN. Temporary headquarters were established in the Hearst Building at Third and Market Streets in downtown San Francisco. Within 24 hours more than 3000 calls were logged through the 20 constantly jangling telephones in the office—volunteers wanted to know where and when they could come to work. Businessmen offered food—5000 quarts of fresh milk, 4000 loaves of bread, a truckload of turkeys. Transportation and warehousing firms offered truck-trailer rigs, forklifts. A little girl wanted to give her allowance to help poor people—and Patty Hearst.

Rachel Hayes, a 28-year-old black woman who had been fielding calls for 18 hours straight, told a reporter: "I don't have any children, and I don't have a job and I thought I could do more here than by staying home and complaining."

But behind the scenes, there also was instant and

deep mutual antagonism and distrust between Kramer and his staff and members of the Coalition. By the time Kramer and Mrs. Maze left San Francisco and PIN, the feelings had escalated into mutual contempt and hatred. Among the volunteer workers in the office and in the warehouse such feelings developed at only a slightly slower pace.

Unlike most of the volunteers, Sara Jane Moore was a professional woman—white, upper-middle-class, an accountant and business consultant. She showed up at the Hearst Building on February 22, the day of the first free food distribution, and volunteered her services, gratis, for a week. She was separated from her husband, had a young son to support, and could not afford to work without income indefinitely.

Kramer quickly determined that Ms. Moore's accounting and managerial skills were sorely needed. Kramer and his staffers, Mrs. Maze and Pat Colton, took her out to dinner the following night. They asked her to stay on throughout the program.

"I think Lud said to me, 'We mean paid staff.' I said I would like to be paid because if I were going to do it for the entire program—at that time we were talking about a two- or three-month program—it would mean I would have to be paid enough to reimburse my expenses. We settled the amount at that time."

Ms. Moore, however, refused to take any salary until after the program was completed.

During the next few weeks she would be privy to much behind-the-scenes maneuvering and feuding.

Almost before she knew where the pencil sharpener was located, she began hearing bitter gripes about Kramer. At first she discounted the complaints. But then, soon, she decided the complaints were often valid.

"The majority in PIN, volunteers who helped bag food, businessmen who sold us things, the majority were really doing it from their hearts," she said. "A lot of them disagreed with what we were doing, but as long as we had decided to do it 'Well, hell. Let's do it.' We had tremendous talent, really willing people. Unfortunately, the management—meaning the people from

Washington State—ranged from the inept to the incompetent. ... There was a lack of communication from them, a lack of any real feeling that PIN could succeed or that it should succeed."

She assessed Kramer as the image maker, the front man, perhaps sincere in his own way—but not above using PIN to promote his political ambitions. But in her view, he knew little about administration, almost nothing about food and food distribution. "The man," she said, "didn't know how to butter bread."

Pat Colton was the idea man on Kramer's staff and Mrs. Maze knew a good deal about the technicalities of getting and distributing food—she had headed Washington State's Neighbors in Need program, on which PIN was based, since 1970. That program had distributed some three million parcels of food.

Technically, the Washingtonians were unpaid volunteers. But they were still drawing salaries from the jobs in Washington, Kramer as Secretary of State, Colton as his chief staff assistant, Mrs. Maze as the head of Neighbors in Need. They commuted between San Francisco and Washington at least 17 times. Air fares were paid by PIN and NIN. Kramer and his staffers stayed in free rooms at the posh St. Francis Hotel, but there were expenses and PIN paid them.

"One day," Ms. Moore recalled, "they handed me a bill for $1268. This was simply meals, laundry and drinks."

Kramer, Mrs. Maze and Colton were seen by members of the Coalition and by many of the volunteer workers as an inseparable, isolated troika—isolated from everyone except the Hearsts and the press.

Fear—based on real and imagined dangers—was a factor. Kramer claimed his life was threatened on seventeen different occasions—twice at gunpoint. He hired two bodyguards to provide around-the-clock protection. The burly guards were always accompanied by a fierce-looking dog. The bodyguards cost PIN $400 a day.

Kramer and his staff were not alone in their fears. Paranoia was palpable in the atmosphere in the stormy

189

meetings with Coalition representatives, in the PIN offices, in the warehouse.

On one occasion—flaring because of something that had happened in the warehouse—an angry black woman invaded Ms. Moore's office brandishing a frozen chicken at her like a warclub. One of Kramer's bodyguards tried to intervene. "I do not need protection from my sister," Ms. Moore told him. The black woman calmed down and the bizarre weapon was not used.

John Walker*, a long-time friend of Patty Hearst and her family, a former neighbor in Hillsborough, worked as a volunteer in the warehouse. And he saw things and heard things that were cause for alarm.

"I saw black girls from Hunters Point [a San Francisco ghetto] with .38 caliber specials," he said. "Playing with them in the middle of the warehouse, showing each other their guns. How did they get through the door [past the security guards]? I don't know. But then you can't frisk people, volunteers."

Walker was convinced, like a number of others, that certain elements of the ghetto underworld had infiltrated the operation to rip off food, to demand protection money to insure delivery of food to distribution points. He shared with others, including Sara Jane Moore (of whom he was no admirer) the conviction that the SLA had planted an informer-observer within the PIN organization or within the Coalition itself. (The SLA's condemnation of PIN rations as "hog food," made on a March tape recording, came within 24 hours after the phrase was used by a PIN warehouse worker in reference to a shipment of beans. Only 3 or 4 others were present when he made the remark in a closed Coalition-PIN meeting.)

But, by Walker's lights, PIN's problems were not principally in the warehouse but in the front office.

"Between Sara Jane Moore being a white savior of the world and Ludlow Kramer being a future president of the United States, and his trusty assistants (who I

---

* Like a number of Patty's friends, this source declined the use of his name. The fictitious name John Walker was his own suggestion.

don't dislike, in fact I really like Peggy Maze) these people could not make a decision," Walker charged. "Everyone was on a fucking hero trip."

He said on one occasion the front office tried, unsuccessfully, to expedite an order for rice. Kramer, he said, assured everyone that the rice would be coming in any moment. "Finally," Walker exploded, "I said to Kramer, 'Fuck you.' That's the only way I could get through to this guy. I said, 'Mr. Kramer, you want some rice, I'll get you some rice. Give me two hours, an hour and a half.' And I went in and I *did* it."

V

A. Ludlow Kramer *was* a politician. A native of New York, a resident of Seattle since 1956, elected to the Seattle City Council in 1961, elected Secretary of State in 1964 as the youngest man ever to serve in statewide office in Washington. Now, at 42, he was widely considered a comer in Republican politics. His eyes—if not focused on the White House—were on Washington State's Third Congressional District seat well before the kidnaping of the media princess in California.

In an interview with one of the authors, Kramer vehemently denied that the inevitable publicity spotlight which would fall on him as a principal figure in the Hearst case—and the political benefits of such exposure—in any way influenced him to take on the top PIN post. He argued that politically his role with PIN damaged him.

"There was no question in my mind that going to California on the Patty Hearst thing hurt me politically," he said. "It hurt, one, from the point of view that in effect, to all intents and purposes, the campaign stopped while I was gone. Two, you're talking about the [Pacific] Northwest—they [the voters] don't understand blacks, they don't understand involvement in that way. You know, [they say] 'You were elected

191

Secretary of State of Washington—why are you down in California dealing with the Hearst case? You let those people rip you off. So, all in all, it is a negative factor by a long shot. I *know* that."

Why, then, did he take the role?

"There was a job to do," Kramer said. "Someone had to do it."

And, he said, he saw his involvement as short-term. No doubt influenced by the shouting matches, recriminations and distrust that quickly became evident in his dealings with the Coalition, he made it clear that so far as the term was concerned, the shorter the better.

"Cecil Williams [the best-known member of the Coalition] made the statement at a press conference, you know, that Kramer was just down here to run for president," Kramer said. "In fact, Cecil Williams was the man we all picked, the Hearsts and ourselves, about the third week of the program, to find our replacement—get us out of there."

"We thought a minority [person] should run it. We thought it should be someone from there [the Bay Area]. We were certainly willing to be in the background, to help where we could, things like that."

No one could be found?

"No black man, or white man, white woman, black woman—could not find anybody. He, of everyone, knew damn well that we had no intention of running the whole program, did not want to be there. We thought it should be handled by the leaders within the community. Most of the time it just comes down to the moralistic factor. I know very few people in the world I'm in, or in the world you're in, that's going to [use] a murder or a kidnaping to advance their political career. There's some real bums in my business, as I guess there are in yours. But you just don't play those [games]."

If the Coalition held Kramer responsible for most of the program's failings, the feeling was reciprocal on his part. He held the Coalition responsible, in large part, for the massive thefts, ripoffs, that plagued the program from the outset. In an interview with a national publication, Kramer estimated that "about one-third" of the food was taken from delivery trucks before it was distributed. In the interview presented here, he estimated that ripoff losses amounted to about $300,000.

Who did the stealing?

"I think it had to come from a number of sources. We had a truck hijacked in the beginning. The driver came back and said it was hijacked. Remember, we [were] operating on a thesis in which the Hearst family and the Coalition asked that we would not call police. It was an SLA request, but we were asked to honor it by everybody. So we did very little about it.

"The next day at the meeting, the Coalition deeply criticized us. 'Whatta ya mean, how did you let that go? You didn't check it out?' The whole smear."

How much was in that truck?

"Oh, that would be probably $20,000 to $30,000 worth of meat. Next time ... in Oakland ... we now have a security company. [Security officers go to the scene]. They have a call from the Oakland Police Department, they have spotted the food, a truckload of food. They know what basement it is in. They know who has swiped it. They asked permission to go get it, and give it back to us, give it to poor people. Okay. The Coalition refused to give that authority. *They* refused. ... We were told we could not go in and get it. The next day at our 'secret meeting' [with the Coalition] we were severely attacked for an hour. 'What's the idea of having snoopers around?' "

The first food distribution, two days after the program was publicly announced, was chaotic. Even in the *Examiner*—where reporters were expressly ordered never to refer to the program as a "giveaway" or to the SLA's demand as "ransom" for fear of offending the recipients or the terrorists—the headline read: "Food Program's Troubled Start."

Food trucks failed to arrive on schedule. Long lines began forming outside designated distribution centers hours before food was to be handed out. Patience wore out; tempers flared. The center in East Palo Alto failed to open at all. In Oakland volunteers tossed food off of their truck to the waiting crowd—and the crowd threw

193

it back. A CBS television camera was smashed. Thirty-five persons were arrested. In San Francisco, at the distribution point in Hunters Point, newsmen were jeered, threatened and chased away.

Many recipients of the free food considered it second-rate or worse. It had been announced beforehand that the rations would be "supplemental," the aim being to bolster diets rather than to provide a full supermarket range of goods. Yet few of those who did get food that first day—and one member of the Coalition reported that as many as half went away empty-handed—were satisfied with the quantity or quality.

Yet some went through the lines two or three times—and before nightfall PIN food was being offered for sale in more than one neighborhood by street hustlers.

Each of the four subsequent distributions improved in efficiency and in food quality, even according to an otherwise sharply critical Coalition report. The last, on March 25, was not without foul-ups, but it was generally conceded, even by some of the program's severest critics, that it went well. Credit was given in large part to the efforts of San Francisco's unique Delancey Street Foundation, a no-nonsense organization of reformed ex-convicts whose members pitched in to work around the clock in the warehouse and on the trucks. PIN claimed that 35,000 boxes of top-quality food were given out in the last distribution.

The SLA was contemptuous of PIN even before it got under way with the distribution on February 21. In a tape delivered to Rev. Cecil Williams the day before, Cinque characterized the program as "a few crumbs" and demanded that an additional $4 million be pumped into PIN within 24 hours.

On February 24 Randolph Hearst was before the cameras and microphones again. "The size of the latest demand of the SLA is far beyond my financial capability," he said in a flat, weary voice. "Therefore the matter is now out of my hands."

Then *Examiner* publisher Charles Gould announced that the Hearst Corporation would put $4 million into the food program provided Patricia Hearst was released unharmed. The money would be placed in escrow (it was on April 1), the agreement would be legally binding. The first $2 million payment would be made immediately upon Patty's release. The rest would be paid in January 1975.

"Neither the Hearst Corporation nor the Hearst foundations are controlled by members of the Hearst family," he said. And he concluded: "No other funds will be committed by the corporation or the foundations under any circumstances."

VI

On March 9, another taped message from the SLA—a slashing attack on the PIN program.

The voice was a woman's. She identified herself as General Gelina (Angela Atwood). There was the usual revolutionary rhetoric, then she bored in on PIN:

The Court of the People requested that $70 worth of top-quality food, including an equal balance of dry stuffs and canned goods and fresh meat, poultry, produce and daily products, be given to poor families and in various Bay Area communities as a gesture of good faith so that negotiations for Patricia Hearst might begin. But Hearst and the Hearst empire contributed $2 million to People in Need, a program set up by Hearst in reaction to the request of the SLA. Instead of issuing a type and quality of food stipulated, PIN showed contempt for the people through disorganization in distribution of surplus commodities instead of top-quality fresh meats, vegetables and produce. PIN also intended to sham the people by trying to distribute *hog food* [authors' emphasis] instead of top-quality dry stuffs. The people had to stand in long lines only to be treated as dogs when the PIN food was thrown at them. Many people were injured by police in East Oakland.

Then the voice of Patty Hearst, and her words were hurt and hurting.

I hear that people all around the country keep calling on the SLA to release me unharmed. But the SLA are not the ones who are harming me. It's the FBI along with your indifference to the poor and your failure to deal with the people and the SLA in a meaningful, fair way.

I don't believe that you're doing everything you can, everything in your power. I don't think you are doing anything at all. You said it was out of your hands; what you should have said was that you wash your hands of it. . . .

I don't know who influenced you not to comply with the good-faith gesture. I know that you could have done it the way the SLA asked, I mean I know that we have enough money. . . .

I've been hearing reports about the food program. So far it sounds like you and your advisers have managed to turn it into a real disaster.

I heard only 15,000 people received food in the first two weeks and each of them received only about $8 worth. It sounds like most of it is low-quality. No one received any beef or lamb, and it certainly didn't sound like the kind of food our family is used to eating.

She struck out verbally at her mother, her sisters, Steven Weed, Willie Hearst. She wanted them to speak out. "You can't be silent."

From the captive's vantage point, the criticism may have been partially justified. But Randy Hearst had never "washed his hands" of the program. Before and after his statement of February 22, he kept in constant contact with PIN officials, met regularly with Coalition members. He argued, cajoled, raged, wheedled, compromised. He wielded his power wherever and whenever he felt it would be effective in moving toward his single-minded goal: freedom for his daughter. When Wilbert "Popeye" Jackson faced revocation of his parole by the California Adult Authority, Editor Randolph Hearst's newspaper carried news stories and an editorial with the same message: Give the man a break. Jackson, president of the United Prisoners' Union, was a member of the Coalition. Randy Hearst wanted him on *his* side. He ordered one of his top executives to intervene directly on Jackson's behalf at the highest levels of state government. It was done. Jackson's parole was *not* revoked. Later Jackson would bitterly condemn Randy Hearst and PIN.

Randy made mistakes. In the face of conflicting advice, he sometimes was indecisive. "Sure," said one who came to know him intimately during the PIN program, "there were times he shilly-shallied."

But none who worked with him doubt that he tried with every fiber of his being to make PIN work.

Sara Jane Moore, one of Randy Hearst's stoutest defenders, commented that the Coalition, the SLA, and Patricia Hearst thought the editor was all-powerful—and he was not. She thought the impact of this reality on Patty must have been stunning.

"You have to remember that Patty was only 20 years old," she said quietly. "When I was 20, I thought *my* father was omnipotent. And Patty, I'm sure, feels that about her father with a great deal more reason than I would. Her father *is* wealthy, powerful, influential. She had gone through life seeing him getting his own way, and she thought he was omnipotent. And he simply is not. So I'm sure there is this tremendous letdown for Patty, and combined with the education she was getting from the people in the revolutionary movement—she must have felt deserted."

PIN ended on March 25. Kramer and his staff returned to Washington State the next day. "We have done the things that we said we would do," Kramer said. The more than 1,000 volunteers who had worked in PIN returned to their ordinary pursuits—the bartender went back to wiping glasses at the Burlingame Country Club; the little old lady who sneaked away from her Hillsborough mansion on the pretense of going to church went back to afternoon teas with her family; the black woman who experimented with the frozen chicken as bludgeon went back to her flat in the ghetto; the street people went back to cadging quarters from tourists.

The $2 million was gone. Another $500,000 in debts was outstanding. Lawsuits were in the works.

People were fed, but PIN was a failure. The SLA never made its claim on the additional $4 million. Patty Hearst was not freed.

And Randy Hearst, at least in public, never said a word against anyone who was involved with PIN.

CHAPTER FIFTEEN

THE REAL PATTY HEARST—II

Hearst's Daughter Castigates Hearst's America,
Attacks Absolute Spiritual Bankruptcy.

————From a 1973 poem by San Francisco poet
Lawrence Ferlinghetti

I

Everyone who knew Patricia Campbell Hearst before
the kidnaping saw her from a slightly different perspective. But not one—family, fiancé, friends, casual acquaintances, teachers—knew her as a political creature.
She did not talk politics; she did not read politics. She
and Steven Weed did not subscribe to a newspaper.
Newspapers bored her, politics bored her. She had no
cause. She never demonstrated against the war in Vietnam, even at a time when many if not most of her peer
group were marching and sometimes rioting against the
most unpopular of all wars.

Yet she was politicized, radicalized, to the point that
she felt compelled to pick up the gun, first figuratively
and then literally, in the cause of political revolution.

She did it figurately in a tape recording on April 3, delivered only one day after the hopeful message from the SLA with a bunch of red roses to an obscure radical newspaper called *the Phoenix*. The message of April 2 was that the time and place of the Patricia Hearst's release would be announced within 72 hours. The message of April 3 was that she was no longer a Hearst. She was Tania, and she had decided to stay and fight with the SLA.

She did it literally two weeks later when, as Tania, she walked into a bank with a gun at the ready.

Why?

II

We still maintain a republican form of government, but who has control of the primaries that nominate the candidates? The corporations have. Who controls the conventions? The corporations. Who own the bosses and the elected officials? Are they representatives of the people or of the corporations? Let any fair-minded man answer that question truthfully.

If the corporations do all this—and they surely do—can we any longer maintain that this is a government by the people? It is a government by a distinct class, not a government for the greatest good of the greatest number but for the special advantage of that class. Laws are passed for the benefit of the corporations, and such laws are not to the advantage of that class. Laws are passed for the benefit of corporations, and such laws as are not to the advantage of the corporations are ignored. The people are neglected because they have ceased to be an important factor into the government.

Except for the absence of jargon, the words might be those of Nancy Ling Perry/Fahizah, the SLA's chief propagandist. The tone of moral outrage is there. The disillusion with the system, the condemnation of the corporate state, the abstract concern for the "people."

The words are those of William Randolph Hearst Sr., founder of the Hearst media empire, grandfather of Patricia Campbell Hearst, in a letter to his chief lieutenant and political mentor, Arthur Brisbane.

The letter was written on February 21, 1906.

Exactly 68 years to the day later, Hearst's diatribe against the corporate state was echoed in amplified, less literate form in a tape recording by a man who called himself Field Marshal General Cinque—except that Cinque's attack was directed not only against the corporate state as a whole, but also at one corporate structure in particular: the Hearst empire. Cinque demanded an additional $4 million from the Hearst empire for free food for the people before he would consider freeing the captive heiress of that empire.

And 41 days after Cinque's message—in words of even greater outrage than *her* political mentor—the heiress herself attacked the corporate state, the Hearst empire and her father and mother. The words are from the Tania tape of April 3:

> Dad, you said that you were concerned with my life, and you also said that you were concerned with the life and interests of all oppressed people in this country, but you are a liar in both areas and as a member of the ruling class, I know for sure that yours and mom's interests are never the interests of the people. Dad, you said you would see about getting more job opportunities for the people, but why haven't you warned the people what is going to happen to them—that actually the few jobs they still have will be taken away.
>
> I should have known that if you and the rest of the corporate state were willing to do this to millions of people to maintain power and serve your needs, you would also kill me if necessary to serve those same needs. How long will it take before white people in this country understand that whatever happens to a black child happens sooner or later to a white child? How long will it be before we all understand that we must fight for our freedom?

Patty/Tania was 20 years old at the time she spoke those words. William Randolph Hearst was 43 when he wrote the letter to Brisbane.

There is not, of course, an exact parallel between the two statements. His makes no personal allusions, contains no racial references, shows no manifestation of paranoia, includes no call to direct violent action. He was in no personal physical danger as he wrote.

But the words of the grandfather, in the context of the time in which he wrote, certainly seem at least as radical as those of the granddaughter in the context of the time in which she spoke.

It would be absurd to suggest that somehow the political attitudes of the grandfather nearly seven decades before were somehow transmitted genetically to the granddaughter's apparent conversion to revolutionary terrorism was in any way influenced by the writings of her famous ancestor.

It is highly unlikely she was aware of the existence of the letter to Brisbane, or knew that her grandfather, who died nearly three years before her birth, had ever flirted with radical thought.

As far as her family, friends and fiancé knew, Patty Hearst had never been interested in her grandfather's fascinating personal life, let alone his public and political life. She had never seen *Citizen Kane,* the Orson Welles film old Hearst so despised, nor W. A. Swanberg's unauthorized but authoritative best-selling biography *Citizen Hearst.*

What does seem significant in this inexact parallelism is that both William Randolph Hearst Sr. and Patricia Campbell Hearst were able to make seismic shifts in their political positions—he from the radicalism of 1906 to the right-wing conservatism of his later years; she from the unformed passive liberalism evident up to the time of her kidnaping to the revolutionary terrorism of her twentieth year.

III

As a child, Patty Hearst was both a leader and a loner in suburban Hillsborough. The Hearst home on Santa Ynez Avenue was a gathering place for neighborhood kids. They liked Patty, got along well with her mother, and were impressed with her father's easy friendliness and informality. (He was remembered vividly by several friends of Patty's as the kind of father who, with his wife beautifully and formally dressed, would sometimes sit down at the dinner table in his pajamas.)

Patty's girlfriend, possibly her best friend as they went through the important years between 9 and 16 together, talked of their shared childhood but would not permit the use of her name.

"Patty," she remembered, "was extremely athletic when she was younger. An excellent swimmer, a good tennis player. Very capable. You know, very attractive and very much of a leader. But always sort of independent. The type that—what everybody else was thinking [privately]—would say it [directly] to the authority figure. She was never antagonistic or hostile; she was outspoken, but never to the point of being antagonistic."

Others saw Patty quite differently.

Lorna Corbetta was a classmate of Patty's at the Convent of the Sacred Heart, a boarding school in Menlo Park. She met Patty when they both were ten, and became close enough to be invited to the Hearst home several times.

She remembered Patty as exceptionally strong-willed, competitive and assertive—the kind of girl who would dispute a referee's call in a friendly game of basketball, the kind of girl who tried to take over in rah-rah activities.

"Most everybody would just sort of shrug it off [a referee's disputed decision] but Patty always had to argue," she said. "And when Patty became a cheerleader she took control of the squad."

At 14, Patty was sent to Santa Catalina School, a strict boarding school run by Dominican nuns in Monterey, California. She couldn't abide the harsh discipline, the scrubbing of toilets for relatively minor infractions. *Newsweek* magazine reported that Patty was expelled from Santa Catalina for smoking marijuana, but her family, the school, classmates and friends vehemently denied the report.

From Santa Catalina, Patty transferred, at 16, to the nonsectarian Crystal Springs School near her home. It was an expensive, private school, more relaxed than the Catholic school. Paradoxically, Patty seemed to seek out discipline in ballet.

She began classes at the Peninsula School of Ballet and worked at mastering the dance with great intensity. Anne Bena, her instructor, thought Patty took it all too seriously and did not encourage her to continue her lessons. "I think she was searching for something," the teacher said. "Searching for herself maybe."

Patty was capable of bending and sliding by rules at home and at school. Before she got her own car, she occasionally sneaked one of the family autos to go joyriding. And, like her older sister, Gina, she often used the excuse of "going to see a movie in San Francisco" to make surreptitious expeditions to forbidden concerts at the Fillmore Auditorium.

John Walker* was several years older than Patty but they were good friends, and they once carried on a mild mutual flirtation. He knew of the Fillmore expeditions firsthand. He dated Patty's older sister Gina. They occasionally took Patty along when they went to the Fillmore.

Walker's affection extended to the entire Hearst family—and he felt that the role of Patty's mother was the most misunderstood in the family. He believed Catherine was not the uptight disciplinarian others have characterized her to be.

"No way," said Walker. "She knew every time that I

* Fictitious name.

would take Gina—or that we would go with Patty to the Fillmore. . . . She just didn't want Randy to know. . . . He cared. That [the thought of his daughter going to the raucous Fillmore] bothered him. Randy is a super nice guy, really is, and I think his girls were *his* girls more than they were Catherine's.

"Her mother was the one who made them play the game—'Tell me you are going to see *Dr. Zhivago*—you can't tell me you're going to the Fillmore, because then I can't let you do it.' I would say she sacrificed herself so that Randy would be close to his girls. . . . My parents were five times stricter than hers ever were. . . . The Hearsts were not the strict disciplinarians they were portrayed to be."

Walker agreed with most of her peers—and with her parents and teachers—that Patty was always very much a person unto herself. "Independent, headstrong," he felt.

To Walker, the Hearst family, and Patty in particular, were never part of what he called Hillsborough's "Brotherhood of Money." Gina Hearst came closest to conforming to Hillsborough's social patterns.

"Gina was much more typical as a young girl," according to Walker. "Patty was much more comfortable in blue jeans and T-shirts than she was in a dress. Gina was more comfortable in a dress than blue jeans."

Gina chose to participate in the Hillsborough rite of the debutante coming-out party. Patty chose not to.

Yet Walker did not see this as deliberate nonconformity or rebelliousness, either social or political, on Patty's part. It was, he thought, more a matter of self-awareness.

"If you put me on the spot, and said, 'Did she rebel?' I'd say no. . . . Patty had found someone that was *her,* which a lot of people don't find in Hillsborough. Because they have a [social] world and they are told they have to live up to this—this is who you are. . . . *She* was never Junior Miss Hearst. She was always *Patty.*"

He paused to refresh his impressions, then went on:

"I think Patty was, has always been, one of the leaders of her peer group. She was a person who would follow what she wanted to do more than she would follow what someone else wanted her to do. . . . In a group, if the conversation wasn't going her way, she would turn away and leave. A lot of people [in that situation] either have bad feelings, get upset one way or another or go through a scene. She never seemed like that kind of girl."

There is general agreement among her friends that during her mid-teen years a rift—even an alienation—developed between Patty and her mother. It is not an uncommon phenomenon, particularly in families in which both mother and daughter are strong-minded, strong-willed. Most attribute it to Patty's love affair with Steve Weed, but a few, like Walker, feel it was due more to Patty's drift away from the Roman Catholic Church, to which she had once been devoted and from which her mother continued to draw strength and solace.

Whatever the cause, the consensus is that the rift was almost completely healed well before the kidnaping. Catherine had at last accepted what Patty's friends had known since shortly after the affair began—that Patty and Weed were deeply in love, that they intended theirs to be a permanent relationship.

IV

Weed was understandably reticent, sometimes dissembling, in talking to reporters about his relationship with Patty. One reporter writing a free-lance "Portrait of Patty" not long after the kidnaping, asked Weed how he met her at Crystal Springs School. He denied having known her there.

"Well, I've changed the emphasis of that story depending on how I felt," he admitted later. "I knew her at Crystal Springs. What I've pretty much been going along with ... is that we started really knowing each other at Menlo College the following year.

"She wasn't in any of my classes ... wasn't my student. I knew her to say hello to, but I knew lots of girls at Crystal Springs. There were only two hundred girls, and I must have known half of them. We saw a lot of each other when she was in Menlo."

In fact, the romance between Weed and Patty was clearly a serious affair by then. Weed's one-bedroom Menlo Park apartment was only a few blocks away from the campus. Patty lived in Howard Hall, a woman's dormitory. Her little blue MG, the birthday gift from her father, became almost a fixture on the street where Weed lived. Sometimes it was there overnight. Friends at school covered for her—Patty wasn't the only coed at Menlo having an affair.

One published story portrayed Patty as the aggressor in the romance—stated that she "pursued" Weed.

"The whole article was snide," said Weed. But, speaking of his relationship with Patty, he added, "I didn't initiate it."

The decison to transfer from Menlo College to UC Berkeley and move in with Weed apparently was largely Patty's—and she made it fairly quickly.

"I know she didn't hesitate very long when she got me," Weed said. "Six weeks doesn't seem like a very long time. ... Once she gets hold of an idea, it's hard to dislodge her."

They set up housekeeping in July 1972, after her six-week tour of Italy and Greece. More because she wanted a break from the scholastic life than because she needed the money, Patty got a sales job at Capwell's Department Store in the neighboring city of Oakland. She earned $2.25 an hour—her first and last salaried job. She left no lasting impression on coworkers. She was just another young working girl.

When she quit Capwell's to begin classes at UC in January 1973, her father boosted her allowance from $100 to $300 a month. She and Weed devoted their time almost exclusively to their studies and to making the apartment comfortable and attractive. By the standards of other UC students, the place was lavishly decorated—scores of houseplants, many prints and paintings (including several from the collection of Patty's grandfather), Oriental rugs, a collection of old California wine bottles, a tenth-century Persian manuscript.

V

No one was indiscreet enough to say it publicly, but when the kidnaping occurred suspicion fell almost immediately on Steve Weed as a possible conspirator in the abduction of his fiancé. And in the minds of some investigators, not to mention amateur whodunit fans, the victim herself was not beyond suspicion.

The suspicion of Patty was based almost entirely on her screams as she was rushed down the path to the kidnap car—"Please! Please! Not *me!*"

Her words were read to mean that she had had foreknowledge that a kidnaping was to take place, but there had been a betrayal or a mistake at the last moment.

If the discovery of the boxful of unfired cyanide-tipped bullets in the apartment by the FBI the day after the kidnaping had been leaked to the press at the time, it seems certain that the Patty-as-conspirator theorists would have had a field day. Cyanide bullets were known to be the trademark of the SLA. They were found *under* a bookshelf. Theorists could spin out beautiful plots from this: both Patty and Weed were members of the SLA, the kidnap was a fake, Weed would rendezvous with his lover after her father had been extorted of his fortune.

Such theorists would have discounted the more likely possibility that the bullets had been dropped accidentally during the scuffle with Weed, or deliberately left behind by one of the kidnapers so the publicity-conscious SLA's feat would not go unrecognized.

By the summer of 1973 Patty's parents had come to accept their daughter's life style. Patty asked for and received money to help with furnishing the Berkeley apartment—$1000. In the fall the Hearsts came up with another $1000 for tuition and school expenses.

Patty and Weed announced their engagement in December. They planned to be married in June. They also planned to go to Europe after the wedding to spend a year of touring and studying. "I was thinking in terms of Germany because I need to study German, but I'd rather be in France," Weed said. Then, quietly, he added, "We were planning on doing something nice."

But "something nice" was not fated for Patty Hearst and Steven Weed.

Airy theorizing aside, there were more substantial reasons for suspecting Weed. His escape from the apartment struck many as implausible. The two men were armed. Possibly the woman was too. All three were ruthless. How, then, could Weed have made his break without being riddled?

There also were strong rumors that Weed had been a member of the radical Students for a Democratic Society (SDS) while he was a student at Princeton.

A stash of marijuana had been found in the Benvenue apartment.

Under initial questioning, he seemed hesitant, even uncooperative.

When he was released from the hospital the Saturday after the kidnaping, he publicly announced that he would not identify the kidnapers in court if they were brought to trial.

All this—plus his cool, intellectual manner—marked Weed in the minds of some investigators and a large cross-section of the public—as a prime suspect.

In an interview with one of the authors, Weed told about his last few moments in the presence of Patty and explained as best he could why he was not gunned down.

Question: When you made the break, you were thinking you had nothing to lose?

Answer: That was exactly my thought. And being hit over the head—I didn't feel like either having my head bashed in or being shot while I was tied up. I was nervous when they started to tie me up.

I was pretty groggy by that time. I just lurched to my feet and I think I crashed into them [one or perhaps two of the kidnapers]. I'd pretty much have to because of the positions we were in.

I ran round the front room—I couldn't really see. I was really groggy and I thought they were going to be shooting at me, so I was just lurching around the room, knocking things over, crashing into things, and getting my hands untied.

Q.—Was the [back] door open?

A.—No. I went out the back door, opened the back door and ran out the back door.

Q.—Were they yelling?

A.—I didn't hear a thing after I got out. I didn't hear shots go off.

Q.—Do you have any idea why they wouldn't have shot you at the time?

A.—They must have planned not to.

Q.—They just didn't want to?

A.—Yeah.

Q.—They wanted a witness to the kidnap?

A.—Whatever. They could have shot at me.

Q.—Then you went over a couple of fences and ...?

A.—And as soon as I realized they weren't chasing me, I ran back to the street [Parker Street, which intersects with Benvenue].

Q.—And you had no idea who the hell it [the kidnap gang] could have been at that time?

A.—No. I was totally confused. Saw no reason for it [the kidnaping] at all.

Q.—Subsequently, have you learned exactly who they [the kidnapers] were?

A.—[Thero] Wheeler, [Donald] DeFreeze—that's who it was believed [to be].

Q.—The girl?

A.—I think it was Angela Atwood, although I didn't see her very well. It is likely that it was her.

Q.—About the [hiding or accidental dropping of the cyanide] bullets, did you hear anything, see anything, sense any activity like that?

A.—No. I have no ideas on that.

Q.—Did you have the feeling that, early on, that the FBI considered you a suspect? Did they treat you as a suspect?

A.—Yeah, certainly they did. But I also realized that that's their way. They treat everyone as a suspect until they find out.

Q.—Did you resent this, get uptight?

A.—No, I didn't resent it. I knew they had to do that, but the only thing I consistently resented about the FBI was the way they would withhold information from people—unreasonably, I think. From me in particular. Things that . . . would have helped us deal with this problem. Yeah, for instance, they wouldn't let me look at the pictures that were taken at [the robbery] of the bank. I asked. I ran all over the stupid Federal Building. And that was a very important thing to know—not just who was there, but what the expressions on *her* face were.

Q.—Do you think you might have been able to read the expression and determine. . . .

A.—I certainly would have known a hell of a lot more than I did, just by reading the newspaper. Which was nothing.

Weed explained that he made the statement about refusing to identify the kidnapers in court as a ploy to gain the confidence of the abductors, to encourage them to release Patty. He said that in fact he was unsure he could have made a positive identification of any of the kidnapers.

Weed was reluctant to discuss the marijuana found in his apartment—he did not think the subject was relevant—but admitted he kept some in the place. "Just say there was a fair amount," he said. He insisted that marijuana was simply part of the Berkeley scene and neither he nor Patty used it except socially, as older people used alcohol.

Weed's involvement with the SDS at Princeton was

checked out thoroughly by the FBI. Agents learned that in 1969 his roommate was Peter Kaminsky, an SDS leader, but that Weed was never a member. He was asked to hand out SDS leaflets and to take part in demonstrations, but refused.

Once, though, he was an athletic ringer for the SDS. The Princeton ROTC had challenged the SDS to a football game. Weed, a track man at Princeton and a footballer in high school, was recruited for the SDS team. He wore a beard at the time, and it was thought he would fit in nicely with the team's radical image. Weed played quarterback. The SDS won.

Weed was questioned again and again by the FBI. His family and friends were questioned. Berkeley radicals and known associates of SLA members were questioned.

All told, the 190 FBI agents who worked on the case at one time or another interviewed more than 20,000 persons. And FBI Agent in Charge Charles Bates has stated without qualification that there was no evidence that either Weed or Patty Hearst was in any way involved with the SLA before the kidnaping.

If Patricia Campbell Hearst was not a secret member of the SLA before the kidnaping, how then was her self-proclaimed transformation from media princess to revolutionary terrorist accomplished?

Countless experts—credentialed and self-appointed —have explored the question from virtually every angle and come up with answers which are often fascinating but unproved and unprovable at this point.

The most popular theory is that of mind manipulation through "brainwashing," drugs, hypnosis or a combination thereof. The theory was put forward long before the Tania tape. And the theory was rejected again and again by the voice of Patty Hearst before and after she took her revolutionary name.

Revolutionaries claimed that the abduction was an educational experience that raised the political consciousness of Patty/Tania and brought her to the realization she was living in an oppressive fascist state she was morally bound to fight against.

Those who choose to believe that virtually every political phenomenon is the produce of convoluted conspiracies saw Patty as a kind of "Manchurian Candidate" of the 1970s. Others believed the real Patty was murdered immediately after the kidnaping and her place taken by a consumate actress-impostor.

Sex was seen by some as a key factor—and Patty/Tania did say that she fell deeply in love with Willie Wolfe/Cujo.

The psychiatrist Frederick Hacker, consultant to the Hearst family, made one of the more cogent analyses in an interview with *People* magazine. He was asked what lure the SLA could have for a young woman like Patty Hearst.

"In spite of everything, the sense of close proximity among these people gives a feeling of family, of community and caring," he said. "There is shared danger and a sense of strong commitment that is very impressive to the uncommitted.

"Everybody asks how voluntary *her* conversion was. I raise the question, 'How intentional was the SLA's conversion of Patricia?' Maybe they didn't want to convert her at first. Let's look at it this way. She's kidnaped, and she's frightened and inclined to believe these people are really monsters. Then they treat her very nicely. She begins to talk to them, to the girls. She finds they are very much the kind of people she is—upper-middle-class, intelligent, white kids. She finds a poetess, a sociologist. They tell her how they have found a new ideal and how lousy it was at home. Perhaps she started to think, 'Well, at my home it wasn't so hot, either.' This may be what happened. There is a strong possibility, of course, she *was* brainwashed. Maybe they did use drugs. . . ."

The only person who may be able to provide the definitive answer is Patty/Tania.

But however desperately they may seek the answer,

to Steven Weed and the Hearst family, it is essentially beside the point. To them the key fact is that Patricia Campbell Hearst was a woman stolen by force—all that followed and will follow stems from that central violence.

CHAPTER SIXTEEN

MARKED FOR EXECUTION—THE SLA DEATH LIST

I

Patty/Tania's message home on April 3, as shocking and distressing as it was to the Hearsts and disheartening to many others, was barely noticed by three people. Cinque had sent a special message to them at the end of the tape recording.

"These subjects are to be shot on sight wherever found and at any time," said Cinque.

The three had been "found guilty of working and informing against the people and therefor death warrants have been issued by this court."

The new SLA targets named were Robyn Sue Steiner, who had been Russ Little's girlfriend before fleeing home to Coral Gables, Florida the previous December; Chris Thompson, the former New York Black Panther and Peking House resident who had been Nancy Ling Perry's lover briefly; and Colston Westbrook, UC communications professor and former outside adviser to the Black Cultural Association at Vacaville.

Westbrook was identified by Cinque as an agent for the CIA who also worked for the FBI. His CIA background was linked to Vietnam, where he was said to have been an interrogator and torturer in the Phoenix program; other unspecified countries had also been his duty areas, Cinque said.

The short, chunky Westbrook had not been shy since the kidnaping, and had set up several press and television sessions. His references to his Southeast Asia activities usually were veiled in joking responses that allowed reporters to infer CIA ties.

With one female reporter, Westbrook kidded that she would make good CIA material. He hinted he knew many ways to persuade a man to tell him anything he wished. Some alternative press reporters and free-lance writers had been told about CIA work on his part. South America was said to have been another of his assignments, according to one specialist in intelligence operations.

About a month after Patty's kidnaping, Westbrook had attempted to set himself up as a contact man between the SLA and Hearst.

A press conference spiced with a slide show of Willie Wolfe and Russ Little attending BCA meetings at Vacaville set the stage for his reading an open letter to Cinque.

"No rich white man is going to know how to talk to a nigger, especially a pure nigger. But maybe a bousjie* nigger and a pure nigger can rap a bit," he said, directing his comments from a three-page letter to Cinque through the media.

His showbiz response to the death warrant was irrepressible and unorthodox. Anyone calling his listed telephone number would be answered by a tape recording that referred to the death threat and making some lighthearted greeting. Reporters who sought interviews were usually granted them only through arrangements that smacked of old movie cloak-and-dagger scripts. Westbrook always made allusions to being in constant touch with some protective force. Few were able to gain any solid answers from him.

* bourgeoisie.

Westbrook sought endlessly to establish that there was no tie between his BCA and SLA, because Cinque had left the group 14 months before the kidnaping. He also promoted the theory that Cinque was not the leader directing SLA operations, that the leader remained to be identified.

Inclusion of Chris Thompson on the death list was more of a surprise than naming Westbrook. Thompson, eight years younger than the 35-year-old Westbrook and a half-foot taller, had not been nearly as vocal. Few knew at the time of his testifying before the Alameda County grand jury in the Foster slaying. Fewer still knew that he had volunteered information about the gun he had sold Little.

Thompson turned to the media readily upon being named an SLA enemy. Appearing on television interviews and talking to newspaper reporters, Thompson pushed an idea for a black people's union modeled after the United Farm Workers. Economic boycotts could become its strongest weapon, because of the size of the black community in the United States, he contended.

Cinque had called Thompson a paid police agent and informer to the FBI. Thompson acknowledged that his apparent access to money had made him suspect. He had helped finance a student newspaper while at Merritt College and arranged financing for a black filmmaking firm.

He explained that he knew how to obtain student loans and worked part-time for the rest of his money. His jobs had been as a low-paid security guard at an elementary school in Emeryville, next door to Berkeley, an aide in the audio visual department at North Peralta Community College and operator of a fruit stand.

Thompson had come to Berkeley in 1972 driving a six-year-old Volvo. He had come from New York where he had worked as a pest exterminator and been a student for three years at Staten Island Community College. While there he had been active in the Huey Newton wing of the Black Panther Party and had been president of a black student group.

Before entering college in New York, Thompson

served a two-year hitch in the marines, after which he toured Africa. He had to be repatriated home from Accra, Ghana in September 1969 when he ran out of funds. A loan for his fare home was later repaid.

Less flamboyant and affecting a quieter style than Westbrook, Thompson admitted he had toyed with the prison movement, but had never attended any of the BCA sessions at Vacaville while living at Peking House. He had moved from the Chabot Road commune to an apartment on Hillegass Avenue in mid-1973 and was operating his roving stand he had dubbed the Black Market Fruit Vending Co.

Least comprehensible was the reason for SLA's having named Robyn Steiner as an enemy. Neither her former boyfriend, Russ Little, or his codefendant Joseph Remiro understood the death warrant. They issued a public statement asking SLA to reconsider on the basis that they knew she had not given the FBI any information.

She had refused to speak to investigators from either the Alameda County Sheriff's office or the FBI after they trailed her to her parents' home in the Greater Miami area. The 21-year-old former University of Florida coed had been too terrified to talk.

Her involvement with the BCA at Vacaville had been as a grammar instructor. Visits to prison inmates like "Doc" Holiday were a little more difficult to explain. She had trimmed her long hair, thrown away granny glasses and bought a miniskirt to wear for her return trip to Florida. Back home she enrolled in nurse's training and threw a wall up around herself to keep strangers and friends away.

Within two weeks, the Black Panther Party newspaper had added a fourth name to the SLA enemy list. Their own Huey Newton was said to be a target. The party newspaper quoted a letter received from a prison group calling itself the Sacramento Solidarity Committee.

"He [Newton] has betrayed the people and become an enemy of the people," the letter was quoted as saying.

Newton had been freed from prison and returned to running his Panther group and attending classes at the University of California at Santa Cruz. His friend J. Herman Blake had been appointed provost of Oakes College at UCSC and had invited Newton to his school.

The SLA death warrant list appeared to be a mixed blessing. To at least one it represented terror, while to others there was a chance for more publicity.

II

Russ Little and Joseph Remiro, who were referred to by Cinque as "our two soldiers who are in the hands of the enemy," received an apology and best wishes.

Cinque apologized for not having equipped them with offensive weapons at the time of their capture. He promised never to relent in an attempt to reach them.

Little and Remiro had waged a broad propaganda war from inside their cells. Alameda County authorities had transferred them to San Quentin for safekeeping while they awaited trial in the Foster slaying. But their handling there won the two wider sympathy.

Prison officials had taken them on a tour of the death house for some reason never fully explained. They were also used by prison officials in an attempt to contact the SLA.

Two hours after the death-house tour, Remiro and Little were taken to a meeting watched over by a dozen heavily armed plainclothesmen. Raymond Procunier, Department of Corrections director, and Clifford "Death Row Jeff" Jefferson, whom Little had visited in prison, were there to see how the SLA might be contacted. The two-hour session reached no conclusion other than a story that the two accused had demanded a live television press conference.

Transferred back to Alameda County jail three days later, the two charged four deputies with physically attacking them during a strip search. In response to their accusations of brutality and poor cell conditions, Randolph Hearst appointed an attorney friend as an ombudsman to check their treatment. SLA communiqués had warned that Patty's accomodations would depend upon treatment of Little and Remiro.

After lengthy negotiations through the courts, their bid for a live television press conference was turned down on the basis it might prejudice their right to an impartial trial jury.

Both Little and Remiro contended the attack on them by deputies had been part of a plot by U.S. Attorney General William Saxbe and FBI Director Clarence Kelley to force SLA retaliation upon Patty.

Just four days before Patty announced she had chosen to stay with the SLA, Remiro and Little mailed a statement predicting she would be freed.

"We share the SLA's concern for the safety of Patty and the element guarding her. They are in grave danger and should deal with the primary task of the safe return of Patty to her fiancé and the safe withdrawal of the SLA element," they wrote.

"We hope that 'everyone' is preparing for the government's massive terrorist assault that will surely follow Patricia Hearst's release. It's obvious that once she is released many people and organizations will be attacked and put behind bars regardless of any guilt or knowledge of the SLA," they said.

III

Despite warnings from the underground not to talk to the FBI and police, there were plenty of informants ready to trade talk. While posters appeared on Berkeley walls cautioning against trusting an investigator, police and FBI officials were being contacted by people eager to become involved. Other contacts were made by former radicals now fearful they might be implicated in a dangerous situation.

Thompson readily admitted having talked to the FBI before and after being placed on the SLA enemy list.

Several former Venceremos members volunteered what they knew about the people on the missing list.

Mary Alice Siem came forward just three weeks after the kidnaping and gave investigators a broad inside view of the workings of the SLA band, but denied that her boyfriend Thero Wheeler had been involved in the kidnaping. She claimed Wheeler and DeFreeze had separated after a dispute over what course to take.

The 25-year-old former Redding woman said she had been involved with SLA in about 20 meetings prior to the Foster slaying, but knew nothing of their involvement in the black educator's assassination.

She portrayed Cinque as a fanatic who would allow no argument with his viewpoint. This had led to the split with Wheeler. She said that DeFreeze, as Cinque, had prepared the statement of principles for the SLA.

The meetings she attended, usually taken blindfolded to a small apartment, were between August and October 1973, she said. The SLA, or something called the Symbionese Federation, was mentioned from the start. Elaborate charts showing communications units, combat units and medical units were shown, but she knew of no other members than those she linked directly to DeFreeze.

She could link only Nancy Ling Perry, Patricia Soltysik whom she knew only as Zoya, and Russ Little.

While she knew Willie Wolfe, Emily Harris and Robyn Steiner, she told interrogators she was unaware of any SLA activities on their part.

Her last meeting with DeFreeze, Nancy and Zoya was a harrowing one for her, because they took $600 cash from her at gunpoint, threatening to kill her, Wheeler and her two-year-old son, Jeremiah Jackson Siem.

Both Nancy and Zoya were said to have been physically attracted to Cinque. Their sexual relations with him had created so much friction that sex was finally abandoned in favor of revolutionary work, she said.

She predicted that SLA would be extremely difficult to penetrate, because they were extremely security-conscious, always taking circuitous routes to reach their hideouts and favoring "safe houses" like the residence in Contra Costa County. Cinque seldom went outside, choosing to read, study and exercise indoors and letting the women to errands and shopping.

Cinque was said to be an alcoholic, favoring plum wine, but also drinking beer and whiskey as well. His inability to abide any criticism had led to the split with Wheeler well before the kidnaping, she said. Wheeler had considered Cinque as infantile in his revolutionary ideas.

She never answered directly an inquiry on how Cinque and Wheeler had come together after their escapes, but denied it was because they belonged to any organization prior to walking away from prison. She told officers she now had taken a fictitious name and moved where Wheeler or anyone else involved with SLA could not find her. She declined to give them any idea what kind of car Wheeler might be driving or where he might go to hide.

Other information had come to investigators from a chain of tipsters set up inside radical groups.

One such informant had named Reese Erlich, a Venceremos member, as a participant in the Symbionese Liberation Army just two days after the kidnap. Another said Erlich had had the original idea to make Foster a target for execution, but whether he participated was not known.

Erlich, a 26-year-old former UC student who was expelled a few days before due to receive his B.A., had been a production worker at National Can Co. in Hayward. While there, he had taken part with Venceremos in several labor disputes.

He also made several trips to San Diego while Venceremos was planning demonstrations at the Republican National Convention, first proposed to be held there. One of his constant traveling companions was former Venceremos Central Committee member, Janet Cooper Weiss, who had left her husband and dropped his name. Erlich dropped out of sight, but Janet Cooper remained in Oakland.

Tipsters also kept investigators up to date on the residents of three Oakland addresses used by Venceremos members. Not only their movements, but their standing in the revolutionary group were reported.

There were crosscurrents of jealousy and suspicion in the tipster network. One of the more fanciful tips came about a former girlfriend of Joseph Remiro, who had been a regular visitor to inmate Raymond Sparks, the man many believed to be the SLA Chief of Staff.

Alicia Englander, a 28-year-old blonde electronics worker, had been Remiro's girlfriend and a regular at a series of Venceremos pads. She had been active in the Chino Defense Fund and several other projects, sometimes being the only one involved in study-criticism sessions for her cadre. One tipster reported to the FBI that Ms. Englander had been reported to fellow revolutionaries as an informer for the FBI.

Cindy Garvey, active in Venceremos for years and a regular visitor to inmate William Carter, an organizer of SLA inside, had her love life well covered by the tipsters. Her affairs with Remiro and Russ Little were thoroughly reported.

None of the tips brought investigators closer to the SLA hideouts or elicited any clues as to their next move. The death warrants issued against the three former SLA friends could not be considered anything more than more stagecraft in their continuing guerrilla theatrics. Their next grand production was bound to be astounding. But they would have a tough time topping their last act, recruiting a revolutionary at the point of a gun and converting her into a legendary figure.

CHAPTER SEVENTEEN

"THIS IS TANIA"

I

April 15, 1974. A fine, bright Monday in San Francisco. Seventy days had passed since the foggy night Patricia Campbell Hearst had been torn from the warm security of her Berkeley apartment and thrust into the uncertain cold of the revolutionary underground.

Twelve days had passed since the the tape-recorded claim that she had changed her name and life style—that Patty the Media Princess had become Tania the Revolutionary Soldier of the SLA.

Three days had passed since revolutionary journalist Regis Debray's letter—written at the urging of Steven Weed—had been published in Randy Hearst's *Examiner*. The intent of the letter was to determine whether the kidnap victim's enlistment in the SLA was a voluntary act or a gun-at-the-head impressment. But in a certain context, the letter could have been read as a personal challenge to Patty/Tania. You say you're a revolutionary: now prove it. Pick up the gun. Use it.

Certain investigators and reporters had been speculating in private since immediately after the Tania tape that the terrorists had put themselves into a position which would virtually force them to demonstrate dramatically and publicly that their putative revolutionary pupil was no longer a captive but a convert.

"It's got to be something really spectacular, really vicious," one *Examiner* reporter brainstormed. "Like ordering her to assassinate Randy or one of the other Hearsts."

Patricide in the name of revolution was beyond the moral boundaries of even the SLA. But the terrorists were planning another spectacular—one that fit their conception of a revolutionary act and at the same time met a practical need for operating funds. Ordinary criminals would have called it a bank job. The SLA called it an expropriation. The planning was meticulous.

On the same day the Tania tape was delivered, a woman customer noticed a goateed black man in the lobby of her neighborhood bank—the Sunset Branch of the Hibernia Bank. She did not recognize the black man then; she would tell bank manager James Smith about it after it was too late.

The black man was DeFreeze/Cinque. He was on an intelligence-gathering mission. An ordinary criminal would have said he was casing the joint.

The Hibernia was one of California's oldest banks. It had been controlled for many years by the Tobin family, and the Tobin family was very big in Hillsborough. Trish Tobin was Patty/Tania's age. Trish and Patty been playmates and best friends when they were kids.

There were 22 banks with branch offices in San Francisco—171 branches in all. Hibernia had 9 branch offices, including the one in the Sunset district.

It could have been pure coincidence. On the other hand, certain members of the SLA had a highly developed sense of irony.

Shortly before five o'clock in the afternoon on Thursday, April 11, two young white women walked into the office of Continental Rent-A-Car at 404 O'Farrell Street in San Francisco. One was a slender blonde, the other a tall brunette. Part-time rental agent Phil

Goldbeck greeted the women and showed them a 1973 red AMC Hornet Sportabout when they asked about renting a car.

The brunette said she'd take the Sportabout. She handed over a California driver's license bearing the name of Janet Cooper. Goldbeck filled in the rental form and the brunette signed it. She told Goldbeck she would keep the car through April 15.

"Everything was in order," Goldbeck said later. "So she paid $40 cash in advance. I gave her the keys and she and her friend drove off."

The SLA had just acquired a getaway car.

On the same evening, or possibly a couple of nights before, a retired machinist named Aldo Ricci noticed a green Ford station wagon near his home in the Sunset district. On three or four subsequent nights, the same car appeared, pulled up near the intersection of 30th Avenue and Lawton Street, sat there four or five minutes with its engine running and its lights on, then drove away.

Ricci thought this odd enough to register the car in his memory. What he had seen was the SLA making dry runs in its second getaway car.

II

The Sunset branch of Hibernia Bank was located in the heart of middle-class San Francisco. A clean, quiet neighborhood. The well-kept homes surrounding the small shopping district along Noriega Street, between 21st and 23rd Avenues, had been in the $30,000 to $40,000 price range a couple of years before; now they were selling for about $50,000. Civil servants, white-collar workers, pensioners with good retirement plans, plus the businessmen along Noriega, did their banking at Hibernia. It was a friendly place. Ed Shea, the 66-year-old guard from Young Patrol Service, made it a practice to stand near the twin front doors and greet regular customers as they came in. Bank manager

James Smith and his 19-member staff also knew most of the customers by name. The branch had opened in the modest, white stucco building at 1450 Noriega Street in 1955. It was equipped with standard alarm systems and twin Mosler automatic motion picture cameras, but none of the security devices had ever gone into operation except in tests. Ed Shea had never pulled his .38 caliber pistol. Bank robberies didn't happen in nice neighborhoods like this.

At 9:40 A.M. on April 15 there were six customers in the bank. Manager Smith was upstairs in the mezzanine employees' lounge finishing a cup of coffee.

Outside, the red AMC Sportabout with four persons in it pulled in and stopped in an abandoned service station directly across from the bank. The green 1973 Ford LTD station wagon parked in the bus zone next to the red-painted curb on 22nd Avenue just off Noriega.

Five people got out of the station wagon and walked briskly around the corner to the bank's swinging glass door—a distance of only 20 paces. Ed Shea watched them come in. They weren't regulars. All were dressed in dark-blue, three-quarter-length coats. One was a black man with a goatee. The others were young white women.

They entered almost as if they were a single organism—Cinque-Fahizah-Mizmoon-Gabi-Tania. They took up prearranged positions, then flung their dark coats open. Each carried a .30 caliber automatic carbine on a military sling.

"This is the SLA," Cinque announced from his spot near the bank vault. He was covering the doors and Ed Shea. Shea raised his hands.

Cinque ordered everyone to get down on the floor. One of the bandits nodded toward the young woman now stationed in the center of the lobby. "This is Tania!"

Cinque moved into the cubicle to the left of the vault area, grabbed the secretary at the reception desk there, pulled her into the lobby and ordered her down on the floor. Shea turned slightly as the black man moved past

227

him. Cinque noticed the pistol on Shea's hip and disarmed the old man.

Shea heard the one called Tania shouting at the people stretched out tensely on the brownish mustard-colored carpet: "Keep down or we'll shoot your motherfucking heads off!"

Upstairs Smith heard the shouting, glanced out the small window overlooking the main floor below and realized instantly what was going on. He saw only two of the robbers—two women. He pulled back and punched the silent alarm. The automatic cameras began rolling. The time was 9:43 A.M.

Mizmoon vaulted deftly over the cream-colored counters on the north side of the lobby and ordered the tellers to turn over their keys. They did. Mizmoon fumbled briefly with the locks on a couple of cash drawers, gave up, moved to unlocked drawers and started scooping up handfuls of currency. She stuffed the bills into a small bag.

Her four companions covered Mizmoon. They seemed to be timing themselves—counting to themselves, checking their watches. Precision, discipline. It was a workmanlike job until the very last moment.

Mizmoon vaulted back over the counter. She had more than $10,000 in the bag. The bandits grouped themselves for their flight.

At that moment 70-year-old Eugene Brennan and 59-year-old Peter Markoff came through the doors. Cinque ordered them down on the floor. "All I saw was a beard and a gun," Markoff said.

The two men disobeyed, turned and started out the doors. Fahizah let go a burst of four shots. Markoff staggered a couple of steps and fell outside on the sidewalk, a slug through his right buttock. Brennan, a bullet through his right abdomen, reeled and lurched out to the street.

Pharmacist Ken Outlander, who had been filling in for the bartender at the nearby neighborhood tavern, heard shots, hurried outside and saw a man down on the sidewalk. The robbers were coming out as he ran toward the fallen Markoff. One of the bandits fired at

228

him and missed. A bullet fragment grazed 54-year-old Frank Cassidy's right leg just above the kneecap as he came around the southeast corner of the bank from the parking lot.*

Cinque and the four women made the dash around the corner to the green station wagon, scrambled in and peeled away north on 22d Avenue. The red Sportabout followed. The "expropriation" had taken less than five minutes.

At 30th Avenue and Lawton Street, the two cars stopped. The occupants shifted quickly into two other cars—a Ford LTD sedan and a Maverick—and drove away. The first two cars, discovered minutes later by police who swarmed through the entire Sunset district, were at the spot where Aldo Ricci had seen the station wagon making the dry runs. The station wagon was parked directly in front of a pink stucco house at 2330 Lawton. It was the former home of San Francisco Police Chief Donald Scott.

III

The two Mosler cameras made 1200 frames of motion picture film of the holdup. The bank had been carefully cased. On the front window was a decal no alert scout could have missed: "Cameras Will Film Any Holdup of Premises." Any one of the five raiders—even Tania, the only one who had not been trained extensively in marksmanship—could have shot out the cameras.

But guerrilla theater was an essential element in SLA's revolutionary melodrama. The film would be yet another media-borne message to the masses: Go and do likewise. The revolutionary troupe even placed their

* Cassidy's wound was slight. He refused medical treatment. Brennan, a pensioner, and Markoff, owner of Noriega Liquors, were hospitalized and recovered. Shea worked at the bank for the next three days, then never returned.

star attraction at center stage and announced: "This is Tania."

The identities of the five bandits were quickly established from the films. Certain frames were released to and published by the media around the world. Several showed Patty/Tania, wearing a long dark wig, with her carbine leveled. Her expression was unreadable. It could not be determined from the films, of course, whether her carbine was loaded with live ammunition. In some frames, it appeared that her companions were pointing their weapons at the star.

The Hearst family and Steve Weed—said they did not doubt that Tania—the young woman in the bank—was Patty. But they took the position that she had somehow been forced or coerced into taking part in the raid, just as they believed she had been in announcing that she had gone over to the SLA.

Randy, just back from a brief vacation in Mexico with his wife, daughters and nephew, took a look at the photos and reacted with angry dismay. "I feel like any father would react to it," he said. "I think it's the most vicious thing that I've ever seen or had happen to me."

The two top federal lawmen in San Francisco—U.S. Attorney James L. Browning and FBI Agent in Charge Charles Bates—cautiously said they had no way of knowing whether Patty had acted of her own free will.

Not so their boss, U.S. Attorney General William B. Saxbe. The nation's chief law enforcement officer had previously made a number of shoot-from-the-hip remarks about the Hearst case. Among other things, he had said that he didn't think Randy Hearst should comply with any ranson demands and that the FBI— which had repeatedly said it would do nothing to endanger the kidnap victim's life—ought to "go in and get her" whenever and wherever they found the SLA. Such remarks won applause from law and order hardliners but did nothing to advance the investigation.

Now, after looking at the bank robbery films, Saxbe called the SLA raiders, including Patty/Tania, "common criminals." On the basis of the films, Saxbe decided that she was "a willing participant." Saxbe's instant analysis embarrassed many other lawyers and lawmen, including several directly involved in the investigation. Randy Hearst, who had been irritated by Sazbe's earlier remarks, was furious at his latest mouthings.

In his public reaction, Randy tried to maintain a cool, measured tone, but didn't quite succeed. "We happen to know our daughter better than Saxbe does," he said. "I don't see that the statement he makes does anything except confirm my original view that the man makes irresponsible statements and obviously talks off the top of his head when he should be listening."

Privately his characterization of Saxbe was considerably more colorful. His mildest comment was, "Saxbe's incredible!" And he added, "Kelly of the FBI agrees with me."

John Kelly, the number-two man in the FBI's San Francisco office had told the *Examiner* he believed the kidnap victim participated in the robbery under duress. He said that she may have been told to go along or "we'll kidnap your sister."

Chesterfield H. Smith, president of the American Bar Association, would not talk about the merits of the case, but did speak out on Saxbe's ethical stance. It was, he stated flatly, unethical for a man in Saxbe's position "to comment on the guilt or innocence of anybody, or to in any way interfere with the process of a fair trial."

IV

In New York, Peter Davies began studying the news photos copied from the bank robbery films and concluded that Patty/Tania had been playacting, going through the motions. Davies was an amateur but expert photo analyst. His studies and reports on photos of the 1970 shooting deaths of four students at Ohio's Kent State University played a large part in the reopening of that controversial case.

Davies convinced himself that Patty/Tania had been forced to carry her carbine in such a way that she could not get rid of the gun—throw it away and surrender—without first removing her coat. If a gun battle started, she would be helpless. "The object was to create a situation in which she would be killed by law enforcement," Davies said.

The photos suggested to him that Patty/Tania's right hand may have been strapped to her side or to the butt of the weapon—that she could not reach the trigger. He also thought the carbine probably was not loaded. In short, he believed the star of the bank raid was playing a reluctant role under threat of death.

Bates of the FBI said only that the photos were "subject to various interpretations." Randy thought Davies's analysis was "interesting" but beside the point because he steadfastly believed that even if his daughter had been able to fire the carbine, she still had been forced by some means to take part in the robbery.

On-the-street veterans looked at the pictures and said Patty/Tania and the others were simply using the old "211-sling." Armed robbers who liked short-barreled carbines or shotguns commonly slung their weapons in that manner, concealing the guns under their coats until confronting their victims. The right-hand coat pocket was cut out so the gunman could reach the trigger. And, in fact, San Francisco police did recover one of the SLA raiders' jackets some time later. The right-hand pocket had been carefully cut out.

V

Late on April 15, federal warrants were issued for the arrest of Donald David DeFreeze, Nancy Ling Perry, Patricia Soltysik and Camilla Hall—Cinque, Fahizah, Mizmoon and Gabi. They were wanted for bank robbery. A warrant also was issued for Patricia Campbell Hearst—Tania. She was wanted as a material witness.

On April 19 it was revealed that a small green notebook found in the burned-out SLA hideout on Sutherland Court in Concord nearly a month before the kidnaping contained references to the intended victim. "Patricia Campbell Hearst" ... "teams" ... "guns" ... "on the night of full moon January 7" ... "at UC—daughter of Hearst" ... "Junior Art Student ..." The notebook also contained the names "David and Margarieta" and "Yolanda and Camilla."

From the notebook it was clear that the kidnap plot had been planned for January 7, but had somehow gone awry and been postponed. On February 4 the moon over Berkeley was in the final phase before full moon.

It was clear, too, that someone had bungled in not alerting the victim or her family, but then the notebook was only one piece in a great pile of evidence found in the Sutherland Court hideout.

"They should have notified us," said Randy Hearst. "But it's possible they had reams of material to go through before they got to this, and this little green notebook didn't come up until it was too late."

To Randy, the notations in the little green notebook was hard evidence that his daughter had not been in on her own kidnaping—and by extension, since she was a captive, not responsible for anything that followed the kidnaping. To investigators, the notebook was reasonably solid evidence she did not cooperate in her own abduction. They would not go beyond that.

On April 25, ten days after the bank robbery, San Francisco police found the second-stage getaway cars (the Ford LTD sedan and the Maverick) in a public parking garage on Geary Boulevard. On the same day, two more tapes came from the SLA.

Cinque made a report:

Greetings to the people and all sisters and brothers behind the walls and in the streets, elements of the Black Liberation Army, the Weather Underground and the Black Guerrilla Family and all combat forces of the community.

233

I am General Field Marshal Cin speaking.

Combat operations: April 15, the year of the soldier.

Action: expropriation.

Supplies liberated: One .38 Smith & Wesson revolver, condition good. Five rounds of 158 grain .38 caliber ammo. Cash: $10,660.02.

Number of rounds fired by combat forces: seven rounds.

Casualties: People's forces, none. Enemy forces, none. Civilian, two.

Reasons: Subject One, Male. Subject was ordered to lay on floor face down. Subject refused order and jumped out the front door of the bank. Therefore the subject was shot. Subject Two, Male. Subject failed or did not hear warning to clear the street. Subject was running down the street toward the bank and combat forces accordingly assumed subject was an armed enemy force element. Therefore subject was shot.

We again warn the public. Any citizen attempting to aid, to inform or assist the enemy of the people in any manner will be shot without hesitation. There is no middle ground in war. Either you are the people or the enemy. You must make the choice.

The words were cold, the style chilling. No human beings were torn by bullets—only "civilians," "subjects," "males." To Cinque, the men who were cut down by SLA slugs were abstractions, not flesh and blood.

Another voice: "Greetings to the people, this is Tania. On April 15 my comrades and I expropriated $10,660.02* from the Sunset branch of Hibernia Bank. Casualties could have been avoided had the persons involved kept out of the way and cooperated with the people's forces until after our departure."

Randy and Catherine Hearst heard the tapes and recognized the voice as their daughter's. She went on to

---

* An FBI audit placed the robbery amount at $10,600. It is possible the additional $60.02 listed in the SLA's accounting was money picked up from a counter before it had been deposited.

explain that she was acting as a free agent, and to rationalize her act:

I was positioned so that I could hold customers and bank personnel who were on the floor. My gun was loaded and at no time did any of my comrades intentionally point their guns at me.

Careful examination of the photographs which were published clearly show this was true.

Our action of April 15 forced the corporate state to help finance the revolution. In the case of expropriation, the difference between a criminal act and a revolutionary act is shown by what the money is used for.

She scoffed at the idea she had been brainwashed. She called Steve Weed a clown, and a sexist, ageist pig. She referred to Vincent Hallinan, the attorney, as a clown, and to her family as the pig Hearsts. She also called her father Adolf.

She closed:

In any case, I hope that the last action has put his [Randy's] mind at ease. If it didn't, further actions will.

To those who still believe that I am brainwashed or dead, I see no reason to further defend my position. I am a soldier in the people's army. Patria o muerte; venceremos.

CHAPTER EIGHTEEN

THE INSECTS LEAD THE WAY

I

The insects were the worst affront. Of all the embarrassing disclosures, mistakes and bad luck that had plagued investigators since Patty was kidnaped, the break that led to the discovery of the SLA's hideout was the worst. Cockroaches were the bird dogs.

There had been all the mouthing about "fascist insects that prey upon the life of the people" and a counter slogan about the SLA being "insects who feed upon the life of the revolution." The cockroach bit seemed the final insult, as if some twisted comic scenarist was pulling the puppet strings.

The housekeeper for Mrs. Lolabelle Evans, a blind black woman who lived in an apartment at 1827 Golden Gate Avenue not far from downtown San Francisco, found the cockroaches. They were swarming down the walls from the apartment above. She called Mrs. Evans's landlord on Thursday, May 2.

Inside the apartment above Mrs. Evans, the landlord found what the insects had been feeding upon; great quantities of debris and food particles. More shocking than the mess left behind by the missing tenants was the writing and a symbol scrawled murallike across the walls.

"Patria o Muerte Venceremos. Tania."

"Freedom is the bread of the land. Cin."

The symbol was made of large sweeps of black in the shape of the seven-headed cobra, insignia of the SLA.

Police entered the filthy apartment cautiously, carefully checking for any booby traps or bombs that might have been rigged like those in the Concord house. After checking its explosive potential, investigators were quickly convinced they had found their first SLA hideout since the kidnaping—less than a mile from FBI headquarters. It had taken only three months and an assist from some cockroaches.

The SLA had strewn the apartment with taunting little slogans about "juicy clues" and warning officers to "remember you are not bulletproof either."

Powder and pellets had been removed from 100 shotgun shells. Powder and slugs had been removed from nearly as many rifle cartridges. Some jumped to the conclusion they were constructing bombs or antipersonnel grenades. But investigators had learned the hard way not to take everything left behind by the SLA at face value.

There were bits and pieces of gun barrels and gun stocks.

"Making little ones out of big ones," one old-timer noted. This was a common method criminals used to reduce the size of rifles and shotguns so they could be slung beneath coats, as the bank robbery squad had done.

Two leather coats had been left behind like those worn at the Hibernia Bank 17 days before. There were hats and sleeping bags and papers, too.

The bathroom contained signs that most of the papers had been destroyed in a brew of potassium cyanide mixed in the bathtub.

A pair of sponges cut out as if they might have been used to convert sunglasses into a blindfold stirred some new theories about Patty's real status in the SLA. A tracking dog helped the investigators conclude that Patty had worn or handled the sponges.

The lack of a full set of fingerprints of Patty hindered investigation. Without these, experts could not be certain prints found in the apartment or anywhere else might be hers.

Mrs. Evans told investigators she had heard the neighbors until about a week before. They had been uncommonly noisy, sounding as if they were trying to saw or drill their way through the floor. They had once tried to use her telephone, but she had been alone and refused to open her door for any strangers.

A neighbor in the building next door, Mrs. Stella Bowles, thought she saw the tenants moving out a week before. A black man and two white women had loaded up a gray or green station wagon. She could not recognize the photos of any of the SLA suspects.

Their statements and other physical evidence analyzed by FBI laboratory technicians gave investigators new hope they might be closer to the group; the cockroach joke might have backfired and placed the trackers only a week behind the SLA.

II

There were many disturbing elements to finding the hideout in the midst of the city, especially since so many people must have seen the SLA soldiers moving about. There had been a growing number of false sightings of Patty and her comrades since the bank robbery, some as far away as North Carolina and Florida. But there was growing evidence their neighbors on Golden Gate Avenue had seen them and decided not to call police.

The four-story brick apartment building where they lived for five weeks was a typical San Francisco structure built in the 1920s on a 40-foot-wide lot and sharing common walls with similar buildings on either side. The sweep of bay windows could be seen on the second, third and fourth floors above the entry and garage on the main floor. A fire escape was tucked down the middle between the bay windows.

The 1800 block of Golden Gate Avenue is in the black ghetto section called the Western Addition, home of the radical Western Addition Project Area Committee that the SLA had insisted help oversee the food giveaway.

The SLA members had moved freely around their neighborhood, even venturing downtown to rent automobiles for bank robberies and buy flowers and cards for special announcements.

The last two cars used in the bank robbery as the transfer vehicles were found abandoned just nine blocks away on Geary Street. A parking garage at Japantown had been the drop point.

Parking tickets on the Ford LTD showed it had been parked the day after the bank robbery. The Maverick had not been parked there until four days afterward. In both cases, the cars had been placed there after wanted bulletins had been issued to all police units in the Bay Area and California. After the tense drive to the garage, there had been a walk back or possibly the use of public transportation.

Whether the SLA's fear of police had diminished with their apparent imperviousness to capture or whether black people were protecting them by looking the other way bothered officials. The police had had their own share of foul-ups after the robbery. Evidence discovered shortly after the bank job had not been turned over to investigators for nine days. If the general public was turning their backs on them, the investigators' job would become unmanageable.

Down the street from the hideout, a corner grocery store provided more troubling insight into why there had been no calls from Golden Gate Avenue.

The gregarious black woman who ran the store—her friends called her "Momma"—admitted that she had seen a girl who looked like Patty Hearst, had asked her about it more than once.

"It wasn't no secret they was here," she said.

"I just asked her was she the Hearst girl. I told her I be praying for her to go back to her parents."

"But she just said: 'Everybody tells me that,' that she looks like Patty Hearst."

"Momma" did not call the police, because "You call the police, they come round askin' you questions, did you see this? did you see that? They treat you like you was the criminal."

The storekeeper remembered a young black man, extra light-skinned with slightly slanted eyes, asking for plum wine. But she thought he was kidding, not believing there was any such thing as plum wine.

The girl who looked like Patty caught the attention of a neighborhood woman, because she spent $11 in the small convenience market. That seemed too much, because most people in the neighborhood would go to a supermarket where they could have saved some precious pennies on a purchase that large.

"The vibes I got was she was tense," she said.

"She was dressed kind of hippie. She looked out of place. She looked like she had class, a lot of class, but she was dressed down."

To counteract this casual response, such an easy acceptance of terrorists in their midst, the FBI issued pleas for assistance from the public. Posters were placed in public gathering places like service stations, post offices and through the media, showing pictures of the key SLA soldiers. The resulting avalanche of telephone calls kept police agencies all over the country busy.

Hardly a day went by when someone did not spot a girl who looked like Patty/Tania or a man who looked like DeFreeze/Cinque or both together. Incalculable police man-hours were spent chasing down one lead after another, before all proved fruitless.

III

The Golden Gate Avenue hideout had been intensively used since March 20 when a young white woman using the name of Louise Hamilton had rented the place for $125 a month. They had cleared out on April 24, using an old gray station wagon and a rented truck.

Their next move was to rent quarters about two and a half miles away in a half industrial-half residential section mostly occupied by blacks. A street-level apartment at 1808 Oakdale Avenue in the Bayview district was rented by a black woman using the name of M. Jackson. She paid $375 cash, which included the first and last month's rent and a $25 cleaning deposit. Rent receipts for the three-room apartment were dated May 1.

This left nearly a week unaccounted for and possibly another hideout.

The second hideout lacked colorful slogans and taunts. There were five mattresses, shoes, jackets, trousers, toothbrushes, wigs and beauty aids, but nothing much more. Flimsy blankets served as drapes, hiding the interior from passersby.

The week-long gap between the hideouts concerned investigators, but not nearly as much as the larger one between the February 4 kidnap and the March 20 rental of the Golden Gate Avenue apartment. Chasing the SLA hideouts, there had been far-ranging theories about that hideout. Theories that had sent officers from the Santa Cruz Mountains to the Redding foothills.

Another division of officers were kept busy on the San Francisco peninsula, the stringy megalopolis that houses some 1.5 million people from the southern city limits to southern San Jose. A chance comment Camilla Hall made and a map found in the Contra Costa County SLA pad made the search there a hopeful possibility.

The Rev. George Hall said Camilla had told him the

last time they talked she was moving from Berkeley to Palo Alto, because she had gotten a job taking care of someone's estate. He was vague about the location. It could have been Palo Alto or Los Altos Hills or Atherton, all in the midpeninsula area.

Investigators working out of FBI's Palo Alto office found a locksmith who had sold a dead-bolt lock to Camilla on February 20. She had been in the company of two black men, one of whom resembled DeFreeze/Cinque.

The map, which contained notations from surveillance of the neighborhood, seemed to point slightly north to the community of Hillsborough, where Patty had grown up.

The map was not sufficiently keyed to existing maps that investigators could be certain of the precise location. Notations on the hand-drawn map could have indicated locations for another planned kidnap, or merely information to prevent any interference with a neighborhood's normal routine, if they planned to hide out there.

DeFreeze once had told SLA friends he had contacts in East Palo Alto, a black enclave squeezed into old homes and apartments between Bayshore Freeway, industrial projects and salt flats at the edge of the bay. None of the haunts of radicals there provided investigators with any leads.

Neither was an estate turned up that might have been the first hideout.

Tracking the SLA through the maze of papers, documents, books and maps left behind in suspects' homes and apartments had used a tremendous amount of the investigators' time. The standard FBI response to kidnaps had been to press as much manpower as possible into use swiftly, using available leads, directories, tips. This often involved patient plodding through dull records and papers for some seemingly insignificant fact or address that might prove useful.

This case had been complicated because the ransom required none of the kidnapers to pick it up personally. Methods used to communicate with the family of the kidnap victim also avoided easy detection. Thus investigators were left to the paperwork. The SLA had been obliging in leaving a lot of potential evidence.

At each of the six residences searched by investigators, there had been something more, some new possibility. From the day Little and Remiro were arrested, there had been a vast cataloging effort and attempts to make some sense out of chaotic situations like they found at the Concord house.

There was such a wealth of leads that looked likely. Inside the Harris apartment, there were photographs of mountain treks and camps, notations on maps of sites in the Sierras, the foothills and the Mt. Shasta area. Even little notations about their hoping to get back there soon. Code books, or series of numbers and names that appeared to be codes kept cryptographers occupied for days. Reference works had been marked in key places. Pencil-drawn maps of Bay Area locations had to be checked out.

There were maps of old mines in the East Bay hills that had notations as if they had been planning to use them. These had to be checked.

All of the clothing, hardware and gun parts had to be analyzed. There was so much evidence, it looked suspiciously like it had been fed into the investigative machinery just to clog it up.

IV

Financing for the SLA was another crucial part of the search, because running was an expensive affair. Before the bank robbery, there had been little visible means of supporting so many people. Some of the papers had indicated places apparently marked for robbery or burglary, but none had been carried out as indicated. None of the known robberies or burglaries had been linked to the SLA.

Mary Alice Siem had told the FBI she had been robbed of $600 by three SLA soldiers, but that had been the previous October. She had also suggested the SLA was financing itself chiefly from funds that Willie Wolfe was able to obtain from his father, who did not know of his SLA ties.

The Harrises had attempted to obtain $1,500 from Bill's mother ten days after the kidnaping. Emily had written to a former sorority sister in Indiana, asking her to forward an enclosed letter to Bill's mother.

The letter to Bill's mother asked her to send him $1,500 in an envelope they had enclosed. It bore the name and address of Janet Cooper, General Delivery, Main Post Office, Santa Clara, California. His mother and stepfather mailed the envelope with only $250 inside on February 19. The envelope was picked up by a young woman bearing indentification of Janet Cooper.

The former Venceremos central committee member, Janet Cooper, told investigators and news reporters that her identification had disappeared when her wallet was stolen the previous October. She said she had reported the theft to Oakland police. When called to testify before the federal grand jury, she refused to appear without her attorney. Her first appearance was inexplicably cut short by the U.S. attorney, but her subpoena to appear was kept alive.

The other source of income investigators could trace was the money withdrawn by Camilla Hall from the bank across from FBI offices in Berkeley. Her $1,565 and the Harris $250 could hardly be enough to support the main SLA squad's expensive operation; it appeared that another source of money still had not been discovered.

V

The SLA's own money problems appeared to have made them forget the $4 million held in escrow for the food giveaway program. The deadline set for May 5 was ignored by the SLA. Despite last-minute reminders that Patty's release could free the money, no sign was given.

The money reverted to the Hearst Corporation and the final section of the ill-fated People In Need program was dissolved.

VI

Whether money was the motive or another step in their self-styled revolution, three of the SLA squad were at work surveying another victim in mid-April, while they still occupied the Golden Gate Avenue apartment.

The daughter and grandchildren of Mayor Joseph Alioto found themselves under scrutiny of Emily Harris and two others that they could not identify. Alioto, who was in the midst of a race for the Democratic nomination for California governor, found out only after the surveillance was cut short.

The Harris woman approached the children of Angela Mia Alioto Veronese in front of their Pacific Heights home one afternoon the second week of April. The next day, when she returned with a nervous young white man, Mrs. Veronese walked out of the house to talk to her.

Several days later, another woman, dressed more like a hippie was parked across the street, studying the Veronese home. Police set up a stakeout inside the Veronese home from April 18 to April 27, but none of the group ever returned nor were spotted in the neighborhood again.

VII

Another group of police organizations just 55 minutes south of San Francisco was more tense than those at the Veronese house. An extra-large crowd of VIPs

245

was gathering for two days of the California Republican State Central Committee convention commencing Friday, April 19, just four days after the Hibernia Bank job. Intelligence officers with the responsibility of protecting the important personages feared the SLA might try yet another headline-hunting session by attacking the convention.

The prizes of such an attack would have been Vice President Gerald Ford, California Governor Ronald Reagan, State Attorney General Evelle Younger, Lieutenant Governor Ed Reinecke and other top state officers.

Federal, state and San Jose security officers took over the hotel chosen as convention headquarters, the just-completed Le Baron Hotel, a glass and stucco affair that had not been completely painted yet. Each corner room on all floors was occupied by a police officer, uniformed men and plainclothesmen roamed through the crowd. Security measures were so stringent some of the convention delegates who had been promised rooms were turned away, some with bitter and often grimly humorous results. One dignified young man was so vociferous about his canceled reservation, he was carted away to jail for his trouble, only to have charges dropped later.

When Reagan arrived, a contingent of plainclothesmen cleared the way for all of his appearances at a television studio where a weekly youth program was taped at a press conference, a luncheon speech and even his journey to the Los Altos Hills home of a major Republican contributor. Officers were taking no chances.

The night of Reagan's keynote address and Vice President Ford's appearance the next day, there was one small group of protesters.

This scraggly crew was kept hidden behind the hotel in a vacant lot seen only by lower-echelon conventioneers who had to walk further to their parked cars. But there was no trouble. The protesters carried signs about Watergate, impeachment, ITT and all the rest of the affairs the Republicans preferred not to discuss.

Otherwise, their protest was kept most decorous. If there were any SLA sympathizers or members among them, they kept their counsel and just watched the police, who were watching them and any other suspicious parties in the vicinity.

VIII

The SLA's "intelligence and surveillance" unit was apparently more concerned with rumors it was receiving of a big police build-up. Equipped with elaborate procedures and codes for contacting fellow members, this unit simply gathered tips and observations from old friends and acquaintances. While the members had the advantage of knowing who to watch in officialdom, they were not so adept at interpreting what they observed.

Plans and moves based upon these faulty observations shifted their direction to new, unfamiliar ground.

CHAPTER NINETEEN

DEATH ROW JEFF AND THE SLA—
GETTING RID OF PATTY

"I could solve this whole thing right now. If I was
Randy Hearst, I'd just put an ad in the paper:
Wanted, seven-headed mongoose."
———Knox Bronson, *Examiner* copyboy.

I

Knox Bronson's surrealistic suggestion was made after several cocktails at the M&M, the saloon where the
Examiner's staff did its drinking, griping and gossiping.
The idea of setting a seven-headed mongoose after the
seven-headed cobra of the SLA was only slightly less
farfetched than many of the thousands of schemes put
forward by thousands of men, women and children
who wanted to help Randy Hearst recover his daughter.

And Randy was willing to listen to almost anyone,
consider any proposal, risk his fortune or his life if
there was even a remote chance his daughter might be
freed as a result. It was a time for desperate measures.

At one point early in the case, he soberly considered
offering himself to the SLA in exchange for Patty. He

finally rejected the idea only after convincing himself the terrorists would turn down the offer, and that the public would misconstrue it as a grandstand play.

At least a thousand mystics and psychics of all persuasions offered their services—about one hundred for substantial fees. Randy did consult at least two psychics in all seriousness. One was a guest at the Hillsborough home for about a week, made field trips to several spots in the Bay Area which gave off "psychic emanations" indicating that Patty was nearby. The field trips were dead ends.

Examiner executive editor Tom Eastham, a cautious believer in extrasensory perception for many years, was contacted by dozens of ESP "sensitives" and kept in communication with several for months after the kidnaping. He was particularly impressed by a woman physician from Bellevue, Washington, and a man who phoned him regularly at his own expense from New Jersey.

The woman—"a knowledgeable, scientific person"— made a number of vision-based predictions which Eastham said were borne out by later events. She received psychic impressions that Patty was being held in San Francisco, and that the prisoner would eventually be taken to Los Angeles, where she would be given more freedom by her captors. She "saw" specific neighborhoods, named specific streets. Eastham assigned a team of *Examiner* reporters to check out one of the streets in Los Angeles (the psychic claimed she had never been there) for a former Baptist church which she believed had been taken over by the SLA. They spent hours cruising the seemingly endless street (Sepulveda Boulevard) but never found a building which fit the description.

The New Jersey man, among other inspirations, suggested a public appeal to Patty/Tania to surrender herself. The appeal was presented in a front-page *Examiner* editorial; the Los Angeles County Bar Association and the Los Angeles Press Club established special phone lines and set up a fail-safe procedure under which she and her comrades could surrender themselves to newsmen instead of police. The appeal fell on deaf ears.

II

Directly or indirectly, the Hearst case—like a successful television crime series—stimulated any number of criminal spin-offs. At least 30 kidnapings occurred in the United States within five months after Patty's abduction. The attempted kidnaping of Britain's Princess Anne on March 20 by 26-year-old Ian Ball, who gunned down four persons during his desperate foray, may have been the most spectacular of them.

Among the splashier kidnapings in this country, which received intense coverage by the media, were those of *Atlanta Constitution* editor Reg Murphy, a bungled inside-out version of the SLA abduction; 8-year-old John Calzadilla of Long Island; Mrs. Eunice Kronheim, the St. Paul banker's wife; Mrs. Betty Van Balen, wife of a Roanoake, Virginia, manufacturer; Philadelphia socialite Annette Friendland—they went on and on. Millions of dollars were paid in ransoms, but in most cases the money was recovered and the kidnapers apprehended.

The Hearsts themselves, tortured by the impossible demands of the SLA, were hit again and again by extortionists who tried to get in on the act. One anonymous weirdo threatened to send Patty's ear—an obvious sick gimmick borrowed from the Getty kidnaping —to authenticate his demand.

Cab driver Nile Dwayne Marx and his wife Shirley Ann were arrested in Los Angeles less than two weeks after Patty's abduction when he made a phony $100,-000 ransom demand by phone to Catherine Hearst. On March 1 and 2 Samuel Lee McGraw tried the same gimmick from San Diego, demanding $10,000. He wound up with a five-to-life term in state prison. Ralph Lee Jones of Van Nuys used the mails to send his demands for $100,000 from the Hearsts in early April.

Jones was indicted by the federal grand jury in Los Angeles after his arrest when he tried to pick up the payoff in Sherman Oaks.

In none of these cases was any link established to Patty's real kidnapers.

Two of Randy Hearst's top executives—Eastham and *Examiner* publisher Charles Gould—were involved directly in a derring-do effort to recover the boss's daughter. Eastham, unclear on the exact dates, told the story:

"A guy called [through the *Examiner* switchboard] and said he was DeFreeze and he was trying to get away. That they wanted to drop Patty. The voice, it was *so* right-sounding. It sounded like the voice on the tapes. He said he only wanted enough for bus fare out of town."

That struck Eastham as fishy—a terrorist who originally wanted millions in free food now willing to settle for bus fare.

"I said, 'You've been asking for two million.' He said, 'Like, man, we got to get away. We're not talking about money for the people, we talking about getting away.'

"I said for him to call back in 20 minutes. I wanted to talk to Charles Gould. It [the demand] was only $250 and we couldn't afford *not* to do it ... This was about two months after the kidnaping. It was logical to believe, and anyhow I got on the thing. I had $80 in my pocket. Charles came up with the rest out of his pocket."

The drop area was in Oakland, near the Berkeley city limits. Eastham put the money behind a bush, as per instructions, then drove down the street a half block and stopped near a gray Volkswagen bus.

"I was to blow the horn twice, and Patricia would get out," Eastham said. "I dropped it—and nothing happened."

He was reminded that office rumor had it there were two drops of cash.

"I was hoping no one would remember that," Eastham said glumly. "The first time I dropped off $100 as a test. Then I came right back to the office. I was with Charles when the second call came. Mary [the switchboard operator] said, 'A black man wants to talk to you and he said it [the payoff] wasn't enough, and so I asked him to put Patricia on the phone.

"A woman's voice came on. I said, 'It doesn't sound like Patricia.' He said, 'It's Patricia all right, and I want you to go do it again.' Charles and I discussed it, and we decided again we couldn't afford not to do it."

The second payoff was as futile as the first. It was a nice day's work for a small-time hustler.

III

Another more serious attempt to establish private contact with the SLA was made through Dennis Banks and Russell Means, leaders of the militant American Indian Movement (AIM) and the dramatic 1973 occupation of the Sioux Indian village of Wounded Knee, South Dakota.

AIM, headquartered in St. Paul, Minnesota, was one of the community organizations specified by the SLA to monitor the free food program. Almost certainly, AIM was named by the SLA at the suggestion of Camilla/Gabi, onetime social worker in the Twin Cities, where thousands of Indians were on the welfare rolls. With its grassroots appeal to Indian pride, its mystical devotion to the traditional Indian culture and wide support among white radicals, AIM could hardly have escaped notice of Camilla Hall whose heart was always with the underdog.

When AIM was named as a principal in the food program, Banks and Means were on trial in St. Paul on federal charges growing out of the historic and sometimes bloody confrontation between the Indians who had occupied Wounded Knee and the federal forces who had besieged them. Randy Hearst personally intervened with Federal Judge Fred Nichol, presiding at the trial. He persuaded the judge to permit Banks and

Means to fly to San Francisco for secret conferences on the food program.

Banks, a Chippewa, and Means, an Oglala Sioux, wore their hair long in the Indian style, with traditional headbands and feathers. But they weren't role-playing; they had rejected the white life style and chosen the Indian way. They also were tough men, hard bargainers, unawed by the rich man in the expensive sports clothes who sat across from them at the negotiating table in the San Francisco Hilton Hotel. Banks was the quiet one, an ex-convict who had become a leader and hero to thousands of Indians across the country. Means was the more flamboyant and outspoken, a man who had found himself in the Indian movement after long battles with the bottle and drugs. Both were reservation born and bred, and both knew poverty and violence at first hand.

Randy quickly established a rapport with the two Indian leaders, men whose experiences and views were almost completely alien to him.

Banks and Means said Indians would not accept free food as long as Patty was held captive—and Bay Area Indians went along. Banks and Means also agreed to help in any way they could to recover the editor's daughter.

Randy was deeply impressed by the attitudes of the AIM leaders. Not long afterward, he personally assigned Examiner reporter Jerry Belcher to cover the Wounded Knee trial. Later he sent the reporter to South Dakota to write a series of stories about conditions on the Sioux reservations.

The assignments were not exactly a quid pro quo arrangement, but coverage of a trial in St. Paul and a series on the Sioux of South Dakota were certainly beyond the boundaries of the *Examiner*'s ordinary journalistic territory.

Randy explained the assignments to the reporter. "I've known for years that the Indians were getting screwed in this country," he said. "But it never really got through to me until this whole thing happened. These people [Banks and Means] have been the only decent ones in this whole mess. I want you to go back

253

there and do the stories, not just straight reporting but the stories *behind* what's going on. Be objective—but be *simpatico* too."

Banks, back in St. Paul, made repeated pleas to the SLA to release their captive—or at least to make contact with him and use him as a mediator of their demands. In April, he announced that he was prepared to go anywhere in the world—he had a private jet plane available at a moment's notice—to meet and work out a deal for Patty's freedom.

Despite the wide publicity given to Banks's pleas, he received only one phone contact from a man who sounded as if he might be an authentic representative of the terrorists. The mysterious caller said he would meet Banks the next day; Banks was cautiously optimistic. He waited through the day and into the night. The caller never showed up, never made another contact.

IV

While Randy and his minions were pursuing futile free-Patty schemes, her fiancé Steven Weed was working a scheme of his own. After the Tania tape, Weed flew to Mexico City and sought out a man who had known the original Tania—the revolutionary French journalist Regis Debray. Weed spent hours persuading Debray to write an open letter to Patty/Tania, urging her to give some sign that she had chosen to join the SLA of her own free will. Both Weed and Debray, after he finally agreed to write the letter, had little confidence that it would be effective. But they tried.

The letter was written and turned over to Weed in Mexico City, but Debray insisted that it not be released until after he returned to Paris and that it be dated as if it had been written from Paris. He didn't want trouble with Mexican authorities. Debray addressed Patty directly:

Steve let me listen to your last message in which you say you have exchanged your name for that of Tania. The name of Tania—or Tamara Bunke—is an integral part of our revolutionary patrimony. It has deep and grave resonance for all national liberation movements of Latin America. And for me also—because I had the honor of working and fighting with her until the last moments of her life in Bolivia. It is because Tania was a comrade and a friend that I want to speak to you . . . ."

I ask you only to assure me that you have consciously and freely chosen to take the name and follow the example of Tania. If such is indeed the case, we can do nothing but respect your decision—no matter how questionable. . . .

If there is a reason of security for yourself or for those in your company that impedes you to appear personally in public, I am sure that, following the example of all the serious and responsible revolutionary movements which operate in secret because they are compelled to, you will find a way to deliver to an anonymous intermediary, without needless publicity, irrefutable proof of your free and conscious choice. This intermediary can be any common friend of Steve and you.

The Debray letter was printed in full in the April 12 editions of the *Examiner*.

With benefit of hindsight, Weed decided it was a mistake to print the letter in the Hearst newspaper. Patty/Tania herself had no respect for the newspaper. "It came out first in the *Examiner*," Weed said, "And the *Examiner* played it up too much. I didn't expect it to be a headline [story]. If I had it to do over again, I wouldn't give it to them."

In a subsequent tape, Patty/Tania flatly rejected the letter as a hoax.

V

Another internationally known figure had been drawn into the confused and confusing efforts to win the return of the media princess less than a month after the kidnaping. Again Randy Hearst's executive editor Tom Eastham was involved at the outset. Eastham had read an analytical article by John Peterson in the weekly *National Observer* in which psychiatrist Dr. Frederick Hacker was quoted at length on the subject of terrorism.

Hacker, author of an authoritative treatise on terrorist tactics and psychology, was one of the men who, through careful negotiation and cautious granting of concessions, successfully won the release of four hostages held by Palestinian terrorists at the Vienna airport shortly before the outbreak of the 1973 Arab-Israeli war.

Eastham mentioned the article to *Examiner* publisher Charles Gould, who in turn got in touch with the 60-year-old founder-director of the Hacker Institute in Beverly Hills.

Hacker's credentials were impeccable. Professor of psychiatry and law at the University of Southern California, president of the Sigmund Freud Society, expert witness on terrorism before the House Committee on Internal Security.

Hacker traveled to Hillsborough at least three times to consult with and advise Randy and Catherine Hearst. In the beginning, the editor seemed put off by the psychiatrist—Randy was more at ease with blunt, plain-spoken men like Banks and Means than with subtle intellectuals like Hacker.

In time, though, he came to trust the psychiatrist and placed great faith in his undeniable expertise.

In brief, Hacker's advice was to take the SLA at its word that it was a deadly serious revolutionary movement fully capable of carrying out its threats, rather than to consider it as a freaked-out band of criminal crazies bluffing their way into notoriety. He urged the Hearsts in their public statements and actions to demonstrate respect for and trust in the SLA's sense of revolutionary honor. At the same time, he advised the Hearsts to make clear to the SLA that in return for every concession or gesture of good faith they made, they expected a concession from the terrorists.

And, ominously, he told the Hearsts well in advance of the Tania tape that their daughter might well identify with and eventually join forces with the SLA. He noted that in more than one case, stewardesses on aircraft skyjacked by terrorists had become deeply involved emotionally with their captors.

In general, the Hearsts' actions and reactions were in line with Hacker's recommendations. And he may have helped to prepare them psychologically for the shattering impact of their bitter rejection by Patty/Tania.

VI

Four and a half months after the kidnaping, executive editor Eastham was musing over his boss's long ordeal. Randy, he thought, had performed much better under stress than anyone could have expected. He did, now and then, fall into deep depression, and occasionally his temper exploded.

"And when he loses his temper" said another colleague, "Randy can really tear your ass out."

On the whole, though, Eastham believed that Randy Hearst had conducted himself well. "Nobly if not always logically," Eastham said.

And at a lower level in the Hearst organization, others shared that view. When a local bi-weekly newspaper implied in a gossipy "exposé" story that Randy and Catherine tried to escape from reality by way of the bottle, *Examiner* reporters were outraged.

One *Examiner* reporter asked Randy about it directly. Randy spoke with a tone of subdued anger in his voice, "Christ, I haven't got stiff *once* since this thing began. God knows if a guy ever needed an excuse to get drunk this is it. But it's a lot of baloney."

The reporter asked if Randy was thinking about suing the bi-weekly's editor for libel. "I wouldn't give that guy the benefit of suing him. It would just make his rag better known. That's something I learned from my pop."

Whatever his staffers thought of Randy's abilities as an editor—and many considered them indifferent at best—few would criticize his human qualities. They remembered that, when he was entangled in his own terrible crisis, he and Catherine had taken the time to send flowers and a card to the terminally ill wife of a former city editor.

If there was a universal professional and personal criticism of Randy by his executives and his news staff, it was that he was too naive, too impressionable, too willing to make himself available to questionable advice, especially since the kidnaping.

"Randy listened to too many people. He listened to anybody, exposed himself to too many people," Eastham said. "He should have found a few people in whom he had a great deal of confidence, and let them act as his advisers. I don't think he was his own best adviser because of the pressures and emotions of a favorite daughter being in jeopardy. I think his choices were wrong in his advisers. He listened to people like Cecil Williams, Popeye Jackson and Death Row Jeff."

Rev. Cecil Williams, controversial, publicity-conscious "pop" preacher of San Francisco's Glide Memorial Methodist Church, and Wilbert "Popeye" Jackson, reformed armed robber parolee and radical founder-chairman of the United Prisoners Union, were two key members of the Community Food Coalition.

Death Row Jeff was Clifford Jefferson, a 48-year-old murderer who was a quarter of a century into a life sentence. He also was a self-styled revolutionary, a friend of DeFreeze/Cinque—and, reputedly one of the founders of the SLA.

Like Rev. Williams and Popeye Jackson, the middle-aged convict was a black man, a charismatic figure and something of a Bay Area celebrity.

To fellow prison inmates Death Row Jeff was almost a legend, a heavy dude, wise in the peculiar folkways of their world behind the walls. To prison officials he was a complex, paradoxical human being.

State Director of Corrections Raymond Procunier, head of the huge California prison system, knew him well—and liked him. "He's a cool guy," Procunier said. "He's really honorable in many ways—honorable in terms of prison honor. And he really feels empathy for the poor and for people he considers to be innocent. His heart is out all the time."

But he also was a man of violence, willing to kill if he was pushed too far.

Prison reformers, and especially revolutionaries, saw Death Row Jeff as a source of power and influence within the prison proletariat. They figured that if Death Row was on their side, other prisoners would follow his lead.

Jefferson entered the California prison system in 1945 as a criminal nonentity on a burglary-auto theft rap. But he had been a boxer on the outside, he was hard and aggressive, and he took nothing from anyone. His reputation began to build.

Paroled in December 1948, he was back less than six months later, this time on an indeterminate life sentence for the second-degree murder of his brother-in-law in Bakersfield, California. He was then 23 years old. If he was a model prisoner, by the standards of the California Adult Authority, he would be a free man again by the time he was 28. If not, death might be his only release. Jefferson was not a model prisoner.

Jefferson became a prison celebrity in 1956 when he and another convict stabbed an inmate named Leonard "Sheik" Thompson.

Thompson survived, but Jefferson was tried and convicted under a California Penal Code section which provided for a mandatory death sentence for any kind of physical assault by a lifer. He took up residence on San Quentin's notorious Death Row. Caryl Chessman,

San Quentin's famous author-inmate, was one of his neighbors on the Row.

Jefferson lived on Death Row for three years. Twice he was given execution dates in San Quentin's gas chamber. Twice he beat the ultimate rap through legal maneuvers. The second date was canceled in June 1959, when then-Governor Goodwin J. Knight commuted Jefferson's death sentence to life imprisonment without possibility of parole. Any man who beat the gas chamber was a hero to prisoners. He became known as Death Row Jeff, a nickname that mixed affection with awe.

In 1968 the violence that lived within Death Row Jeff erupted again—an inmate was shot to death with a zip gun. This time the victim died. Death Row Jeff at first claimed he had been framed but later pleaded guilty to murder. By then the death penalty had been abolished. He was given another life sentence.

When radicals shifted their focus from antiwar activities to politicizing the prison system, Death Row Jeff was one of the hundreds of inmates drawn into the movement. Although he was no revolutionary scholar, the widely accepted story was that while in Folsom, Death Row Jeff conceived some of the basic ideas that would one day emerge as SLA doctrine.

Prison authorities were aware of Death Row Jeff's revolutionary sympathies, even if they were ignorant of the specifics. After the Marcus Foster assassination and the Hearst kidnaping, when the names of some of the suspected terrorists became known, checks were made of prison visitor logs. The names of Nancy Ling Perry, Emily Harris, Willie Wolfe and Russell Little appeared again and again in the 1973 logs as visitors of Death Row Jeff. Albert Taylor and Raymond Lee Scott, both murderers, both friends of Death Row Jeff, both believed to be at least peripheral behind-bars members of the SLA, also had been visited by the young revolutionaries.

On February 21 Procunier arranged a secret midnight meeting at San Quentin Prison between Death Row Jeff and Russell Little and Joe Remiro, SLA members then awaiting trial for the Foster murder. Procunier doubted that much would come out of the clandestine session, but there was a possibility. He wasn't convinced Death Row Jeff had the "juice" he claimed with Remiro, Little and Cinque. But he *was* convinced Death Row Jeff did want Patty released, did want the SLA to get out of the whole mess unharmed, did want poor people to get free food.

What came out of the three-hour meeting was a series of complaints by Remiro and Little about their treatment in prison, a demand that they be allowed to go on a live, national television hook-up to explain their position, and a three-point list of conditions for the release of the SLA's prisoner. The key condition was that authorities come up with $1 million in cash, aircraft for Cinque and his band, and a guarantee that they be allowed to fly to a friendly nation for asylum.

Procunier thought the conditions were impossible. He did turn them over to a law enforcement agency— apparently the FBI. The list of conditions never reached Randy Hearst.

On March 19 Superior Judge Sam Hall of Contra Costa County—in whose jurisdiction Remiro and Little faced trial on charges that came out of the January 10 shoot-out in Concord—turned down the request for the national television press conference.

On March 28, in a letter to Berkeley radio station KPFA and picked up by the rest of the media, Little and Remiro complained that their plan to free Patty, developed with Death Row Jeff at the secret meeting, had been thwarted by Procunier and the FBI. But their letter referred to the plan only briefly and in the broadest of terms:

"We share the S.L.A.'s concern for the safety of Patty and the element guarding her. They are in grave danger and should deal with the primary task of the safe return of Patty to her fiance and the safe withdrawal of the S.L.A. element." The rest of the seven-page handwritten letter was largely revolutionary rhetoric.

Meantime, in Vacaville, Death Row Jeff, encouraged

by a prison psychologist named Wesley Hiler was trying to get through to Randy Hearst on his own. Hiler considered the convict a frustrated idealist and a humanitarian. He too was convinced Death Row Jeff sincerely wanted to see Patty Hearst set free.

On March 10 Hiler went to Sunday services at Glide Memorial Church in San Francisco, met the Reverend Williams afterward and explained Death Row Jeff's position. He suggested that Death Row Jeff might make a direct television appeal to the SLA for Patty's release.

As a leading member of the Food Coalition, Williams had ready access to Randy Hearst. He arranged for a conference between Hiler and Randy that night at the San Francisco Hilton Hotel. Randy agreed that Death Row Jeff might be helpful. There also was general agreement that attorney Vincent Hallinan would be the best man to mediate the delicate negotiations between Randy and Death Row Jeff.

From that point on, partly because prison authorities apparently objected to Hiler's role (they believed he had an inflated idea of his importance in bringing Randy and Death Row Jeff together), the psychologist was eased offstage.

It was now largely Hallinan's show.

Hallinan was 78 years old, a millionaire, and radical to the core. He was physically and intellectually fearless. He had done time in prison. He was widely respected as one of the toughest, most erudite and imaginative criminal lawyers of the twentieth century. In 1952 he had been the Progressive Party candidate for president of the United States. He called himself a revolutionary, although he was by no means universally acclaimed by either the doctrinaire Old Left or the mystical Marxists of the New Left.

He definitely was not sympathetic to the tactics of the SLA.

"The SLA," he said, "are a bunch of juvenile delinquent maniacs, counterrevolutionaries, extremely dangerous to any progressive movement because they afford the repressive forces the excuse to destroy legitimate, sensible, ordered revolutionary movements." He nominated the Black Panther Party as one of the legitimate, sensible movements.

But despite his views of the SLA—and his generally pessimistic outlook on virtually all human endeavors—Hallinan thought there was a chance that something positive might result from Randy's encounter with Death Row Jeff and from the proposal that he himself act as a go-between in establishing private communications between Cinque's SLA band and the Hearst family.

Hallinan arranged a series of four meetings between the millionaire and the murderer. Randy appeared in an elegant, expensive sports jacket, slacks and tie, Death Row Jeff in proletarian prison denims. Somehow, they hit it off well. Randy was a good listener. Death Row Jeff was a good talker. At the end of one long session, they hugged one another.

Hallinan observed the interaction closely. He came away with the impression of Death Row Jeff as "decent in many ways" and absolutely sincere in his desire to see Patty freed, his SLA comrades escape from the country, and the poor given needed groceries. His impression of Randy was of a man who was simple, honest, open and terribly vulnerable in his naïveté.

"I think that sweet are the uses of adversity," Hallinan commented, "and that Randy's eyes have been opened pretty much in this episode to the general injustices of our culture. And I think he's a pretty badly smashed man by it."

Death Row Jeff's friends Taylor and Scott sat in on at least one session—and Scott tried to take over from the outset.

"Hearst," said Hallinan, "is an innocent. They brought in a man named Scott. Well, I took one look at Mr. Scott and concluded that Mr. Scott was completely insane. So Mr. Scott is asking things, and Hearst is explaining. And Scott is asking things like, 'Well, then, why did the mouse run up the wall?' "

Randy listened as if transfixed, as if Scott's words carried some deep, significant meaning he could not quite grasp.

"So I kicked Hearst," Hallinan recalled.

He took the editor out into the corridor and told him privately, "For Christ's sake, Randy, the man is insane. What the hell are you wasting your time with him for? Let Jefferson make his statement and let's get the hell out of here. If you're going to start with this poor crazy bastard, you'll be here all day."

Another man who participated in some of the discussions—he would not allow the use of his name—also got the feeling of Death Row Jeff's utter seriousness and sincerity. His impression of Randy was similar to Hallinan's.

"I got the feeling that his head wasn't there," he said, "that maybe he wasn't too smart. I got the feeling that all he wanted was some way of waving a magic wand and making it all go away, returning everything to the way it was before. His daughter back, everything the way it was. And things can never be the same. He was waiting for someone to save his ass. I wanted to tell him, 'That's not going to happen. This is the real world, and that's not going to happen.'"

On March 29 Death Row Jeff, Scott, Taylor and Randy had their last formal meeting at Vacaville. Rev. Williams, Procunier and FBI Agent-in-Charge Charles Bates also took part. It was agreed that Death Row Jeff would write a statement addressed directly to the SLA, and Scott and Taylor would join in signing it.

Death Row Jeff worked all night composing the statement in longhand. The next morning he turned it over to Randy Hearst. The editor, a hunt-and-peck typist, punched out a transcription of the statement on a prison typewriter. He thanked the convicts, said good-bye, went directly to The Examiner city room and watched over the rewriteman's shoulder as he pounded out a story for the next day's Sunday editions. The statement itself was run separately and in its entirety:

Greetings to the poor and oppressed people of the world.

Greetings to Comrade Field Marshal Cinque and to the combat units of S.L.A.

Greetings to comrade Russell J. Little and Joseph M. Remiro now prisoners in the tiger cages of the Alameda county jail.

Your comrade Death Row Jeff wishes to express solidarity with the comminqué issued by my comrade Russell J. Little and Joseph M. Remiro on March 28, 1974. You brothers and sisters are truly soldiers of the people and are more beautiful than life itself to me.

In furtherance to my comrades communiqué of March 28, 1974, I hereby suggest to General Field Marshal Cinque that it would be for the best interest of the poor and oppressed people to start negotiations as soon as possible with Randolph Hearst to release prisoner of war Patricia Hearst.

I have been assured that upon the release of the prisoner of war four million dollars will be placed in the appropriate organization for the purpose of feeding the poor as per the instructions of the S.L.A.

Negotiations should deal with any combat unit that may be pinned down in the field.

Dare to struggle ... Dare to win but do not forget the cry of the people.

Love in the struggle.

Death Row Jeff's statement was acknowledged in passing in a subsequent SLA tape but never acted upon. On May 2 the convict made another try. He telephoned Randy from prison. At his request, his words were tape recorded and released to the media. Again he urged the SLA to release the editor's daughter and explained why:

"It's my belief that Comrade Tania would better serve the SLA above ground, go around the country and around the world teaching the people, talking with peoples, let the peoples know what the SLA's goal is and what the SLA stands for. . . ."

Again the SLA ignored his advice.

Whether Death Row Jeff's influence on the SLA was exaggerated, whether his pleas would have been more effective if they had been televised as Hiler suggested, can only be the subject of conjecture.

For Randy Hearst the only positive result of the Byzantine episode with Death Row Jeff was his assurance that Patty/Tania had not been a member of the SLA before her kidnaping.

VII

Examiner city editor Larry Dum and rewriteman Sam Blumenfeld were drawn into a caper which sounded more promising than most of the other ventures, if considerably more bizarre.

On May 10, Tommy Mann*, a 28-year-old black man, a parolee and a prison associate of both De-Freeze/Cinque and George Jackson, walked into the sumptuous office of well-known San Francisco attorney Hall Pettison*. The two men knew, and within limits, trusted each other. Mann was working at a menial job now, but he still had contacts in the underworld.

He laid a strange story on the attorney. Mann said he had been shacking up with a woman who was in direct contact with Cinque and his band.

"The Man [Cinque] want to get rid of this Hearst girl," Mann told the attorney. "She's too hot. He don't want to kill her."

Mann mentioned the $50,000 reward Randy Hearst was offering for information leading to the return of his daughter. Mann was very interested in fifty Big Ones. He did not mention a split with Cinque.

Mann wanted to know if Pettison was interested, whether he could get in touch with the Hearsts.

*The names Pettison and Mann, for obvious reasons, are fictitious.

Pettison was—and could. All right, then, Mann would get together with the SLA and see if they were still interested in dealing.

Pettison called his old friend Blumenfeld at home; the rewriteman was on vacation. Blumenfeld thought the deal sounded unlikely. But then the whole Hearst case was unlikely. He broke off his vacation, went back to the *Examiner* city room and briefed Dum. He stressed to Dum that nothing should get to the police or the FBI. Because Dum knew the phone lines into the Hearst home were tapped and monitored, he drove to Hillsborough and filled Randy in. Randy gave him the go-ahead.

Three days later, Mann was back in the lawyer's office. "The Man is interested," he told Pettison. The lawyer called Blumenfeld and Dum in to meet Mann. Mann repeated the story to the *Examiner* men. He mentioned an address on the Great Highway along San Francisco's Ocean Beach.

On May 16 Mann told Pettison, "The Man wants to meet you."

Pettison agreed. "Tell him I'll meet him anywhere."

Later that day, three black men walked boldly into the lawyer's office, located in San Francisco's bustling financial district. Pettison had seen DeFreeze/Cinque's image in the newspapers and on television. He was convinced the leader of the trio was Cinque. He thought he saw suspicious bulges under the jackets of each of the three.

Their story was basically the same as Mann's. They were under too much pressure in San Francisco. The girl was a burden; they wanted to dump her. They wanted $250 upfront to get out of town. They told Pettison they would contact him later and set up a rendezvous in Flagstaff, Arizona. There final arrangements would be made to turn over the hostage. The three men left as boldly as they had come, leaving Pettison puzzled and suspicious over the petty cash demand. Still, the leader *really* looked like Cinque.

Pettison's secretary watched the three blacks leave, then went to the attorney. "I may be crazy," she said, "but that one guy looked just like the pictures of Cinque."

Meanwhile, Blumenfeld and Dum had been doing some checking on Mann. Blumenfeld determined that Mann "had all the credentials—a long record, time in Soledad, everything." Dum, who had never been on a major investigative story before his elevation to city editor, tried his hand at journalistic sleuthing. In the early morning hours, he checked out the Great Highway address, scribbling down the license numbers of cars parked in the area. One of the numbers, he thought, might be linked to someone in the SLA. He had the numbers checked through the State Department of Motor Vehicles. If there was a link, Dum didn't find it.

On the afternoon of May 16, Blumenfeld and Dum met Pettison in a downtown coffee shop. Pettison explained that Mann was to make the $250 payment for travel expenses that night in North Beach, San Francisco's nightclub district. Blumenfeld, like Pettison, was bothered by the pettiness of the initial payoff. It wasn't logical. But *nothing* was logical about the SLA. He and Dum agreed it was worth a try. Dum arranged for the cash to be delivered to Pettison's office. The attorney gave it to Mann. Later Mann reported he had made the payoff, and Pettison informed Blumenfeld by phone.

Shortly before three o'clock on the morning of May 17, Tommy Mann was shot in the left hand at the corner of Columbus and Grant Avenue in North Beach. Mann refused to talk to San Francisco policemen who questioned him at Mission Emergency Hospital. He also refused to talk to FBI agents who questioned him later the same day after he had been transferred to Mt. Zion Hospital.

On the same day, 400 miles to the south in Los Angeles, there occurred a greater violence—witnessed by millions—that cancelled the proposed sale of Patty

Hearst. Pettison, Blumenfeld, Dum and Randolph Hearst would never know whether the transaction was real or merely another round in the game of Ripping Off Randy.

CHAPTER TWENTY

A BLAZE OF GLORY

I

Götterdämmerung in the ghetto.

Death—viewed live and in flaming color by millions of Americans from the comfort of their homes.

The date was May 17, 1974. It was late afternoon in California. Hundreds of thousands heard the news bulletins on their car radios as they fought their way homeward on jammed freeways. Police had moved into a black ghetto in South Central Los Angeles. No official confirmation, but police believe they have the Symbionese Liberation Army surrounded. No word whether Patty Hearst is among them.

By the time the commuters got home and snapped on their TV sets, portable minicameras were in action, feeding the scene directly to the tubes at home. Then the national networks tied in and the whole nation focussed on a little yellow stucco house, fascinated as the instant documentary flickered across its consciousness.

As always, what the nation saw was individually perceived in countless different ways. To some it was a rerun of the same confused violence they had been seeing on the tube for years—Vietnam again, except this was *here,* this was *now.* For others, the latest, climactic episode in a continuing serialization, the Good Guys versus the Bad Guys. For some, Law and Order in Action, for others another Fascist Pig Massacre. For a few, the End of the Beginning of the New American Revolution.

And for a handful scattered across the country—a millionaire in Hillsborough, a black woman in an Ohio ghetto, a physician in Pennsylvania, a philosophy student in San Diego, the families, lovers and friends of the young men and women who made up the SLA—a horror of suspense. None knew as they watched whether son, daughter, loved one, comrade, was inside that riddled flaming little yellow house.

II

The first and last stand of DeFreeze/Cinque's band came about through strategic miscalculation—and possibly sentimental impulse—on the part of the SLA's chief, and an incredible blunder on the part of his second-in-command.

After the April 15 robbery of the Hibernia Bank, San Francisco got too hot for the SLA. According to the later taped testimony of Bill Harris/Teko, the SLA war council dispatched an intelligence team to Los Angeles sometime in April. Then on May 1, the remaining SLA soldiers made their strategic withdrawal from the "massive pig encirclement" in San Francisco and moved south.

However, evidence discovered three days after the shoot-out, indicated that at least several of the band had remained in San Francisco until May 10. Acting on information from Los Angeles investigators, FBI agents and San Francisco police discovered an abandoned SLA safe-house in the city's black Bayview District. San Francisco Police Lieutenant Bill Koenig said an eyewitness later identified Patty/Tania as one of the occupants. A copy of the *San Francisco Chronicle,* dated May 10, also was found in the apartment.

Further doubt was cast on Harris/Teko's claim of a May Day moving date when it was learned that the 1970 red and white Volkswagen van used by three SLA members in an ill-fated shopping expedition in Los Angeles had been purchased in San Francisco on May 6. A black man, about 35, nearly six feet tall and 175 pounds, and using the name "Ricky Delgado," bought the van for $1800 in cash from the Golden Gate Garage. The garage was on Golden Gate Avenue, four blocks from the FBI's regional headquarters.

And on May 13, in San Francisco's financial district, a black man who looked startlingly like DeFreeze/Cinque was arranging a deal to "sell" Patty/Tania.

Whatever the exact date of the SLA's withdrawal to Los Angeles, it was a strategic error. On its face, the move seemed sound. Theoretically the enormous urban sprawl of Los Angeles was a better place to hide than San Francisco because the guerrillas would be less susceptible to "pig encirclement." There were black ghettos in Los Angeles—and they had successfully blended into San Francisco's black community for weeks.

But the SLA misjudged the black community of Los Angeles. A black reporter in Los Angeles analyzed it this way: "We—the black community here—we are a lot more conservative than in San Francisco. Politically and socially. The support wasn't here. Whites running with blacks—they stand out more here than in San Francisco."

III

Harris/Teko blew it. At 4:10 P.M. May 16, he and his wife, Emily/Yolanda went shopping in Mel's Sporting Goods Store at 11425 South Crenshaw Boulevard in Inglewood, one of 74 cities in the urban complex of Los Angeles County. They bought $31.50 worth of heavy-duty outdoor clothing. The woman paid cash.

But before the young woman went to the cash register, a 20-year-old clerk named Tony Shepherd noticed something suspicious. He thought he saw the young man stuff a pair of socks into his heavy jacket. Shepherd went to the back of the store, armed himself with a snub-nosed pistol and a pair of handcuffs.

He alerted other employees: a shoplifter. He followed the pair out as they left the store, tried to stop Harris/Teko, who grabbed for the .38 pistol tucked in his waistband.

Shepherd lunged at the gunman—Emily/Yolanda leaped on the clerk's back. Other employees rushed to Shepherd's aid. The gun was wrestled from Harris/Teko, Shepherd snapped one ring of the handcuffs on his left wrist. He was struggling to snap the other bracelet on the right. . . .

Then from the red and white Volkswagen van in the parking lot across the street, Patty/Tania opened up with a long, ripping burst of automatic gunfire—33 shots. Shepherd dived for the scant cover of a concrete light pole, other employees scrambled to safety.

Harris/Teko and Emily/Yolanda broke for the van, dived in and it roared off north on Crenshaw. Shepherd fired twice at the van, missed, then ran for his car and took off after them.

On Ruthelen Street, the van screeched to a halt. Shepherd pulled up several car lengths down the street.

Harris/Teko and one of the women came out carrying automatic rifles and went to a black and yellow Pontiac car parked at the curb "We're from the SLA," he told the couple inside. "We need your car." The couple fled to a nearby home. A second woman emerged from the van.

As the two women got into the Pontiac, Harris/Teko walked toward Shepherd, his M-2 carbine leveled. Shepherd threw his car into reverse and backed out of range. He gave up the chase. The Pontiac sped away.

At 115th Street and Cimarron Avenue in Hawthorne, the Pontiac stalled. Harris/Teko tried unsuccessfully to restart it. The three took Thomas Patin's light blue 1963 Chevrolet Nova station wagon from

273

him at gunpoint. "We're from the SLA and we need your car," Harris/Teko told him. "We need it right now." Patin surrendered his keys, the three piled into the station wagon and drove east on 115th Street.

One-third of the little revolutionary band was on the run. And in their panicky escape, they had made another blunder—one that would cost the lives of six of their comrades.

IV

In the abandoned VW van on Ruthelen Street the three fugitives had left behind a parking citation issued by the Los Angeles Police Department at 8:40 A.M. May 13 in front of 835 West 84th Street, near Pepperdine University.

Inglewood police, contacted by young Shepherd, located the VW van late in the day of May 16 and immediately notified the FBI. It was quickly established that the van belonged to the SLA. The flimsy sheet of paper found in the van was the hardest, hottest intelligence lead to fall into the FBI's hands since the case began. Yet the information was not passed on to the Los Angeles Police Department until 2:30 A.M. on May 17, not acted upon until three hours after that.

When a Los Angeles policeman slapped the parking ticket on the VW van, it was parked one door away from the SLA's hideout, a one bedroom white frame cottage at 833 West 84th Street. It had been rented the week before by a young white woman with long, brown hair. She called herself "Ms. Rivera."

"Ms. Rivera" was cool and charming. She persuaded the rental agent to reduce the rent from $75 to $70 a month. She paid in cash and declined to sign a receipt.

No one was quite sure when the new tenants moved in. Neighbors saw at least three, possibly as many as seven people going in and out of the cottage. Maybe it was one of those black-and-white communes. Three vans were seen parked near the place at one time or another, a 1966 Chevrolet, a 1964 VW and the red and white VW. One of the other two vans was parked on the street as late as 8:40 Thursday night, four and a half hours after the shooting spree at Mel's Sporting Goods Store.

At 5:30 A.M. Friday May 17, a combined task force of FBI agents and black-uniformed members of the Los Angeles Police Department Special Weapons and Tactics team (SWAT) sealed off the 800 block of West 84th Street. From a man moving through the police lines to go to work, the SLA hideout was pinpointed as the cottage at 833.

A 8:50 A.M., a LAPD sergeant with an electronic bullhorn announced:

"To those inside the house at 833 West 84th Street, this is the Los Angeles Police Department. We want you to come out the front door with your hands up. We want you to come out immediately. You will not be harmed."

There was no response. The SWAT team fired a barrage of tear gas into the front of the house, the FBI charged in through the rear door. No one was in the place. But they did find evidence of the SLA's recent presence. There was a notepad listing survival rations—beef jerky, chocolate bars, dried fruits, kippers. Beside each item was an estimated weight figure. The weights were totaled and divided by nine, as if the rations were to be equally divided and distributed for backpacking.

All of this strongly suggested that the SLA had been planning a back-country expedition to the mountains of Southern California. Or perhaps into the desert country of Arizona or Baja California.

Another page in the notepad contained a numerical guard-duty roster—each of the SLA band with a designated number. Another listed addresses of possible safe-houses, and yet another outlined a complicated system of making contacts at pay telephone booths.

Clothing, wigs, food, boxes of shotgun shells also were left behind. The short-time tenants had left 84th Street in a hurry.

One other item was picked up in the flat—a poem by
Camilla/Gabi or Angela/Gelina. It closed with these
lines:

> Now's the time
> We're all alive!
> Eat it, Pig
> In our minds
> the bigger the trigger
> the better the target!
> The cool
> calm palm
> will smear heavy on the hit.
> Sucker Pay—
> Malcolm
> We're here to stay.

V

While the FBI and SWAT were preparing themselves for the rush on the vacant cottage on West 84th
Street, three soldiers of the SLA were in the Hollywood
hills, dumping one kidnap victim and taking another.
The remaining six were trying to relax in the little yellow house at 1466 East 54th Street.

At about 7:00 the night before, Emily/Yolanda was
at the front door of a home at 10871 Elm Street in
Lynwood, due east of the spot where the VW van was
abandoned. Eighteen-year-old Tom Matthews came to
the door—yes, the '69 Ford van outside was his, yes it
was for sale just as the sign said, and yes, he could give
her a test ride.

Matthews got in, the woman beside him in front. He
drove a short distance, stopped at Pine Street and Pen-
dleton Avenue. The woman told him, "There's two of
my friends. Maybe they want to come along." Across
the street Matthews saw a man and a woman standing
by a light blue Chevrolet station wagon.

Harris/Teko moved to the Ford van, showed Matthews a .45 automatic. "We're from the SLA. Get in

the back and do what you're told and you won't get hurt." Matthews obeyed—and for the next eleven and a half hours the SLA's second kidnap victim rode with the terrorist band's first kidnap victim and her two comrades.

Harris/Teko performed the introductions. "You know who this is?" he asked. "This is Tania."

For the first hour, Emily/Yolanda drove around on another shopping tour, stopping several times to go into stores. She finally came back with a hacksaw. Matthews, literally under the gun, helped cut the handcuff off Harris/Teko's wrist.

Patty/Tania and Harris/Teko talked freely with young Matthews. As she spoke, Patty/Tania idly loaded and unloaded her automatic carbine. Yes, she was Patty Hearst. She said she had joined the SLA of her own free will, helped rob the bank of her own free will, and laid down the covering fire which allowed her friends to escape from Mel's Sporting Goods. Harris/Teko scoffed at the radio report that he had shoplifted a 49-cent pair of socks—it was a canvas ammo pouch.

At 10:30 P.M. the van pulled in at a drive-in movie. A cops-and-robbers film, *The New Centurions,* was on the bill. Harris/Teko made several trips to the snack-bar for food and drinks. Matthews also had the idea he was trying to arrange a rendezvous by telephone.

After the movie, the van moved aimlessly through the Hollywood hills, then parked. Matthews, with ultimate coolness or from tension-induced exhaustion, fell asleep.

He woke up to hear his captors discussing a plan to commandeer another car; the women would pose as hitchhikers. A few minutes later, Matthews heard a car approaching, the women got out while Harris/Teko wrapped the weapons in a blanket. As he left, Harris/Teko told Matthews to stay where he was for ten minutes. Matthews obeyed.

Frank Sutter was driving along Outpost Drive near Mullholland Drive at 6:40 A.M. when he spotted the two women hitchhikers and eased his big 1973 Lincoln

Continental up beside them. Both drew automatic pistols. "We need your car for a couple of hours," Emily/Yolanda told him. "You're not going to get hurt if you do exactly what I tell you. We will hurt you if you don't."

Sutter was a prisoner of the SLA for six hours. They stopped several times to make phone calls, and to ask directions. At one stop, Harris/Teko took Sutter's wallet, removed the cash and returned it. "I counted $250," he said. "You can figure this as a loan, but you won't get it back."

At 1:15 P.M. Friday Sutter was released in Griffith Park. He was told he would find his car left for him down the road. He did. His captors were gone.

VI

Minnie Lewis rented the yellow house, a cramped two-bedroom place set back five feet behind a low rock wall fronting on the south side of East 54th Street. She lived there with her five children. Her cousin Christine Johnson lived next door, and spent much of her time at Minnie's.

Accounts vary as to exactly when DeFreeze/Cinque and his heavily armed outfit arrived, exactly how many people were with him, and exactly who he paid to provide them with temporary refuge.

Minnie Lewis, Christine Johnson, their friends Tate Southard and Leola Barnes* were riding the tail end of a long drinking party. Cinque and the SLA may have arrived any time between 9:00 P.M. Thursday and 4:00 A.M. Friday.

By one account he paid Minnie Lewis $100 in cash. By another, the money went to Christine Johnson. But a bargain was struck and the SLA started moving in— bags, baggage, guns, ammo and bombs. The arsenal was stored in the kitchen at the rear of the house.

*Leola Barnes and Tate Southard are fictitious names.

Sometime before dawn, Tate Southard volunteered to show Cinque a good spot to park the two vans in which his group had arrived. They left the vans in front of a boarded-up apartment building at 1451 East 53rd Street and returned to the yellow house about 6:00 A.M.

The yellow house had a reputation in the neighborhood as a free and easy place. Drop in at almost any hour and there was wine, domino games, card games. It was a free and easy place that Friday too—people in and out all morning and afternoon.

Through incredible luck, everyone who was in the house when the SLA arrived—and the half-dozen others who visited while the band occupied the place—lived to tell their stories. But they were garbled, conflicting and sometimes purely fictitious stories.

One story—told later to a local newspaper reporter —was that Patty/Tania had been with the SLA band at the house, that they had arrived some time Thursday evening and that she had been taken away later that night by two black men in a car. The tale-spinner subsequently disavowed the story.

Leola Barnes was more convincing. Her story was verifiable, at least in part. She said she saw seven strangers in the yellow house—but none was Patty/Tania.

"I went down to Minnie's early Thursday evening to play some cards and drink a little," she said. "I fell asleep early and when I woke up around two in the morning, I saw four white women and three dudes—two black and a white one.

"I saw guns spread out all over the floor, so I asked them why they had guns—more than I'd ever seen in my life, everywhere."

The strangers offered no explanation but one black man introduced his companions. She couldn't remember the names or recognize the faces. "All white folks look the same to me," she said. "All the women had their hair cut short."

She was awakened again at 6:00 Friday morning. "The black dude [DeFreeze/Cinque] gave me twenty dollars to go to the store for some beer, food—you know, lunch meat—and two packs of Camels.

"He told me to be cool 'cause he was going to watch me. And he did, too."

Leola bought the stuff at Sam's, a liquor store-delicatessen at East 56th and Compton, and returned to the yellow house. One of the women made sandwiches. The black man told Leola they planned to leave that night—and might take a hostage with them.

Around 11:00 the taller of the two black men left the yellow house. He told Leola, "I'll be back after I get a car." He never came back.

Terri Ring*, who lived across the street, went to the Minnie's house to borrow some money from her friend Leola.

"When I came in I saw all those guns on the floor and a black dude with a beard was trying to get things together," she recalled.

The SLA was preparing for battle.

DeFreeze/Cinque asked if she had any ammunition or weapons at home. She said she didn't and went back home—only to return not long afterward.

At about the same time, DeFreeze/Cinque sent Leola out for more beer and food. She remembered that 8-year-old Tony Lewis, one of Minnie's children, was in the kitchen with two of the white women; that DeFreeze/Cinque was at the kitchen door; and the white man, Willie Wolfe/Cujo was in the bedroom twirling a pistol on his finger.

This time Leola Barnes did not return. Police stopped her and told her not to go back.

By this time police were infiltrated throughout the neighborhood. Beanie of the 'Jects*, street-wise self-proclaimed mayor of Compton, said he had known something heavy was going down as early as 7:30 Friday morning, but he wasn't quite sure what.

By 9:30 he said the word was definitely out that the

*Terri Ring is a fictitious name.
* Beanie of the 'Jects (for the nearby San Pablo Housing Project) is the young black man's street name. He asked that his true name be withheld.

police were looking for some important people. By 11:00 they knew exactly who and where the people were.

Afternoon—DeFreeze was getting nervous. He had given Tate Southard $500 earlier in the day with instructions to buy a station wagon or a van. Southard went to a phone booth in the neighborhood, tried to negotiate a deal with friends, failed, and returned to the yellow house.

A woman visitor overheard DeFreeze/Cinque tell one of the white women, "Trish, we got to get out of here. It's getting too hot." The SLA leader turned to Henry Dandridge*, another visitor who had been drinking with Southard, and told him, "The station wagon should be here by now."

Incredibly, the ebb and flow of visitors continued. Minnie Lewis's children came home from school. Her 11-year-old son met and recognized DeFreeze/Cinque and asked him his name. The SLA leader denied his identity and told the boy to get into the bathroom and lie in the bathtub if he didn't want to die. Instead the boy slipped out the back of the house and ran down the alley.

Donnalee Forbes* arrived shortly after Mary Carr, Minnie Lewis's mother, came in to take two of her young grandchildren out of the place. She was unaware that her 8-year-old grandson, Tony, was still in the house, and she could not rouse her sleeping daughter.

Donnalee had come to the house because she had heard the SLA was there. She was curious and had a certain sympathy for the terrorists' goals.

She talked to DeFreeze/Cinque—and he outlined the SLA's aims and tactics. Kidnaping rich white girls, getting money from their parents, helping the poor. He had done this, he said, with Patty Hearst—and she had joined his army. She was one of his "children," as were the other white women here. And he knew his fate.

"I know I am going to die, and all my people know

*Henry Dandridge and Donnalee Forbes are fictitious names.

they will also, but we are going to take a lot of mother-fucking pigs with us," DeFreeze/Cinque told her.

Donnalee said he was drinking—not imported plum wine—but domestic Boone's Farm.

Just before Donnalee departed for the last time, De-Freeze/Cinque showed her the SLA's array of weaponry. Then he confided a secret. One reason he had led the SLA to Los Angeles, he told her, was to find his wife and six kids. If he meant what he said, De-Freeze/Cinque's fatal decision to withdraw the SLA to Los Angeles was not uninfluenced by his own personal sentimental motives. If he knew that Gloria DeFreeze and their children were halfway across the country in Cleveland, he gave no hint of the knowledge to Don-nalee Forbes. She left the house and did not come back.

Terri Ring returned, stayed briefly, and went home again. This time she telephoned the FBI.

As the afternoon wore on and tensions built, the yellow house became less and less free and easy, and people edged out. By 5:45 P.M. only Southard, Dandridge, 8-year-old Tony Lewis, the sleeping Christine Johnson and the six members of the SLA remained in the house.

VII

Two members of the SWAT team that had raided the vacant cottage on West 84th Street—now back on regular duty as plainclothesmen—spotted the '64 VW and the '66 Chevrolet vans on East 53rd Street at 12:20 P.M. The location was one of their routine checkpoints, a well-known drop for stolen cars.

Two undercover agents inspected the vans. From information developed earlier by the FBI, they knew these were the SLA vans. Both were registered under phony names and addresses. The Chevrolet had been purchased May 1, the VW six days later, both in San Francisco. The undercover men also found ignition keys hidden in both vans. A stakeout was put on the vehicles.

Anonymous phone calls were coming in on the switchboards of the FBI and the LAPD's Newton Division. There were white people in a house at 1462 East 54th Street. They had guns.

By 4:00 P.M., a police command post had been set up four blocks from Compton and East 54th. An hour later Mary Carr, with one of her grandchildren in tow, stopped a traffic patrolman at 55th and Compton. She told him a black man, a white man and several white women were in her daughter's house at 1466 East 54th. They were heavily armed. She correctly identified De-Freeze/Cinque and Camilla Hall/Gabi from photos. She looked at a picture of Patty/Tania and erroneously identified her as one of the white women in the yellow house. The information was passed on to the command post.

Thirty minutes before Mary Carr talked to the traffic cop, the neighborhood had been sealed off by the Los Angeles Police Department, which was in overall charge of operations this afternoon. FBI agents also were on the perimeter. Two of the LAPD's nine-man SWAT teams and a seven-man SWAT team of the FBI were dispatched from the command post to take up positions near the yellow house. The FBI team was held in reserve.

Another SWAT team took up positions around the place on East 53rd, where the vans were still parked. By now newsmen and women were swarming into the area. One blonde television newswoman, Christine Lund, in a moment of bravura stupidity, walked up to the door of the boarded-up apartment building, knocked and waited for an answer. None came. The place was empty. The real action was about to begin a block away.

VIII

The time was 5:44 P.M. A flak-jacketed, black uniformed SWAT squad leader made an announcement over the bullhorn: "Occupants of 1466 East 54th Street, this is the Los Angeles Police Department speaking. Come out with your hands up. Comply and you will not be harmed." He repeated the message. A minute later, another: "People in the yellow frame house with the stone porch, address 1466 East 54th Street, this is the Los Angeles Police Department. Come out with your hands up. Comply immediately and you will not be harmed."

Some of those inside heard the announcements. Tony Lewis emerged from the front door. A SWAT officer, in a crouching run, dashed to the boy's side and took him off toward Compton Avenue. Then Dandridge and Southard came out and were taken away.

A dozen spectators would claim later no surrender announcements were ever made, but the LAPD said at least 18 were broadcast before a SWAT man kneeled and fired two tear-gas projectiles through the front window of the yellow house. The time was 5:53 P.M.

Now, at last, there was a reply from the house—a long staccato burst of automatic weapon fire. Both SWAT teams immediately returned fire—their semiautomatic AR 180's pop-popping, 12-gauge shotguns booming.

Reporters and cameramen hit the deck but continued recording the sights and sounds.

Stuttering rapid fire from the house, punching holes in the face of the apartment house across the street, in the tires of cars at the curb. Black-clad SWAT men firing methodically again and again and again. Helicopters flapping overhead, dogs howling, thousands of spectators surging against the police lines, trying to get closer to the action, then surging back when drifts of tear gas began to choke them.

An FBI man, crouching behind the yellow house, watching in amazement as a barefoot man in shorts went trotting by. "Who is he, a jogger?" the FBI man asked.

The gunfire becoming sporadic now—most of the rounds coming out of the house are going high. The SLA has gone to ground behind the 18-inch high concrete foundation of the little house.

Some SWAT members broke away from the firefight to remove householders from six homes on the edges of the battle. There had been an advance evacuation plan, but the fight erupted before it could be put into effect. Some civilians, like the old black woman cowering in the bedroom at 1447 East 54th, were simply overlooked. She lay there throughout the fight, more than 20 bullets tearing through the flimsy walls of her cottage.

Later there would be bitter criticism. "There was total disregard for black life," an angry black businessman commented. But no bystanders were hit—and no policemen—by any of the more than 6000 rounds fired that afternoon.

By 6:00 P.M. the SWAT teams were running low on ammunition and tear gas. The FBI's seven-man SWAT team moved into action for the first time, firing semiautomatics and tear-gas projectiles. They were on the firing line for thirty minutes, long enough to pump 60 rounds from their rifles, 16 rounds from gas guns.

As the FBI team moved in, the SWAT officer in charge made a radioed request for four fully automatic weapons. Two M-16s and two 9 mm Schmeissers were immediately dispatched from Metropolitan Division downtown, but did not get to the SWAT teams for nearly 45 minutes. A minute after his call for the automatics—worried that the SLA might try to tunnel out of the house or make a wild counterattack break for freedom—he requested fragmentation grenades. The order was denied.

Shortly afterward, radio communications broke down between the two SWAT teams and the command post. Contact was restored 30 minutes later.

Automatic and semiautomatic fire was still coming from the house, breaking off for as long as a minute at a time. At 6:40 P.M. a SWAT man threw two cannisters of powerful riot gas through a broken window on the east side of the yellow house. Sixty seconds later dense black smoke began billowing out of the rear of the house.

The squad leader of SWAT Team One bullhorned: "Come on out. The house is on fire. You will not be harmed."

Orange flames were burning through the roof at the back of the house four minutes later when Christine Johnson appeared at the front door. The cease-fire order was given. She staggered past the wall, into the arms of a SWAT man and, half-dragged, half-stumbling, was roughly hustled to cover. Live television cameras were on her when the SWAT officer in charge put his boot in the middle of her back to keep her down. She was taken to California Hospital for treatment of minor buckshot wounds, cuts, bruises and burns.

At 6:45 P.M. the fully automatic weapons arrived. Team One, in front of the house, took the two .223 M-16s. The Schmeissers went to Team Two at the rear.

Within five minutes the whole house was blazing. A palm tree nearby flared like an enormous pyrotechnic display. In the fire's heart, the temperature burst up to 2000 degrees Fahrenheit. Still the SLA fought on, firing now from crawl-holes in the foundation.

Then Nancy Ling/Fahizah was coming out of one of the crawl holes at the rear of the house, followed by Camilla Hall/Gabi. The poet came out firing an automatic pistol. The Schmeissers opened up on her and she fell. She was dragged back through the hole. Perry fired her revolver, then fell under the deadly fire of the Schmeissers. There was a burst of automatic fire from the crawl-hole, returned by the ripping Schmeissers. The SLA's guns went silent.

At 6:58 P.M. the little yellow house collapsed on itself. Ammunition was heard popping beneath the roaring flames. Firemen, at the scene since 5:30 P.M., went to work on the blaze. The last flames died at 7:30 P.M.

The last of the six guerrillas in the yellow house had died thirty minutes before.

IX

But the horror did not die. The suspense went on and the myth-making began.

Steven Weed flew to Los Angeles while the flames still roared through the yellow house. He arrived at the scene while the smoke and stink were still rising from the ruins. He was there when crews from the coroner's office carried away five body bags—and he did not know whether his fiancé's remains were enclosed in one of those black plastic shrouds.

Saturday morning, while Los Angeles coroner Dr. Thomas Noguchi and 20 forensic experts were working in the morgue to identify the bodies, shoppers at the Co-op supermarket in Oakland, 400 miles to the north, were reading a freshly painted graffito on the wall of the building:

"Viva Cinque—Camilla Hall lives."

On ghetto streets, black kids were telling one another, "It took 500 pigs to get Cinque." (The Los Angeles Police Department, in a report two months later, would say only 410 officers were involved in the operation—and only 29 members of its SWAT teams and seven FBI men were actually directly engaged in the firefight.)

In white working men's bars, drinkers were making cracks about "The Cinque Barbecue."

In the blackened pile that once was the yellow house, technicians were sifting for evidence. Across the street, a Los Angeles policeman assigned to hold back the growing crowd of curious onlookers was asking a reporter a rhetorical question straight out of a "Dragnet" script.

"Do you think," he intoned solemnly, "that justice was done here?" He answered himself. "We saved the 'Frisco cops a lot of trouble. And we saved the taxpayers two and a half million dollars for a trial."

Shortly before two o'clock Saturday afternoon, Dr. Noguchi phoned Randolph Hearst in Hillsborough to inform him privately that his daughter was not among the dead. Then, in a jammed press conference, he identified four of the five bodies—Donald David DeFreeze, William Wolfe, Nancy Ling Perry, Patricia Mizmoon Soltysik. Later in the day the fifth was identified as Angela Atwood.

Sunday—another agonizing surge of suspense—a sixth body found in the ruins. Beside the body lay the skeleton of a cat. Camilla Hall and her beloved pet.

Five days later, in another crowded press conference, the media-conscious little Los Angeles coroner detailed his findings and elaborated his outspoken opinions on why the six SLA soldiers died.

All had worn gas masks throughout the fight, Dr. Noguchi said, and all had fought on even as flames were scorching their flesh and searing their lungs. "In all my years as coroner, I've never seen this kind of behavior in the face of flames . . . a fantasy of guerrilla warfare."

He ran down the casualty list: Angela Atwood, dead of smoke inhalation and burns; Patricia Mizmoon Soltysik, smoke inhalation, burns, multiple gunshot wounds; William Wolfe, smoke inhalation and burns; Nancy Ling Perry, two gunshot wounds, one severing the spinal cord, the other puncturing the right lung; Camilla Hall, a single gunshot wound in the forehead.

And Donald David DeFreeze—Cinque, the last to die. There were two nonfatal gunshot wounds in his midsection. The fatal wound was made by a single .38 caliber slug fired into the right temple. Powder burns were found deep within the wound. He was found face down. Beneath the body was a snub-nosed .38 caliber revolver.

Dr. Noguchi concluded that General Field Marshal Cinque of the Symbionese Liberation Army died a suicide.

CHAPTER TWENTY-ONE

OUT OF THE ASHES—
REBORN OR BURIED?

I

Patty/Tania's fate was as irrevocably sealed as her six dead comrades. Police switchboards throughout the Los Angeles basin flashed thousands of tips, dozens of sightings. Patty/Tania was seen here, there, everywhere. She was always smiling, that engagement picture-turned-wanted poster smile. The Patty legend was becoming the Tania myth.

The first solid lead came from Mrs. Anita Alcala, a Hollywood apartment manager. Two black men and a white woman resembling the smiling Patty/Tania offered her $500 for one night's use of an apartment. When she refused, one of the blacks slashed at her with a knife, cutting only her dress.

Some 24 hours later in Newhall north of Hollywood, two white women and a white man in a red and white Chevrolet like Mrs. Alcala's attackers had been driving stopped to ask directions. Eighty-three-year-old retired army sergeant Richard Wallis told police they had asked about a place to spend the night. Motorists spotted them near Bakersfield, further north on Interstate Five and all over the state. Sightings soon were reported from Idaho, New York and Florida. Police checks of all the reports failed to turn up Patty/Tania.

Randy Hearst's plaintive reminder that "the child is still a victim" could not prevent her slipping away into a half-life underground, a world already peopled by dozens who had disappeared during the past decade of protest.

Pleas were broadcast immediately from Patty's parents, sisters and friends as well as the families and friends of the Harrises, urging them go give themselves up, rather than suffer the same fate as their six comrades. Families of the dead SLA six joined the plea. Only silence answered them for 20 days.

II

Another tape recording from the SLA was delivered on Friday, June 7. A telephone call about 6:30 A.M. to Los Angeles radio station KPFA, sister station to the Berkeley outlet that had received previous communiqués, led to the tape being found beneath a mattress behind the station. Patty was the spokesman who read the eulogy to the dead.

Greetings to the people. This is Tania. I want to talk about the way I knew our six murdered comrades, because the fascist pig media has, of course been painting a typical, distorted picture of these beautiful sisters and brothers.

She opened her eulogy with a declaration of love for Willie Wolfe, who had adopted the name Cujo inside the SLA. Her five-minute, impassioned speech was interwoven with references to the tall, handsome youth from Pennsylvania and the parallels that had been drawn between her own family and Wolfe's parents. Her growing disillusionment with her parents had been reinforced by what she called the Wolfes' refusal to "betray" Willie Wolfe/Cujo. A similar parallel had been drawn between the response of Rev. Hall to Camilla, who had adopted the name Gabi.

> I was ripped off by the pigs when they murdered Cujo, ripped off in the same way that thousands of sisters and brothers in this fascist country have been ripped off of people they love. We mourn together, and the sound of gunfire becomes sweeter.

Her recitation of love for Willie Wolfe/Cujo, Angela Atwood/Gelina, Camilla Hall/Gabi, Mizmoon Soltysik/Zoya, Nancy Ling Perry/Fahizah was filled with romantic phrases.

Fahizah was "wise and bad, and I'll always love her." Zoya had "perfect love and perfect hate reflected in stone-cold eyes." Gabi "loved to touch people with a strong—not delicate—embrace." Gelina "taught me how to fight the enemy within, through her constant struggle with bourgeois conditioning." But Cujo held a special place. "Neither Cujo or I had ever loved an individual the way we loved each other."

DeFreeze/Cinque, who along with Wolfe/Cujo had given her the name Tania, also received a special tribute. She credited him with saving her life on February 4. Patty/Tania continued:

> He taught me virtually everything imaginable, but wasn't liberal with us. He'd kick our asses if we didn't hop over a fence fast enough or keep our asses down while practicing. Most importantly, he taught me how to show my love for the people. He helped me see that it's not how long you live that's important, it's how we live; what we decide to do with our lives.

She explained that the squad, which she now called the Malcolm X Combat Unit of the SLA, had been a leadership training cell to prepare its members to become advisors to other units.

"All of us were prepared to function on our own if necessary, until we connected with other combat units."

William Harris/Teko had been second in command under DeFreeze/Cinque, who was the personal leader of the unite, she asserted. She berated the official contention that DeFreeze/Cinque had committed suicide.

"What horseshit! Cin committed suicide the same way that Malcolm, King, Bobby, Fred, Jonathan and George did."*

She saved her most biting sarcasm for her own parents.

One day just before making the last tape, [sent after the bank robbery] Cujo and I were talking about the way my parents were fucking me over. He said that his parents were still his parents, because they had never betrayed him, but my parents were really Malcolm X and Assata Shakur.** I'll never betray my parents.

"Her response to her natural parents' plea for surrender was brutally blunt:

The pig lies about the advisability of surrender have only made me more determined. While I have no death wish, I have never been afraid of death. For this reason, the brainwash/duress theory of the pig Hearsts has always amused me. I would never choose to live the rest of my life surrounded by pigs like the Hearsts.

William Harris/Teko, who presumably had assumed command of the decimated unit, spent nearly all his

---

* Malcolm refers to Malcolm X, the name taken by the ex-hustler, pimp and narcotics pusher who became the messiah of the black revolution and was assassinated in 1965; King is Rev. Martin Luther King, who was assassinated April 4, 1968 by James Earl Ray; Bobby is Bobby Hutton, 17, one of the original Black Panthers who was shot by Oakland police while standing naked at their command April 6, 1968; Fred is Fred Hampton, a Chicago Black Panther leader slain while asleep during a police raid on December 4, 1966; Jonathan Jackson, 17, was killed during the August 7, 1970 attempt to take over the Marin County courthouse in a try to free his brother, George; George Jackson was slain inside San Quentin walls on August 21, 1973.
** Assata Shakur is the "liberated name" of Joanne Chesimard, a black woman from New York City, who was charged with killing a New Jersey state trooper in 1973 while serving in the Black Liberation Army.

time on the tape explaining, almost as if rationalizing mistakes to some superior officer who might be listening to the broadcast.

"It had become clear from intelligence reports from other SLA elements and from people in the community that the pigs were preparing to trap us in the San Francisco peninsula," he said.

An intelligence and reconnaisance team made a survey of the Los Angeles area and returned with information about more favorable terrain and "vast oppressed communities," he said, so they had "left the San Francisco Bay Area in a successful effort to break a massive pig encirclement."

William Harris/Teko theorized that the six inside the house on 54th Street had split up in a move to break out forcibly, using the fragmentation grenades they had built in the Golden Gate Avenue pad.

He denied having attempted to shoplift anything at Mel's Sporting Goods store, observing that SLA policy was to avoid such escapades "because of the heavy risk involved to the whole unit."

He insisted that the SLA's whereabouts would not have been learned by police "if a collaborator named Mary Carr had not snitched to the enemy," which William Harris/Teko asserted had lead to a "CIA-directed force attacking their stronghold.

Mrs. Carr, mother of the woman in whose house the group had spent the night, had tipped police when her suspicions were aroused by all the guns.

Their tape-recorded words, which attempted to both eulogize and rationalize the fates of their dead comrades, were the last to be heard from the fugitives for a long time.

III

Warrants were issued charging Patty/Tania, William Harris/Teko and Emily Harris/Yolanda with a long list of law violations, making Patty/Tania officially a wanted fugitive for the first time.

Federal officials and a federal grand jury seemed to be placing their official stamp on the Patty/Tania switch. The kidnaped had become officially a kidnaper. The night and morning of May 16-17 had resulted in one count of kidnaping, another of kidnaping with purpose of robbery, three counts of driving without owner's consent, four counts of robbery and five counts each of assault with intent to commit murder and assault with a deadly weapon. Patty/Tania had become an official fugitive. She was charged June 6 by a federal grand jury in San Francisco with armed robbery in the Hibernia Bank holdup.

IV

The chillingly efficient SWAT team and the televised spectacle of the stucco house being allowed to burn to the ground stirred swift and sharp criticism. While Wolfe's father was the most vehement of all the parents, families of all six expressed angry disbelief that the fire power needed to be so deadly. Many residents of the ghetto could not help wondering what tactics would have been used if the SLA had holed up for its last stand in the Hearst mansion in affluent Hillsborough. Most saw it as a horribly graphic object lesson in the double standard of police protection in the rich and poor sections.

Police and political leaders joined in backing the police action as necessary and routine "under the circumstances." FBI Chief Clarence Kelley, California Attorney General Evelle Younger and San Francisco Mayor Joseph Alioto praised the police handling.

Los Angeles Mayor Tom Bradley, a former policeman and a black who had only recently taken office by beating conservative Sam Yorty, promised the city would pay for property damages suffered in the shoot-out. He also ordered a complete probe and report on what happened.

The police department turned out a 138-page report that confirmed most of the early, off-the-cuff versions, but cleaned up the department's act in evacuation of neighboring houses. This was explained away by asserting that many residents refused to be evacuated until after the shooting started. The study was crammed with statistical details about costs, manpower expenditures and property damages.

During the shootout, 5,371 rounds of .38 caliber, .223 caliber, .243 caliber, 9mm, 12-gauge double-O buckshot and rifle slugs were fired by SWAT officers at a cost of $1,010.13.

The 83 rounds of tear gas cost $1,074.60. Total cost of vehicles used by police was $1,435.98. Manpower costs were meticulously broken down rank by rank for the day of the shoot-out as well as the mopping-up investigation; a total of $26,966.27 was spent, mostly for overtime, on May 17 with a grand total of $59,581.81 required for the three full days and nights spent on the SLA case. There were also miscellaneous expenses like $3,386 worth of departmental equipment damaged, flares for traffic control cost $472.50 and 70 box lunches furnished line personnel during the shoot-out cost $175, or $2.50 each.

Three houses in the neighborhood were totally destroyed. The SLA pad and houses on each side were wiped out at an estimated cost of $35,600. Bullet holes caused most of the damage to another 20 houses and 2 automobiles, bringing total real and personal property damages to $48,842.47.

Hidden by the dry statistics were the human dramas suffered by neighborhood families. Mrs. Mattie Morrison sat for hours in the debris of her house, surrounded by the few dishes and kitchen utensils that she could salvage. Tears filled her eyes; her three pet dogs had burned to death in the flames.

Mrs. Morrison told another black woman police had crept into her house about 4:15 P.M. and ordered her to stay inside. When the fire from the SLA pad next door spread to her house, she was finally evacuated. Her pets were left inside. The value of the house may not have been high by comparison with other neighborhoods, but it had been Mrs. Morrison's home for 20 years.

A considerable amount of the report was spent justifying the tactical decisions. News accounts that the shootout had required the largest manpower in the history of Los Angeles were denied.

The Watts riots in 1965 and the service of warrants on Black Panther headquarters in 1969 were cited as two incidents requiring greater manpower. The Black Panther confrontation had taken 584 officers, it was noted.

While the report discussed the close cooperation between the FBI and the Los Angeles Police Department in handling the SLA, there was only passing mention of the presence of Secret Service officers. None of these officers sustained any damage to their equipment, the report noted. Although the SWAT officers often furnished men as security guards when President Nixon visited Los Angeles, the president was across the continent at Key Biscayne at the time of the shoot-out. There was no explanation of their presence on 54th Street.

A careful search of the house debris enabled investigators to locate a small arsenal of weapons used by the SLA. Near the corner were Camilla Hall/Gabi, Angela Atwood/Gelina and Nancy Ling Perry/Fahizah were found, investigators found a fully automatic M-1 .30 caliber carbine, a .244 semiautomatic Remington rifle, 9-mm Mauser automatic pistol and the .38 caliber Rossi revolver that Chris Thompson told the Oakland grand jury he had sold Russell Little.

At the other rear corner of the house, where DeFreeze/Cinque, Willie Wolfe/Cujo and Mizmoon Soltysik/Zoya were found, searchers unearthed a 12-gauge shotgun and a .38 caliber Smith & Wesson revolver. Between the two groups, there lay three shotguns, a .30 caliber automatic M-1 carbine and a 9-mm Mauser automatic pistol. Abandoned nearer the front of the house were two other M-1's, a Browning .30-06, a Colt .45 caliber automatic pistol, a 9-mm Browning automatic pistol and another shotgun.

In their grimly meticulous scorekeeping, investigators noted that they found 4,247 cartridges inside the house, but only 668 had marks showing they had been fired. Primers from 3,772 had melted in the blaze, making it impossible to tell how many others had been fired by the SLA.

V

SWAT's summary disposal of the six rebels short-circuited answering the big question of who really led the SLA—Cinque or some hidden, mad revolutionary. Rumors still reverberated that DeFreeze/Cinque had been an agent of the Los Angeles Police Department that had killed him, a charge they denied emphatically.

One radical writer-researcher, Mae Brussell, had predicted a month before the shootout that DeFreeze/Cinque would be killed in just such a manner. In a long, twisting essay in the *Berkeley Barb,* she had theorized that he would become the first black Lee Harvey Oswald. Her thesis was that he was one in a long chain of police agents whose masters had assassinated them after they finished their dirty work. She considered him part of a military-intelligence takeover of the nation.

She had been one of the team that had worked with former police spy, Louis Tackwood, when he left the LAPD Criminal Conspiracy Section.

Donald Freed, a former teacher who now writes screenplays and books, was another Tackwood collaborator. He called several press conferences to announce that he had proof that DeFreeze/Cinque was a police agent and had been working for the Los Angeles Police Department from the days when Tackwood had served. Freed declined to outline his proof, sidestepping such questions with a promise that one of his forthcoming books would contain the necessary documentation.

Police denied Freed's charge, asserting they had never had anything to do with helping DeFreeze get light sentences or tender handling in his numerous brushes with courts in their jurisdiction.

The Black Panther newspaper did not take the LAPD's denial as gospel, pointing out that DeFreeze's arrests on gun charges had come during a period when police agencies were in "a state of hysteria" about blacks with guns.

His record of activity "strongly suggests that for at least from 1967 through 1969, he operated under the protection and with the guidance of California police authorities," the newspaper reported.

DeFreeze's activities with the Black Cultural Association at Vacaville were also seen as suspicious. He had formed his own unit, Unisight, after failing a bid to win leadership of the BCA. His "escape" from Soledad Prison less than three months after his transfer there was equally suspect. Most inmates with histories of radical work are seldom made trustys and placed in jobs where they can simply walk away unnoticed.

His presence in an all-white band of revolutionaries also made him a suspect to many black radicals. After Patty's kidnaping, he and women squad members were the only ones to make public appearances. There had been two other unidentified blacks around the house in Los Angeles, but they took part only in diversionary tactics after the holocaust.

Police agent accusations were readily accepted in radical circles, because of the experiences around Oakland and Berkeley among those who had met DeFreeze before the Foster murder and the kidnaping. Most experienced radicals thought his brash talk and ideas must come from a provocateur. Police agents and provocateurs were on everyone's mind because of recent disclosures that the FBI had had counterintelligence forces at work in radical groups since 1967. Most were in the midst of efforts to identify such provocateurs and link them to any destructive actions that might have divided radicals. One memo was found that linked the FBI's Palo Alto office with a counterintelligence operation aimed at fouling up Bruce Franklin's work in Revolutionary Union. Thus everyone on the radical inside had been super cautious in their dealings with De-Freeze.

After the kidnaping, as radical leaders cast about for ideas on who and what the SLA might be, some theorized that this cool response to DeFreeze might have pushed him into a lunatic fringe that absorbed him. The more naïve and frustrated and inexperienced could have been drawn to ideas of immediate action. There had been so much talk for so long. Organized and disciplined groups like Venceremos and Revolutionary Union were losing their steam, leaving such people no alternative to the romantic vision of instant revolution.

None of the six dead soldiers fit the mold of lunatics. While some had their instabilities and others flitted from one fanciful goal to another, they were little different from many other young people their ages.

Willie Wolfe/Cujo had been a wanderer, whose doting father nourished his restlessness with accessible funds and permissive acceptance of most any new project.

Emily Harris/Yolanda, Angela Atwood/Gelina, Nancy Ling Perry/Fahizah and Mizmoon Soltysik/Zoya had been submissive followers for most of their lives, vacillating from one interest to another. One or two of their friends had observed some leadership qualities, but most had detected impressionability as being their chief characteristic. Joining a revolutionary squad so deep into the black movement that they adopted black speech patterns and sounds, though, seemed more than just being impressionable and easily influenced.

Few insights were available into their conversion until a letter was found from Camilla Hall/Gabi to her parents. The letter was never delivered; it was found beneath her body in the charred ruins of the 54th Street house. While many had thought her a late recruit, drawn by emotion and the influence of her former lover, Mizmoon/Zoya, there were signs of a careful, thoughtful consideration of the consequences.

"You know well that I have worked for changes all my conscious life. I went through many stages of development, attacking the enemy on many different fronts, only to see changes coopted into reformism. I exhausted all the possibilities before finally deciding that this was the only way to actually get the revolution going in realistic terms.

"It has become increasingly obvious (or rather I used to be incredibly naïve) that the ruling class, the corporate state, have no intention of giving up any power voluntarily, (the contortions Nixon has gone through to stay in power); that the capitalistic system is an evil that must be destroyed," she wrote.

She told of the squad trying to purge themselves of "this putrid disease of bourgeoisie mentality" by constant self-criticism.

As for the radical leaders that "stumbled all over each other trying to get on the other side of the fence to denounce" the SLA, Camilla/Gabi told her parents such people were only protecting their own self-interests.

The truth is that they are scared witless because we have put them in a situation that calls for action to fulfill the courage of their convictions. Our support is from the people and will continue to grow with each victory as we prove to the people that the revolution can indeed happen, and will indeed be successful. We intend to be around for quite a while to live to see the victories.

I know you trust my sincerity even if you haven't come to agree with the course of action I have committed myself to. I am young and strong and willing to dedicate my courage, intelligence and love to the work. I feel really good about what I am doing— want you to also.

She outlined writings, an alternative newspaper and other ways for her parents to prepare themselves to better understand what she was doing. She also cautioned

301

them to avoid using the telephone or talking about her near the phone, fearing it might be bugged.

I want you to remember that I'm with really good people, that we've trained ourselves in a great many ways because we realize the importance of the People's Forces surviving, gaining victory after victory (you know I never do anything half-assed).

While Patty/Tania's last words had perpetuated the image of DeFreeze/Cinque as their leader, there were still considerable doubts. The unanswered questions about the unidentified black who had fled the house before the shoot-out. The unexplained dropping of Thero Wheeler from official statements about the SLA. All this complicated analysis.

Many analysts inside and outside of police agencies contended that the real leader of the SLA squad was William Harris/Teko. His military background and experience came through in so many details. The knowledge necessary to convert easily available hunting rifles and surplus weapons into automatic rifles and submachine guns did not come out of books. Construction of grenades and bombs had not been in any of the courses the college kids in the squad had taken. While DeFreeze's past had been involved with gunrunning, he had never demonstrated a talent for ordinance that was displayed by the Malcolm X combat unit of the SLA.

The other techniques of the squad, the references to medical units and intelligence units and communications units sounded military enough, but were really an extension of radical practices during the previous decade. Large demonstrations and confrontations had grown so complicated that they had adopted establishment tactics. There were separate brigades, each with separate responsibility for the tasks of intelligence, first aid, keeping tabs on those arrested and in need of bail, gathering funds for bail and circulating communications between units and to the media.

But the real leader of the SLA could have been someone away from the center of action, someone Harris/Teko felt compelled to advise through his tape recorded communiqués. Among all of the past attempts at prison revolt and social revolution, there were sufficient candidates. But investigators were slow to find the link.

VI

Canonization of the dead six SLA soldiers took many forms. The Weather Underground used an explosive method, bombing Evelle Younger's Los Angeles headquarters and then notifying alternative newspapers it had been in honor of the SLA "freedom fighters."

Younger, who was trying to forestall an end to his political career in a potential Democratic landslide in November, attempted to use the bombing and SLA affair in political speeches. But he found a lukewarm response and interest even among conservative audiences.

The guerrilla theater the SLA had spawned was too powerful, too emotional to be bothered with politicians. The spectacle of thousands of blacks trooping past De-Freeze/Cinque's coffin in Cleveland, Ohio, was too disturbing.

His brother Delano had failed to attract any radical or revolutionary leaders to the funeral. He vowed he would carry his brother's banner without them. He had placed an old photo of his brother atop the coffin, not because the body had been so badly burned, but because the head and hands were missing. The Los Angeles coroner's office had retained those parts for some reason that was never explained.

Lifting DeFreeze/Cinque to the revolutionary hero status of George and Jonathan Jackson took a nationwide organizational effort. Some of the same faces and names appeared at all the memorial services.

Popeye Jackson, leader of the United Prisoners Union, was a regular as was Halvorsen. Arnold Townsend, chairman of the Western Addition Project Committee, turned up at the San Francisco rally with the two and pronounced the SLA efforts "a beginning."

In Berkeley, the memorial for Angela Atwood was held in Willard Park, just three blocks from where Patty was kidnaped four months earlier. The dead woman's friends urged the fugitive trio to "keep fighting" because "we're with you."

In Santa Rosa, the family of Nancy Ling Perry held a 15-minute ceremony at the Presbyterian Church of the Roses. Her radical friends and ex-husband spoke their words in Fremont, south of Berkeley.

A young man carrying a single red rose tied by a ribbon inscribed "Venceremos" was turned away in Santa Rosa. Her family had asked that instead of flowers, donations be sent to Friends of the Children of Vietnam. A family friend, who had never met Nancy, read an elegy to the dead woman he had written at the Lings' request. Her body was cremated and the ashes scattered over the Pacific Ocean off Gualala, where the family had vacationed in happier times.

Both the Lings in Santa Rosa and Perry in Fremont suggested that perhaps the rest of society should investigate some of the social problems Nancy had attacked so violently.

A rising spirit of radical anger was expressed at services for Willie Wolfe and Patricia Mizmoon Soltysik. Only at the services for Camilla Hall, which were held in the Lincolnwood, Illinois Lutheran Church where her father is pastor, had love as the keynote.

VII

The Weather Underground took the lead among revolutionary groups backing the SLA actions. Where others had criticized the SLA as being without proper credentials or doctrine, the Weather Underground urged immediate support:

304

Many members of the SLA are still free. They must be defended, publicly and privately. Anyone who is in a position to help them directly should give them encouragement, support, shelter and love. Empty your pockets. Struggle with them. Learn from them. We must protect our fighters.

The Weather Underground exhortation was unnecessary because SLA imitators had sprung up all over the country. Some maintained a revolutionary guise, others were unabashedly self-seeking. The very day of the shootout in Los Angeles, a quintet was arrested in Nashville, Tennesee, and accused of plotting a bank robbery they hoped to blame on the SLA by dressing one of their number as Patty/Tania and arming her with a submachine gun.

Five days after the shoot-out, a new group announced itself, claiming to be the United Peoples Liberation Amry under the command of someone calling herself General Field Marshal Cabrilla. A tape recording was sent to Radio Station KPFA announcing plans to continue the SLA cause.

Several minor robberies and fire bombings were followed by letters to editors or tape recordings to radio stations claiming to be some form of "liberation" organization.

As suddenly as this imitative phenomenon arose, it subsided, leaving many of the old questions still unanswered.

VIII

At the same time authorities were congratulating each other for wiping out the SLA, pressures from the long siege were starting to spring some troublesome leaks between police agencies involved as well as from the prisons from which this had emerged. Old enmities were trotted out. Old friends became contenders for the spotlight. Hardest hit was the FBI, whose carefully cultivated image of infallibility in kidnap solutions had been badly blemished.

California Attorney General Evelle Younger, who had been an FBI man before he was Los Angeles district attorney and attorney general, led the pack in potshots. Younger, who had been noticeably silent during the SLA chase, came out swinging after the Los Angeles shoot-out. He lauded the officers at the scene, chided the FBI as having defaulted on its "invincible image," and dropped a group of legislative proposals into the hopper at Sacramento. After having been overly solicitous of the Hearsts when the food ransom demands were made, Younger now sought legislation that would make it unlawful for corporations and trusts to pay ransoms, void any pardon granted by a public official to meet kidnapers' demands and outlaw possession of money or property that had been extorted. If these laws had been enacted before the People in Need program, those receiving such food would have become felons.

Younger also contributed a 12-page "study" of the SLA that blamed the entire affair on radicals who had turned from college turmoil to prisons. Echoing work done previously by the California Department of Corrections, Younger listed several secret inmate organizations he considered dangerous. His study also took a leaf from inmate Ron Beaty's testimony and blamed Venceremos activities inside prisons as laying the foundation for the Symbionese Liberation Army. Nowhere did his material—which some attributed to electioneering—assess any blame or responsibility upon state officials who had been keeping track of the prison revolt for more than four years.

Raymond Procunier, department of Corrections director, had identified the inmate organizations as creators of dissension and more serious crimes several years earlier. He had also suggested it was all the fault of outside agitators like Venceremos and the National Lawyers Guild.

Both Younger the politician and Procunier the bureaucrat and political appointee carefully avoided any mention of the long, sad history of prison mismanagement and the investigative ineptitudes in handling the internecine plotting that raged constantly between black, brown and white inmates. Their own personal involvement in counterplots remained hidden in secret files.

Neither talked about their responses to the triple killing of inmates at Soledad Prison in January 1970, or the unusual leniency for ex-con James Carr's transgressions, or involvement of their staffs in the Marin County courthouse shooting in August 1970 and the 1972 Chino escape of convict Ron Beaty from Chino prison.

Procunier did complain to the state senate subcommittee of State Senator Dennis Carpenter that he lacked proper "intelligence forces" to keep track of new radical disruptions. Testimony was also furnished to the sub-committee from some of Procunier's pet inmate informers about workings of the radical groups. But this testimony only demonstrated the lack of any alternatives or suggestions from within his staff. Inmate informers testimony clearly demonstrated the convicts' readiness to say anything the senators or prison staffers wanted to hear, especially if such cooperation might mean a soft job inside the walls or earlier consideration for parole.

Neither did Younger or Procunier admit their prior knowledge of organizing that led to the SLA. Tips from Beaty the escapee and Westbrook, the Black Cultural Association adviser, were conveniently forgotten. Their failure to answer early warnings was glossed over. Such admissions in an election year could be fatal at the polls.

Younger and Procunier had ignored advice within their own departments and backed renewal of the death penalty in select cases, especially those involving prison guards and attacks. This had failed to act as a deterrent. Murderous assaults inside prisons continued to increase.

They had been unable to find any way to control the politicization of prison inmates. Radicals had easily influenced prisoners into considering themselves victims of society. The standard radical description of inmates as "political prisoners," rather than common crooks, inflated egos. A new status system soon grew inside the walls, one that gave even lifers new hope. Those who had been doomed to life without hope of parole could gain new respect and pride as revolutionaries.

Where once men like Eldridge Cleaver, whose talents and skill with words enabled them to express visions, once dreamed of being another Malcom X, lifers could construct daydreams with material fed from urban guerrilla proselytizers like Willie Wolfe/Cujo and William Harris/Teko.

Younger, Procunier and the judicial system they both served fed the revolution with their own fears. Courts after the Marin County attack became armed camps. No private citizen could enter many courtrooms without going through a search of his person as intimate as that suffered by prison inmates. With each succeeding confrontation, the armed camp attitude grew. Judges began carrying weapons beneath their robes. Special alarms and closed circuit television cameras were installed for their protection. All made a deep impression upon lay jurors serving one of the courts for the first time, leaving in doubt the principle of fair trial, creating more recruits for the revolutionaries.

IX

Patty/Tania had slipped underground to join all the other young people who kicked over the family traditions and easy affluence for some romantic vision. No longer could the media princess, art student and collector of fine prints and exquisite designs go for a carefree walk in the Wyntoon woods or along the shore beneath San Simeon. Like so many others, she had been caught up in a visceral excitement, a missionary zeal to save the world from itself.

There had been black men like Jimmie Johnson, son

of a New York nurse, who had forsaken a matchless opportunity at Stanford University to go underground. He had wound up on a Caribbean island, living in a cave and disillusioned for his troubles.

There had been white men like Stephen Bingham, scion of a New York fortune, who became so enmeshed his disappearance left behind on rumors of death, kidnaping and escape.

But there seemed to be more women than men fed into the anonymous reaches of the underground. Bernardine Dorhn. Kristin Hind. Nan Goldie. And dozens more seemed to testify to the revolution in feminine thinking or reinforce old prejudices that some women would go to any length to escape the boredom of a future as predictably safe and secure as their parents had provided. Generations ago the only escape was marriage or running away to a career on the stage. The protest generation had opened new vistas.

Nan Goldie and Kristin Hind were two who were caught up by the excitement of the new ideas. Nan was from the old Rainier brewery family lineage. Kristin was daughter of an associate dean of students at Stanford, where both were students.

Their tearing away from family traditions and life styles was not recorded in glaring headlines, because neither was a media princess. No one noted the arguments with fathers, the disagreeable names used at emotional moments. But there had been a radical cause mixed with emotional attachment to men who displaced their fathers and led them into new adventures.

The two girls wound up living in a commune in British Columbia, one of several thought to have been connected to the Weather Underground's bomb manufacturing training camps. The commune finally broke up in the fall of 1971 and the girls notified their parents they were coming home. Neither arrived home.

Nan's bones were found in August 1973 in the mountains near Spokane, Washington. Kristin has never been found.

Bernardine Dorhn's move underground has been well documented elsewhere. Her Illinois family has not seen her since she disappeared over five years ago. The Weather Underground communiqués sometimes appear, using her signature. Sometimes the communiqués are disavowed by later communiqués. And no one has seen her or admitted seeing her.

Investigators have been unable to penetrate too deeply into this level of secrecy. The network of communes and safe-houses that radicals use to shift people out of the country are only partially known. A few fugitives have been traced part way, because police agents sometimes feed people into the underground in an effort to uncover this network.

The effort to prevent Patty/Tania and the Harrises from disappearing into this bottomless mystery world began for investigators with the funny paper specialists, the experts who turn out false identification papers. In Anaheim, just down the street from where Emily Harris had worked when she was about Patty's age, police raided a large cache of phony papers. There were false Social Security cards, drivers' licenses, credit cards and check cashing cards by the score. Investigators declined to say whether the suspect caught on the premises, Garrett Zwart, 32, had anything to say about recent customers, or whether any telltale negatives had been found. They had found Zwart's shop a full week after the shoot-out.

Neither a saturation of investigative manpower or keeping constant pressure on suspected SLA supporters turned up any definitive leads.

Subpoenas had been issued for three people to testify before federal grand juries about their SLA acquaintances. None had produced any information, because all balked at cooperating.

Paul Halvorsen, a San Francisco State graduate student in philosophy, had been called ostensibly because he and his wife knew Camilla/Gabi. Some purchases of ammunition about the time of the bank robbery had been investigated in connection with the Halvorsens.

Cindy Garvey, girlfriend of Joe Remiro and Russ Little as well as visitor of prison inmates, had been called. Her mother's cabin in the Santa Cruz mountains had been subject of close scrutiny early in the case, because a station wagon matching the description of one used in the kidnaping had been seen parked there.

Both Halvorsen and Garvey were sent to jail for contempt of court for refusing to testify.

Janet Cooper, the former Venceremos central committee member, had been called to furnish firsthand information about the theft of her purse and identification, which had been used in the SLA forays. Investigators were also interested in one of her close friends, Reese Erlich, for questioning. Erlich's activities in the early stages of SLA had never been explained. When Ms. Cooper declined to testify without first asking her attorney a question, the grand jury dismissed her suddenly without an explanation. Her subpoena was kept open, leaving the possibility of her testifying later.

No one expected any of the people being questioned to furnish clues to Patty/Tania's route underground or whether she might return in some new guerrilla theater scenario.

X

Life returned to normal reluctantly at the Hearst mansion, because Randy still sought ways to touch some responsive chord in Patty/Tania, some nerve or emotion he might have overlooked. The possibility he could have missed some opportunity still haunted him.

Catherine Hearst, who had been reappointed to another 16-year term on the University of California Board of Regents, missed a couple of meetings, once because of a broken wrist suffered when a rug slipped beneath her, another time because of the emotional stress of Patty/Tania's disappearance.

Emily Brubach, the cook who had become a favorite of all the newsmen encamped at the mansion, finally took the vacation to Germany she had planned for so long. There were no more newsmen camped out front.

Their tangle of wires and cameras and vehicles had departed.

The mansion itself was put up for sale again. The Hearsts had planned before the kidnaping to sell, but had taken it off the market during the harrowing months after February 4. Their $345,000 asking price did not deter prospective buyers. A realtor was kept busy by a steady stream of interested mansion shoppers.

Randy had trouble keeping his mind on such business details, still clinging to any straw of hope.

Both father and daughter sat in the secret corners of their minds, pondering the inexplicable things the other had done, the words that could not bridge the filial chasm of distrust and injured pride. Few daughters had left the nest with such trauma. Few fathers had so tried to move the immovable mass of bureaucracy, penetrate the myths of power and reach across a generation. He clung still to the miniscule hope Patty/Tania might give herself up or be surrendered safely.

"But I guess that's not realistic. The only realistic prospect now is that she will be captured. I hope to God she will be all right."

Appendix A

CHRONOLOGY OF THE SYMBIONESE LIBERATION ARMY

November 6, 1973—Oakland Schools Supt. Marcus Foster slain and his aide, Robert Blackburn, wounded in an ambush by three people.

November 7, 1973—Symbionese Liberation Army issues its Communiqué No. 1 claiming responsibility for killing Foster and warning that school board members would be killed for supporting student ID's and police on campus.

November 17, 1973—SLA Communiqué No. 2 lifts death warrants on school board members three days after controversial programs dropped.

January 10, 1974—SLA literature found in van following arrest of Joseph Remiro and Russell Little after shoot-out in Concord; guns tied to Foster slaying allegedly found; later in day firemen find more SLA material at house in same neighborhood where arson attempted.

January 11, 1974—Arson warrant issued for Nancy Ling Perry for attempt to torch Concord house, explosives, cyanide equipment and SLA maps, literature and execution/kidnap target list found.

January 17, 1974—Philosophy of SLA explained in

"Letter to People" mailed to media by Nancy Ling Perry now using name of Fahizah.

January 25, 1974—Investigators on trail of SLA search apartment occupied by Emily and Bill Harris, Angela Atwood and possibly Robyn Steiner; find another kidnap/execution list.

February 4, 1974—Patricia Hearst kidnaped, Steven Weed beaten, but escapes as two black men and a white woman invade their apartment.

Investigators immediately begin check of possible SLA link to kidnaping, begin checking associates of known members.

February 7, 1974—SLA sends Communiqué No. 3, announcing that Patricia Hearst is being held as a "prisoner of war."

February 8, 1974—Frederick Schwartz calls FBI in Chicago and tells his suspicions that daughter Emily and her husband Bill Harris involved in Hearst kidnap.

February 10, 1974—Investigators compile list of missing radicals associated with Remiro, Little, Harrises and Perry.

February 12, 1974—SLA mails tape recording to Berkeley Radio Station KPFA containing voice of Miss Hearst and General Field Marshal Cinque. Cinque demanded $70 worth of free food for all poor and elderly as gesture of good will before negotiations can begin for her release. Experts estimate this would cost $400 million.

February 13, 1974—Patricia's father, Randolph Hearst, answers SLA, saying he cannot provide $400 million worth, but he will commence a food distribution plan as soon as possible.

February 15, 1974—Cinque is identified by media as escaped Soledad convict, Donald DeFreeze; second man in kidnap identified as Thero Wheeler, another escaped black convict who had known DeFreeze when both attended Black Cultural Association meetings at Vacaville.

February 16, 1974—SLA sends second tape, this one to the Rev. Cecil Williams, accepting Hearst move as reasonable prelude to negotiations.

February 19, 1974—Randolph Hearst announces $2 million food program, naming Ludlow Kramer of Seattle to head People in Need (PIN) project.

February 20, 1974—Patricia Hearst's birthday. News media used date to speculate she might be released. She was not.

February 21, 1974—SLA tape delivered night before to the Rev. Williams is made public; Cinque denounces $2 million food program as "a few crumbs" and demanded $4 million worth more within 24 hours;

Department of Corrections Director Raymond Procunier sets up midnight meeting between Remiro, Little and Death Row Jeff; proposal is made to give SLA aircraft and $1 million cash for getaway in return for Patty; Procunier gives demands to "proper authorities," but Hearst is never told.

February 22, 1974—Hearst counterproposal made to SLA: an extra $4 million placed in escrow for food if Patty is released safely by May 5; first PIN food distribution marred by riots, confusion.

February 25, 1974—FBI learns that Nancy Ling Perry and Camilla Hall have accounts at bank across street from their Berkeley offices, notify bank officials, but do not establish stakeout.

February 28, 1974—Second day of PIN food distribution held at 10 locations, mostly smooth operations, few ripoffs; Hearst asked SLA response.

March 1, 1974—Camilla Hall walks into bank across from FBI, withdraws sizable savings account and disappears; teller has not been notified Camilla is wanted.

March 5, 1974—Third day of PIN food handout goes smoothly, a few more ripoffs; still no SLA word.

March 7, 1974—Remiro and Little ask for nationally televised pressed conference to reveal plans they insisted would free Miss Hearst.

March 8, 1974—PIN distributes more food, quieter now.

March 9, 1974—SLA sends its fifth tape recording; PIN roundly criticized; Patty statement FBI wants her dead, but she wants out.

March 10, 1974—Wesley Hiler, prison psychiatrist, opens negotiations that lead to four meetings between Randolph Hearst and Death Row Jeff in effort to secure Patty's release.

March 19, 1974—Little and Remiro request for nationally televised press conference is turned down by court.

March 25, 1974—Final PIN food distribution made.

March 28, 1974—Remiro and Little letters to media state their confidence SLA will release Miss Hearst.

March 29, 1974—Randolph Hearst and Death Row Jeff hold final meeting.

March 30, 1974—Death Row Jeff issues statement urging SLA to open negotiations for release of Patty.

April 1, 1974—Hearst Corp. places $4 million in escrow for more food to be distributed when Patty is released.

April 2, 1974—Roses and announcement arrive indicating time and place of Patty's release will come within 24 hours.

April 3, 1974—SLA tape arrives at San Francisco Radio Station KSAN with Patty announcing she had decided to stay with SLA and become revolutionary "Tania"; she denounces PIN program as sham, calls father names; death warrants name three former friends of SLA.

April 4, 1974—Parents and Weed announce disbelief Patty statement free and voluntary; brainwash theory is voiced.

April 12, 1974—Letter from French revolutionary journalist Regis DeBray, as requested by Weed, is published asking Patty not to defame real Tania and if she is revolutionary, to prove it.

April 15, 1974—SLA robs Hibernia Bank with Patty carrying automatic rifle in middle of six-member squad; two customers wounded; $10,000 taken.

April 24, 1974—SLA bank robbery getaway cars found in parking garage beneath Japantown on Geary Boulevard.

May 2, 1974—SLA hideout found a mile from FBI headquarters in apartment on Golden Gate Avenue; evidence of bomb making and gun ordinance work discovered with slogans and poetry.

May 10, 1974—Friend of Cinque makes first contact and offers to "sell" Patty for $50,000 reward from parents because police pressure is too hot.

May 16, 1974—Cinque and two friends make appearance to arrange to turn over Patty for money; next meeting set for Flagstaff, Arizona; at 4:30 P.M., Patty and Harrises caught in confrontation at Los Angeles sporting goods store, Patty shoots way out and they begin round of car heists and kidnapings.

May 17, 1974—Friend of Cinque who made first "sell" contact shot at 3 A.M. on San Francisco street corner; Los Angeles police receive call from Mrs. Mary Carr about a group of white women and a black man with guns in her daughter's house, begin operations and surround house; gunfire leads to house being burned to ground; five bodies are found in wreckage.

May 18, 1974—A sixth body is found in wreckage; first five identified include Cinque; Patty and Harrises still at large; citizen sightings increase; another SLA hideout in San Francisco found.

June 7, 1974—Tape recording sent to Los Angeles radio station; Patty/Tania eulogizes six dead comrades, Harrises explain what happened at sporting goods store and in house, and announce plans to continue the fight.

Appendix B

SYMBIONESE LIBERATION DOCUMENTS AND RULES

The following material was sent by the SLA to media representatives and as part of the required "print in full" directives issued during the early stages of the kidnaping:

This seven-headed cobra is the symbol of the Symbionese Liberation Army. The seven heads represent self-determination, cooperative production, creativity, unity, faith, purpose and collective responsibility.

TO THOSE WHO WOULD BEAR THE HOPES AND FUTURE OF OUR PEOPLE, LET THE VOICE OF THEIR GUNS EXPRESS THE WORDS OF FREEDOM.

UMOJA—LA UNIDAD—UNITY—To strive for and maintain unity in our household, our nation and in The Symbionese Federation.

KUJICHAGULIA—LA LIBRE DETERMINACION —SELF-DETERMINATION—To define ourselves, name ourselves, speak for ourselves and govern ourselves.

UJIMA—TRABAJO COLLECTIVO Y RESPONSA-BILIDAD—COLLECTIVE WORK AND RE-SPONSIBILITY—To build and maintain our nation and the Federation together by making our brothers' and sisters' and the Federation's problems our problems and solving them together.

UJAMAA—PRODUCCION COOPERATIVA— CO-OPERATIVE PRODUCTION—To build and maintain our own economy from our skills, and labor and resources and to insure ourselves and other nations that we all profit equally from our labor.

NIA—PROPOSITO—PURPOSE—To make as our collective vocation the development and liberation of our nation, and all oppressed people, in order to restore our people and all oppressed people to their traditional greatness and humanity.

KUUMBA-CREATIVO—CREATIVITY—To do all we can in order to free our nation and defend the Federation and constantly make it and the earth that we all share more beautiful and beneficial.

IMSNI—FE—FAITH—To believe in our unity, our leaders, our teachers, our people, and in the righteousness and victory of our struggle and the struggle of all oppressed and exploited people.

THE SYMBIONESE FEDERATION & THE SYMBIONESE LIBERATION ARMY DECLARATION OF REVOLUTIONARY WAR & THE SYMBIONESE PROGRAM
AUGUST 21, 1973

The Symbionese Federation and The Symbionese Liberation Army is a united and federated grouping of members of different races and people and socialist political parties of the oppressed people of The Fascist United States of America, who have under black and minority leadership formed and joined The Symbionese Federated Republic and have agreed to struggle together in behalf of all their people and races and political parties interest in the gaining of FREEDOM and SELF-DETERMINATION and INDEPENDANCE* for all their people and races.

The Symbionese Federation is NOT A GOVERNMENT, but rather it is a united and federated formation of members of different races and people and political parties who have agreed to struggle in a UNITED FRONT for the independence and self determination of each of their races and people and The Liquidation of the Common Enemy.

And who by this federated formation represent their future and independant pre-governments and nations of their people and races. The Symbionese Federation is NOT A PARTY, but rather it is a Federation, for its members are made up of members of all political parties and organizations and races of all the most oppressed people of this fascist nation, thereby forming unity and the full representation of the interests of all the people.

The Symbionese Liberation Army is an army of the people, and is made up of members of all the people. The S.L.A. has no political power or political person over it that dictates who will fight and die if needed for the freedom of our people and children, but does not risk their life or fight too for our freedom, but rather

* All spelling, punctuation and capitalizations have been retained.

the S.L.A. is both political and military in that in the S.L.A. the army officer, whether female or male is also the political officer and they both are the daughters and sons of the people and they both fight as well as speak for the freedom of our people and children.

The Symbionese Federation and The Symbionese Liberation Army is made up of the aged, youth and women and men of all races and people. The name Symbionese is taken from the word symbiosis and we define its meaning as a body of dissimilar bodies and organisms living in deep and loving harmony and partnership in the best interest of all within the body.

We of the Symbionese Federation and the S.L.A. define ourselves by this name because it states that we are no longer willing to allow the enemy of all our people and children to murder, oppress and exploit us nor define us by color and thereby maintain division among us, but rather have joined together under black and minority leadership in behalf of all our different races and people to build a better and new world for our children and people's future. We are a United Front and Federated Coalition of members from the Asian, Black, Brown, Indian, White, Women, Grey and Gay Liberation Movements.

Who have all come to see and understand that only if we unite and build our new world and future, will there really be a future for our children and people. We of the People and not the ruling capitalist class, will build a new world and system. Where there is really freedom and a true meaning to justice and equality for all women and men of all races and people, and an end to the murder and oppression, exploitation of all people.

We of the Symbionese Federation and The S.L.A. are the children of all oppressed people, who have decided to redefine ourselves as a Symbionese Race and People. Yet, recognizing the rich cultures of each and enforcing our rights to existance of our many cultures within a united federation of independant and sovereign nations, each of them flourishing and protected by its own laws and codes of self determination.

We are of many colors, but yet of one mind, for we all in history's time on this earth have become part of each other in suffering and in mind, and have agreed that the murder, oppression and exploitation of our children and people must end now, for we all have seen the murder, oppression and exploitation of our people for too long under the hand of the same enemy and class of people and under the same system.

Knowing this, the Symbionese Federation and The S.L.A. know that our often murderous alienation from each other aids and is one of the fundamental strengths behind the ruling capitalist class's ability to murder and oppress us all. By not allowing them to define us by color, and also recognizing that by refusing ourselves to also internalize this false division definition, knowing that in mind and body we are facing the same enemy and that we are all comrades of one people, the murdered and oppressed, we are now able to become a united people under the Symbionese Federation and make true the words of our codes of unity that TO DIE A RACE, AND BE BORN A NATION, IS TO BECOME FREE.

Therefore, we of the Symbionese Federation and The S.L.A. DO NOT under the rights of human beings submit to the murder, oppression and exploitation of our children and people and do under the rights granted to the people under The Declaration of Independance of The United States, do now by the rights of our children and people and by Force of Arms and with every drop of our blood, *Declare Revolutionary War* against The Fascist Capitalist Class, and all their agents of murder, oppression and exploitation. We support by Force of Arms the just struggles of all oppressed people for self determination and independence within the United States and The World. And hereby offer to all liberation movements, revolutionary workers groups, and peoples organizations our total aid and support for the struggle for freedom and justice for all people and races. We call upon all revolutionary black and other oppressed people within the Fascist United States to come together and join The Symbionese Federation and fight in the forces of The Symbionese Liberation Army.

THE GOALS OF THE SYMBIONESE LIBERATION ARMY

1. To unite all oppressed people into a fighting force and to destroy the system of the capitalist state and all its value systems. To create in its place a system and sovereign nations that are in the total interest of all its races and people, based on the true affirmation of life, love, trust, and honesty, freedom and equality that is truly for all.
2. To assure the rights of all people to self determination and the rights to build their own nation and government, with representatives that have shown through their actions to be in the interest of their people. To give the right to all people to select and elect their own representatives and governments by direct vote.
3. To build a people's federated council, who will be a male and female of each People's Council or Sovereign Nation of The Symbionese Federation of Nations, who shall be the representatives of their nations in the forming of trade packs (sic) and unified defense against any external enemy that may attack any of the free nations of the federation and to form other aids to each others' needs.
4. To aid and defend the cultural rights of all the sovereign nations of The Symbionese Federation, and to aid each nation in the building of educational and other institutions to meet and serve this need for its people.
5. To place the control of all the institutions and industries of each nation into the hands of its people. To aid sovereign nations of the federation to build nations where work contributes concretely to the full interest and needs of its workers and the communal interest of its communities and its peo-

ple and the mutual interest of all within the federation of nations.

6. To aid and defend the rights of all oppressed people to build nations which do not institute oppression and exploitation, but rather does institute the environment of freedom and defends that freedom on all levels and for all of the people, and by any means necessary.

7. To give back to all people their human and constitutional rights, liberty, equality and justice and the right to bear arms in the defense of these rights.

8. To create a system where our aged are cared for with respect, love, and kindness and aided and encouraged to become assets in their own ways to their nations and to their communcal community. That the life that moves around them is not a frightening and murderous one and where life is not a fear, but rather one of love and feeling and of unity.

9. To create a system and laws that will neither force people into nor force them to stay into personal relationships that they do not wish to be in, and to destroy all chains instituted by legal and social laws of the capitalist state which acts as a reinforcing system to maintain this form of imprisonment.

10. To create institutions that will aid, reinforce and educate the growth of our comrade women and aid them in making a new true and better role to live in life and in the defining of themselves as a new and free people.

11. To create new forms of life and relationships that bring true meanings of love to people's relationships, and to form communes on the community level and bring the children of the community into being the responsibility of the community, to place our children in the union of real comradeship and in the care and loving interest of the revolutionary community.

12. To destroy the prison system, which the capi-

talist state has used to imprison the oppressed and exploited, and thereby destroy the love, unity, and hopes of millions of lives and families. And to created (sic) in its place a system of comradeship and that of group unity and education on a communal and revolutionary level within the community, to bring home our daughters and sons, and sisters and brothers, fathers and mothers and welcome them home with love and a new revolutionary comradeship of unity.

13. To take control of all state land and that of the capitalist class and to give back the land to the people. To form laws and codes that safeguard that no person can own the land, or sell the land, but rather the nations' people own the land and use it for their needs and interest to live. No one can own or sell the air, the sky, the water, the trees, the birds, the sun, for all of this world belongs to the people of this earth.

14. To take controls (sic) of all buildings and apartment buildings of the capitalist class and fascist government and to totally destroy the rent system of exploitation.

15. To build a federation of nations, who shall formulate programs and unions of actions and interests that will destroy the capitalist value system and its other anti-human institutions and who will be able to do this by meeting all the basic needs of all of the people and their nations. For they will be all able to do this because each nation will have full control of all its industries and institutions and does not run them for profit, but in the full interest of all the people of its nation.

16. To destroy all forms and institutions of Racism, Sexism, Ageism, Capitalism, Fascism, Individualism, Possessiveness, Competeviness and all other such institutions that have made and sustained capitalism and the capitalist class system that has oppressed and exploited all of the people of our history.

By this means and the mutual aid and unity of

325

each nation within The Symbionese Federation, will each nation be able to provide to each person and couple and family free of cost the five basic needs of life, which are food, health care, housing, education and clothing, and in this way allowing people to be able to find and form new values and new systems of relationships and interests based on a new meaning to life and love

IF THE QUEST FOR FREEDOM IS DEATH
THEN BY THE DEATH OF THE ENEMY WILL
BLACK AND OTHER OPPRESSED PEOPLE
FIND AND REGAIN THEIR FREEDOM

CODES OF WAR OF THE UNITED SYMBIONESE LIBERATION ARMY
PENALTY BY DEATH
ALL CHARGES THAT FACE A DEATH PENALTY SHALL BE PRESENTED TO A JURY TRIAL MADE UP OF THE MEMBERS OF THE GUERRILLA FORCES. THE JURY SHALL BE SELECTED BY THE CHARGED AND THE JUDGE CONDUCTING THE TRIAL SHALL BE SELECTED BY THE CHARGED ALSO. THE CHARGED SHALL SELECT HIS OR HER DEFENSE, AND THE TRIAL JUDGE SHALL SELECT THE PROSECUTOR. THE JURY SHALL NUMBER AT LEAST 3/4THS OF THE REMAINING MEMBERS OF THE CELLS, AND THE VERDICT MUST BE UNANIMOUS.
1. THE SURRENDER TO THE ENEMY.
2. THE KILLING OF A COMRADE OR DISOBEYING ORDERS THAT RESULT IN THE DEATH OF A COMRADE.
3. THE DESERTING OF A COMRADE ON THE FIELD OF WAR.
a. LEAVING A TEAM POSITION, THEREBY NOT COVERING A COMRADE.
b. LEAVING A WOUNDED COMRADE.
4. THE INFORMING TO THE ENEMY OR

SPYING AGAINST THE PEOPLE OR GUERRIL-
LAS.

5. LEAVING A CELL UNIT OR BASE CAMP
WITHOUT ORDERS.

Any comrade may leave the guerrilla forces if she or
he feels that they no longer feel the courage or faith in
the people and the struggle that we wage. A comrade,
however, must follow the CODES OF WAR in doing
this: that is, he or she must inform the commanding
guerrilla of their wish to go from the guerrilla force.
Thereupon, the guerrilla in command will release them
in a safe area. The ex-combatants may only leave with
his or her personal side-arm. REMEMBER, this is the
ONLY way a comrade may leave the S.L.A., any other
way is deserting, punishable by death.

6. ALL PAID OR UNPAID INFORMANTS
OPERATING WITHIN THE COMMUNITY
AGAINST THE PEOPLE AND THE GUERRILLA
FORCES ARE SENTENCED WITHOUT TRIAL TO
IMMEDIATE DEATH.

PENALTY BY DISCIPLINARY ACTION

DISCIPLINARY ACTION SHOULD BE PRI-
MARILY TO AID THE COLLECTIVE GROWTH
OF THE CELL, SO THAT THROUGH POSITIVE
ACTION THE MISTAKE IS UNDERSTOOD. ALL
CHARGES THAT FACE DISCIPLINARY ACTION
SHALL BE UNDER THE FULL CONTROL OF
THE GUERRILLA IN COMMAND, AND SHE OR
HE SHALL WEIGH ALL EVIDENCE AND
SHALL DECIDE THE VERDICT, AND IF
NEEDED, DIRECT THE DISCIPLINARY AC-
TION TO BE TAKEN BY THE CHARGED COM-
RADE NECESSARY TO DIRECT HIM OR HER.
EXAMPLES OF DISCIPLINARY ACTION ARE:
THE CLEANING AND MAINTENANCE OF ALL
CELL ARMS, AMMUNITION AND EXPLOSIVES
FOR ONE WEEK, THE UP KEEP OF OUTHOUSES,
THE FULL SUSPENSION OF WINE OR CIGA-
RETTES, AND EXTRA DUTIES SUCH AS ADDI-

TIONAL WATCHES, PRACTICE AND STUDY PERIODS, CORRESPONDENCE, FILING, TYPING, WASHING, CLEANING, COOKING, AND PHYSICAL EXERCISES.

1. LACK OF RESPONSIBILITY AND DETERMINED DECISIVENESS IN FOLLOWING ORDERS.

2. NONVIGILANCE OR THE LEAVING OF AN ASSIGNED POST WITHOUT ORDERS.

3. LACK OF RESPONSIBILITY IN MAINTAINING EQUIPMENT OR PROFICIENCY IN ALL GUERRILLA SKILLS, ESPECIALLY SHOOTING.

4. THE USE OF ANY UNMEDICALLY PRESCRIBED DRUG:

THIS RULE RELATES TO THE USE OF SUCH DRUGS AS HEROIN, SPEED, PEYOTE, MESCALINE, REDS, PEP PILLS, WHITES, YELLOW JACKETS, BENNIES, DEXIES, GOOF BALLS, LSD, AND ANY OTHER KIND OF HALLUCINARY (sic) DRUGS. HOWEVER, PERMISSION IS GRANTED FOR THE USE OF ONLY TWO TYPES OF RELAXING DRUGS: THESE ARE MARIJUANA, AND/OR BEER AND WINE AND OTHER ALCOHOL. THIS PERMISSION IS ONLY GRANTED WHEN APPROVED BY THE GUERRILLA IN COMMAND, AND WITH VERY RESTRAINING USE ONLY. NO OFFICER MAY GRANT THE USE OF ANY OF THESE SAID DRUGS TO THE FULL NUMBER OF FORCES UNDER HIS OR HER COMMAND. IF THIS PERMISSION IS GRANTED ONLY HALF THE FORCE WILL BE ALLOWED TO TAKE PART, WHILE THE OTHER HALF WILL STAND GUARD DUTY.

THE PAST HAS SHOWN ONCE TRUE REVOLUTIONARIES HAVE SERIOUSLY UNDERTAKEN REVOLUTIONARY ARMS STRUGGLE, MARIJUANA AND ALCOHOL ARE NOT USED FOR RECREATIONAL PURPOSES OR TO DILUTE OR BLUR THE CONSCIOUSNESS OF REALITY, BUT VERY SMALL AMOUNTS FOR

MEDICINAL PURPOSES TO CALM NERVES UNDER TIMES OF TENSION, NOT TO DISTORT REALITY.

5. THE FAILURE TO SEVER ALL PAST CONTACTS OR FAILING TO DESTROY ALL EVIDENCE (OF IDENTIFICATION OR ASSOCIATION.

PENALTY BY DISCIPLINARY ACTION

6. KILLING OF AN UNARMED ENEMY: IN THIS INSTANCE THE ENEMY REFERS TO MEMBERS OF THE USA RANK AND FILE ONLY AND NOT TO ANY MEMBERS OF THE CIA, FBI, OR OTHER SPECIAL AGENTS OR ANY CITY POLITICAL POLICE STATE AGENTS. MEMBERS OF THE USA MILITARY RANK AND FILE ARE TO BE ACCORDED THIS DISTINCTION BECAUSE WE RECOGNIZE THAT MANY OF THEM HAVE BEEN FORCED INTO MEMBERSHIP EITHER DIRECTLY, THROUGH THE DRAFT, OR INDIRECTLY DUE TO ECONOMIC PRESSURES.

7. TORTURES OR SEXUAL ASSAULT ON EITHER A COMRADE OR PEOPLE OR THE ENEMY.

8. CRIMINAL ACTS AGAINST THE POOR COMRADES OR GUERRILLA FORCES.

9. MALICIOUS CURSING OF ANY KIND OF DISRESPECT TO THOSE IN COMMAND, A COMRADE, OR THE PEOPLE.

10. DECEIVING OR LYING TO FELLOW COMRADES OR THE PEOPLE. IF ANY OF THESE ACTS ARE COMMITTED ON A CONTINUOUS BASIS, THE CHARGED COMRADE SHALL BECOME A PRISONER OF THE CELL AND SHALL REMAIN IN THIS PRISONER STATUS UNTIL SUCH TIME AS SHE OR HE IS ABLE TO PROVE THEIR RENEWED COMMITMENT TO REVOLUTIONARY DISCIPLINE AND REVOLUTIONARY PRINCIPLES OR THE

CHARGED MAY REQUEST TO BE DISHONOR-
ABLY DISCHARGED.

CONDUCT OF GUERRILLA FORCES TO-
WARDS THE ENEMY SOLDIERS AND PRIS-
ONERS

1. PRISONERS OF WAR SHALL BE HELD UN-
DER THE INTERNATIONAL CODES OF WAR.
THEY SHALL BE PROVIDED WITH ADEQUATE
FOOD, MEDICAL AID, AND EXERCISES.
2. ALL USA MILITARY RANK AND FILE
FORCES SHALL BE ALLOWED TO SURRENDER
UPON OUR CONDITIONS OF SURRENDER, AND
THEREUPON THEY SHALL BE CAREFULLY
SEARCHED AND INTERROGATED. ALL PRIS-
ONERS ARE TO RECEIVE INSTRUCTIONS ON
THE GOALS OF THE SYMBIONESE LIBERA-
TION ARMY, THEN RELEASED IN A SAFE
AREA.
3. ALL WEAPONS, MEDICAL AND FOOD
SUPPLIES, MAPS, MILITARY EQUIPMENT AND
MONEY ARE TO BE CONFISCATED AND
TURNED IN TO THE GUERRILLA IN CHARGE.
4. UNDER NO CONDITIONS SHALL ANY
RANK AND FILE ENEMY SOLDIER BE RE-
LIEVED OF HIS OR HER PERSONAL PROP-
ERTY.

CONDUCT OF GUERRILLA FORCES TO-
WARD THE PEOPLE

ALL GUERRILLA FORCES SHALL CONDUCT
THEMSELVES IN A MANNER OF RESPECT
TOWARD THE PEOPLE, AND SHALL WHEN
ABLE AND SAFE TO DO SO, PROVIDE FOOD
AND OTHER AID TO THE PEOPLE. THEY
SHALL, WHEN POSSIBLE, INFORM THE PEO-
PLE OF THE GOALS OF THE UNITED SYM-
BIONESE FEDERATION AND ENCOURAGE
OTHER WOMEN AND MEN TO JOIN OUR

FORCES AND TO SERVE THE PEOPLE IN FIGHT FOR FREEDOM.

ALL COMRADES HAVE ONE MAIN RESPONSIBILITY, THAT IS TO STRUGGLE AND WIN AND STAND TOGETHER, SO NO COMRADE STANDS ALONE. ALL MUST LOOK OUT FOR EACH OTHER, ALL MUST AID THE OTHER BLACK, BROWN, RED, YELLOW, WHITE, MAN OR WOMAN, ALL OR NONE.

THIS DOCUMENT MAY CHANGE FROM TIME TO TIME, SO OFFICERS ARE REQUESTED TO FOLLOW THE CHANGES WITH DISCIPLINE. AND FUTURE OF THE PEOPLE LET THE VOICE OF THEIR GUNS EXPRESS THE WORD OF FREEDOM.

Gen. Field Marshall
S.L.A.
Cin

Appendix C

COMPLETE TEXTS ON PATTY/TANIA RECORDINGS SENT BETWEEN FEBRUARY 12 AND JUNE 6, 1974

The first transcript was received by Berkeley Radio Station KPFA on February 12; the tape also included the voice of Donald DeFreeze using the name of Cinque. The following is Patty/Tania's portion:

Mom, Dad. I'm okay. I had a few scrapes and stuff, but they washed them up and they're getting okay. And I caught a cold, but they're giving me pills for it and stuff.

I'm not being starved or beaten or unnecessarily frightened. I've heard some press reports and so I know that Steve and all the neighbors are okay and that no one was really hurt.

And I also know that the SLA members here are very upset about press distortions of what's been happening. They have nothing to do with the August 7th movement. They have not been shooting down helicopters or shooting down innocent people in the streets.

I'm kept blindfolded usually so that I can't identify anyone. My hands are often tied, but generally they're not. I'm not gagged or anything, and I'm comfortable.

And I think you can tell that I'm not really terrified or anything and that I'm okay.

I was very upset though to hear that police rushing in on that house in Oakland and I was really glad that I wasn't there and I would appreciate it if everyone would just calm down and try not to find me and not be making identifications because they're not only endangering me but they're endangering themselves.

I'm with a combat unit that's armed with automatic weapons and there's also a medical team here and there's no way that I will be released until they let me go, so it won't do any good for somebody to come in here and try to get me out by force.

These people aren't just a bunch of nuts. They've been really honest with me but they're perfectly willing to die for what they are doing.

And I want to get out of here but the only way I'm going to is if we do it their way. And I just hope that you'll do what they say, Dad, and just do it quickly.

I've been stopping and starting this tape myself, so that I can collect my thoughts. That's why there are so many stops in it.

I'm not being forced to say any of this. I think it's really important that you take their requests very seriously about not arresting any other SLA members and about following their good faith request to the letter.

I just want to get out of here and see everyone again and be back with Steve.

The SLA is very interested in seeing how you're taking this, Dad, and they want to make sure that you are really serious and listening to what they're saying.

And they think that you've been taking this whole thing a lot more seriously than the police and the FBI and other federal people have been taking it.

It seems to be getting to the point where they're not worried about you so much as they're worrying about other people. Or at least I am.

It's really up to you to make sure that these people don't jeopardize my life by charging in and doing stupid things, and I hope you will make sure that they don't do anything else like that Oakland house business.

The SLA people really have been honest with me and I really I mean I feel pretty sure that I'm going to get out of here if everything goes the way they want it to.

And I think you should feel that way too and try not to worry so much. I mean I know it's hard but I heard that Mom was really upset and that everybody was at home. I hope that this puts you a little bit at ease so that you know that I really am all right.

I just hope I can get back to everybody really soon.

The SLA has ideological ties with the IRA, the people's struggle in the Philippines and the Socialist people in Puerto Rico in their struggle for independence, and they consider themselves to be soldiers who are fighting and aiding these people.

I am a prisoner of war and so are the two men in San Quentin. I am being treated in accordance with the Geneva Convention, one of the conditions being that I am not being tried for crimes which I'm not responsible for.

I am here because I am a member of a ruling-class family and I think you can begin to see the analogy. The people, the two men in San Quentin are being held simply because they are members of the SLA and not because they've done anything.

Witnesses to the shooting of Foster saw black men. And two white men have been arrested for this. You're being told this so that you'll understand that whatever happens to the two prisoners is going to happen to me.

You have to understand that I am held to be innocent the same way the two men in San Quentin are innocent, that they are simply members of the group and had not done anything themselves to warrant their arrest.

They apparently were part of an intelligence unit and have never executed anyone themselves. The SLA has declared war against the government and it's important that you understand that they know what they're doing and they understand what their actions mean.

... And that you realize that this is not considered by them to be just a simple kidnaping and that you don't treat it that way and say "Oh, I don't know why she was taken."

I'm telling you now why this happened so that you will know and so that you'll have something to use, some knowledge to try to get me out of here.

If you can get the food thing organized before the 19th, then that's okay and it would just speed up my release.

Today is Friday the 8th and in Kuwait the commandos negotiated the release of their hostages and they left the country.

'Bye.

TEXT OF THE PATTY/TANIA TAPE OF FEBRUARY 16

Dad, Mom, I'm making this tape to let you know that I'm still okay and to explain a few things, I hope.

First about the good-faith gesture. There was some misunderstanding about that and you should do what you can and they understand that you want to meet their demands and that ... they have every intention that you should be able to meet their demands.

They weren't trying to present an unreasonable request. It was never intended that you feed the whole state.

So whatever you come up with basically is okay.

And just do it as fast as you can and everything will be fine.

But the SLA is really mad about certain attempts to make the feeding of food be the receiving of goods that were gotten by extortion.

They don't want people to be harassed by the police or by anybody else, and I hope you can do something about that and if you can't, well, I mean they'll do something about it.

So . . . you shouldn't worry about that too much.

Also, I would like to emphasize that I am alive and that I am well and that in spite of what certain tape experts seem to think, I mean I'm fine.

It's really depressing to hear people talk about me like I'm dead. I can't explain what that's like. What it does, also, is that it . . . it begins to convince other people that maybe I am dead.

If everybody is convinced that I am dead, well then it gives the FBI an excuse to come in here and try to pull me out. I'm sure that Mr. Bates understands that if the FBI has to come in and get me out by force that they won't have time to decide who not to kill. They'll just have to kill everyone.

I don't particularly want to die that way.

I hope you will realize that everything is okay and that they'll just [have to] back off for a while. There'll be plenty of time for investigating later.

I am basically an example and a symbolic warning, not only to you but to everyone that there are people who are not going to accept your support of other governments and that faced with suppression and murder of the people . . . and [that] is a warning to everybody.

It's also to show what can be done. When it's necessary the people can be fed, and to show that it's too bad it has to happen this way to make people see that there are people who need food.

Now maybe something can be done about that, so that things like this won't have to happen again.

Also, the SLA is very annoyed about attempts by the press and by authorities to turn this into a racial issue. It's not. This is a political issue and this is a political action that they've taken.

Anyone who really reads the stated objectives of the SLA can see very clearly that this is not a racial thing. I hope there won't be any more confusion about that.

I turned over my notes there, so . . .

I am being held as a prisoner of war and not as anything else and I'm being treated in accordance with in-

336

ternational codes of war. And so you shouldn't listen or believe what anybody else says about the way I'm being treated. I'm not left alone and I'm not just shoved off. I mean, I am fine.

I am not being starved and I'm not being beaten or tortured. Really.

Since I am an example, it's really important that everybody understand that I am an example and a warning. And because of this, it's very important to the SLA that I return safely. So people should stop acting like I'm dead.

Mom should get out of her black dress. That doesn't help at all.

I wish you'd try to understand the position I'm in. I'm right in the middle, and I have to depend upon what all kinds of other people are going to do.

And it's really hard for me to hear about reports, you know, and . . . I hope you understand and try to do something.

I know that a lot of people have written and everyone is concerned about me and my safety and about what you're going through, and I want them all to know that I'm okay.

And [it's important] for them to understand that I'll be okay as long as the SLA demands are met, and as long as the two prisoners at San Quentin are okay.

And as long as the FBI doesn't come in here.

That is my biggest worry. I think I can get out of here alive as long as they don't come busting in and I really think you should understand that the SLA does have an interest in my return.

And try not to worry so much and just do what you can. I mean, I know you're doing everything.

Take care of Steve and hurry. 'Bye.

TEXT OF THE PATTY/TANIA TAPE OF APRIL 3

To those who would bear the hopes and future of our people, let the voice of their guns express the words of freedom.

I would like to begin this statement by informing the public that I wrote what I am about to say. It's what I feel. I have never been forced to say anything on any tape. Nor have I been brainwashed, drugged, tortured, hypnotized or in any way confused. As George Jackson wrote, "It's me, the way I want it, the way I see it."

Mom, Dad, I would like to comment on your efforts to supposedly secure my safety. The PIN giveaway was a sham. You attempted to deceive the people. You were playing games—stalling for time—which the FBI was using in their attempts to assassinate me and the SLA elements which guarded me. You continued to report that you did everything in your power to pave the way for negotiations for my release—I hate to believe that you could have been so unimaginative as to not even have considered getting [Russell] Little and [Joseph] Remiro released on bail. While it was repeatedly stated that my conditions would at all times correspond with those of the captured soldiers, when your own lawyer went to inspect the "hole" at San Quentin, he approved the deplorable conditions there —another move which potentially jeopardized my safety. My mother's acceptance of the appointment to a second term as a UC regent, as you well knew, would have caused my immediate execution had the SLA been less than "together" about their political goals. Your actions have taught me a great lesson, and in a strange kind of way, I'm grateful to you.

Steven, I know that you are beginning to realize that there is no such thing as neutrality in time of war. There can be no compromise, as your experience with the FBI must have shown you. You have been harassed by the FBI because of your supposed connections with so-called radicals, and some people even have gone so far as to suggest that I arranged my own arrest. We both know what really came down that Monday night but you don't know what's happened since then. I have changed—grown. I've become conscious and can never go back to the life we led before. What I'm saying may seem cold to you and to my old friends, but love doesn't mean the same thing to me anymore. My love has expanded as a result of my experiences to embrace all people. It's grown into an unselfish love for my comrades here, in prison and on the streets. A love that comes from the knowledge that "no one is free until we are all free." While I wish that you could be a comrade, I don't expect it—all I expect is that you try to understand the changes I've gone through.

I have been given the choice of one being released in a safe area, or two joining the forces of the Symbionese Liberation Army and fighting for my freedom and the freedom of all oppressed people. I have chosen to stay and fight. One thing which I have learned is that the corporate ruling class will do anything in their power in order to maintain their position of control over the masses, even if this means the sacrifice of one of their own. It should be obvious that people who don't even care about their own children couldn't possibly care about anyone else's children. The things which are precious to these people are their money and power—and they will never willingly surrender either. People should not have to humiliate themselves by standing in line in order to be fed, nor should they have to live in fear for their lives and the lives of their children as Tyrone Guyton's mother will sadly attest to.

Dad, you said that you were concerned with my life, and you also said that you were concerned with the life and interests of all oppressed people in this country, but you are a liar in both areas and as a member of the ruling class, I know for sure that yours and Mom's interests are never the interests of the people. Dad, you said you would see about getting more job opportunities for the people, but why haven't you warned the people what is going to happen to them—that actually the few jobs they still have will be taken away.

You, a corporate liar, of course will say that you don't know what I am talking about, but I ask you then to prove it, tell the poor and oppressed people of this nation what the corporate state is about to do, warn black and poor people that they are about to be murdered down to the last man, woman and child. If you're so interested in the people why don't you tell them what the energy crisis really is. Tell them how it's nothing more than a manufactured strategy, a way of hiding industry's real intentions. Tell the people that the energy crisis is nothing more than a means to get public approval for a massive program to build nuclear power plants all over the nation. Tell the people that the entire corporate state is, with the aid of this massive power supply, about to totally automate the entire industrial state, to the point that in the next five years all that will be needed will be a small class of button pushers; tell the people, Dad, that all of the lower class and at least half of the middle class will be unemployed in the next three years, and that the removal of expendable excess, the removal of unneeded people has already started. I want you to tell the people the truth. Tell them how the law and order programs are just a means to remove so-called violent [meaning aware] individuals from the community in order to facilitate the controlled removal of unneeded labor forces from this country, in the same way that Hitler controlled the removal of the Jews from Germany.

I should have known that if you and the rest of the corporate state were willing to do this to millions of people to maintain power and to serve your needs, you would also kill me if necessary to serve those same needs. How long will it take before white people in this country understand that what ever happens to a black child happens sooner or later to a white child. How long will it be before we all understand that we must fight for our freedom?

I have been given the name Tania after a comrade

who fought alongside Che in Bolivia for the people of Bolivia. I embrace the name with the determination to continue fighting with her spirit. There is no victory in half-assed attempts at revolution. I know Tania dedicated her life to the people. Fighting with total dedication and an intense desire to learn which I will continue in the oppressed American people's revolution. All colors of string in the web of humanity yearn for freedom!

Osceola and Bo, even though we have never met I feel like I know you. Timing brought me to you and I'm fighting with your freedom and the freedom of all prisoners in mind. In the strenuous jogs that life takes, you are pillars of strength to me. If I'm feeling down, I think of you, of where you are and why you are there, and my determination grows stronger. It's good to see that your spirits are so high in spite of the terrible conditions. Even though you aren't here, you are with other strong comrades, and the three of us are learning together—I, in an environment of love and you in one of hate, in the belly of the fascist beast. We have grown closer to the people and become stronger through our experiences. I have learned how vicious the pig really is, and our comrades are teaching me to attack with even greater viciousness, in the knowledge that the people will win. I send greetings to Death Row Jeff, Al Taylor and Raymond Scott. Your concern for my safety is matched by my concern for yours. We share a common goal as revolutionaries knowing that Comrade George lives.

It is in the spirit of Tania that I say, "PATRIA O MUERTE. VENCEREMOS."

TEXT OF THE PATTY/TANIA TAPE OF APRIL 18

Greetings to the people, this is Tania. On April 15 my comrades and I expropriated $10,660.02 from the Sunset Branch of Hibernia Bank. Casualties could have been avoided had the persons involved kept out of the way and cooperated with the people's forces until after our departure.

I was positioned so that I could hold customers and bank personnel who were on the floor. My gun was loaded and at no time did any of my comrades intentionally point their guns at me.

Careful examination of the photographs which were published clearly shows this was true.

Our action of April 15 forced the corporate state to help finance the revolution. In the case of expropriation, the difference between a criminal act and a revolutionary act is shown by what the money is used for.

As for the money involved in my parents bad faith gesture to aid the people, these funds are being used to aid the people, and to insure the survival of the people's forces in their struggle with and for the people.

To the clowns who want a personal interview with me —Vincent Hallinan, Steven Weed and Pig Hearsts—I prefer giving it to the people in the bank. It's absurd to think that I could surface to say what I am saying now and be allowed to freely return to my comrades. The enemy still wants me dead. I am obviously alive and well.

As for being brainwashed, the idea is ridiculous to the point of being beyond belief. It's interesting the way early reports characterized me as a beautiful, intelligent liberal, while in more recent reports I'm a comely girl who's been brainwashed.

The contradictions are obvious.

Consciousness is terrifying to the ruling class and they will do anything to discredit people who have realized that the only alternative to freedom is death and that the only way we can free ourselves of this fascist dictatorship is by fighting, not with words but with guns.

As for my ex-fiance, I'm amazed that he thinks that the first thing I would want to do, once freed, would be to rush and see him. I don't care if I ever see him again. During the last few months Steven has shown himself to be a sexist, agist pig.

Not that this is a sudden change from the way he always was. It merely became blatant during the period when I was still a hostage. Frankly, Steven is the one who sounds brainwashed. I can't believe that those weird words he uttered were from his heart.

They were a mixture of FBI rhetoric and Randy's simplicity.

I have no proof that Mr. DeBray's letter is authentic. The date and location he gave were confusing in terms of when the letter was published in the papers.

How could it have been written in Paris and published in your newspapers on the same day, Adolf?

In any case, I hope that the last action has put his mind at ease. If it didn't, further actions will.

To those people who still believe that I am brainwashed or dead, I see no reason to further defend my position. I am a soldier in the people's army. Patria o muerte; venceremos.

TEXT OF THE PATTY/TANIA TAPE OF JUNE 6

Greetings to the people. This is Tania. I want to talk about the way I knew our six murdered comrades because the fascist pig media has, of course, been painting a typical distorted picture of these beautiful sisters and brothers.

Cujo was the gentlest, most beautiful man I've ever known. He taught me the truth as he learned it from the beautiful brothers in California's concentration camps. We loved each other so much, and his love for the people was so deep that he was willing to give his life for them. The name Cujo means "unconquerable." It was the perfect name for him. Cujo conquered life as well as death by facing and fighting them. Neither Cujo or I had ever loved an individual the way we loved each other, probably because our relationship wasn't based on bourgeois, fucked-up values, attitudes and goals. Our relationship's foundation was our commitment to the struggle and our love for the people. It's because of this that I still feel strong and determined to fight.

I was ripped off by the pigs when they murdered Cujo, ripped off in the same way that thousands of sisters and brothers in this fascist country have been ripped off of people they love. We mourn together, and the sound of gunfire becomes sweeter.

Gelina was beautiful. Fire and joy. She exploded with the desire to kill the pigs. She wrote poetry—some of it on the walls of Golden Gate, all of it in the LA pig files now—that expresses how she felt. She loved the people more than her love for any one person or material comfort, and she never let her mind rest from the strategies that are the blood of revolution. Gelina would have yelled "Fire Power!" to the people if there wasn't the need to whisper the words of revolution. We laughed and cried and struggled together. She taught me how to fight the enemy within, through her constant struggle with bourgeois conditioning.

Gabi crouched low with her ass to the ground. She practiced until her shotgun was an extension of her right and left arms, an impulse, a tool of survival. She understood the evil in the heart of the pig and took the only road that could demoralize, defeat and destroy him. She loved to touch people with a strong—not delicate—embrace. Gabi taught me the patience and discipline necessary for survival and victory.

Zoya wanted to give meaning to her name, and on her birthday she did. Zoya, female guerilla, perfect love and perfect hate reflected in stone-cold eyes. She moved viciously and with caution, understanding the peril of the smallest mistake. She taught me, "Keep your ass down and be bad."

Fahizah was a beautiful sister who didn't talk much but who was the teacher of many by her righteous example. She, more than any other, had come to understand and conquer the putrid disease of bourgois mentality. She proved often that she was unwilling to compromise with the enemy because of her intense love for freedom. Fahizah taught me the perils of hesitation —to shoot first and make sure the pig is dead before splitting. She was wise, and bad, and I'll always love her.

Cinque loved the people with tenderness and respect. They listened to him when he talked because they knew that his love reflected the truth and the future. Cin knew that to live was to shoot straight. He longed to be with his black sisters and brothers, but at the same time he wanted to prove to black people that white freedom fighters are comrades-in-arms. Cinque was in a race with time, believing that every minute must be another step forward in the fight to save the children. He taught me virtually everything imaginable, but wasn't liberal with us. He'd kick our asses if we didn't hop over a fence fast enough or keep our asses down while practicing. Most importantly, he taught me how to show my love for the people. He helped me see that it's not how long you live that's important, it's how we live; what we decide to do with our lives. On February 4th, Cinque Mtume saved my life.

The Malcolm X Combat Unit of the SLA was a leadership training cell, under the personal command of General Field Marshall Cinque. General Teko was his second in command. Everything we did was directed toward our development as leaders and advisers to other units. All of us were prepared to function on our own if necessary, until we connected with other combat units. The idea that we are leaderless is absurd as long as any SLA elements are alive and operating under the command of our General Field Marshal.

It's hard to explain what it was like watching our comrades die. Murdered by pig incendiary grenades. A battalion of pigs facing a fire-team of guerillas, and the only way they could defeat them was to burn them alive. It made me mad to see the pigs looking at our comrades' weapons—to see them holding Cujo's .45 and his watch, which was still ticking. He would have laughed at that. There is no surrender. No one in that house was suicidal—just determined and full of love.

It was beautiful to hear Gabi's father. He understands. Gabi loved her father and I know that much of her strength came from the support he gave her. What

345

a difference between the parents of Gabi and Cujo, and my parents. One day, just before making the last tape, Cujo and I were talking about the way my parents were fucking me over. He said that his parents were still his parents because they had never betrayed him, but my parents were really Malcolm X and Assata Shakur. I'll never betray my parents.

The pigs probably have the little old man monkey that Cujo wore around his neck. He gave me the little stone-face one night.

I know that the pigs are proud of themselves. They've killed another black leader. In typical pig fashion they have said that Cinque committed suicide. What horseshit! Cin committed suicide the same way that Malcolm, King, Bobby, Fred, Jonathan and George did. But no matter how many leaders are killed, the pig can't kill their ideals.

I learned a lot from Cin and the comrades that died in that fire, and I'm still learning from them. They live on in the hearts and minds of millions of people in fascist America. The pig's actions that Friday evening showed just how scared they really are. They would have burned and bombed that entire neighborhood to murder six guerillas.

The SLA terrifies the pigs because it calls all oppressed people in this country to arms to fight in a united front to overthrow the fascist dictatorship. The pigs think they can deal with a handful of revolutionaries, but they know they can't defeat the incredible power which the people, once united, represent.

It's for this reason that we get to see—live and in color—the terrorist tactics of the pigs. The pigs saying "You're next." This kind of display, however, only serves to raise the people's consciousness and makes it easier for our comrade sisters and brothers throughout the country to connect. I died in that fire on 54th Street, but out of the ashes I was reborn. I know what I have to do. Our comrades didn't die in vain. The pig lies about the advisability of surrender have only made me more determined. I renounced my class privilege when Cin and Cujo gave me the name Tania. While I have no death wish, I have never been afraid of death. For this reason, the brainwash/duress theory of the Pig Hearsts has always amused me.

Life is very precious to me, but I have no delusions that going to prison will keep me alive. I would never chose to live the rest of my life surrounded by pigs like the Hearsts. I want to see our comrades in this country's concentration camps, but on our terms as stated in our Revolutionary Declaration of War, not on the pigs' terms.

Patria o muerte ... Venceremos! Death to the Fascist Insect that Preys Upon the Life of the People.

Excitement Reading

Self help & reference

are you missing out on some great Pyramid books?

You can have any title in print at
Pyramid delivered right to your door!
To receive your Pyramid Paperback
Catalog, fill in the label below (use a
ball point pen please) and mail to
Pyramid . . .